THE WELL OF BEING

SUNY series, Early Childhood Education: Inquiries and Insights
Mary A. Jensen, editor

The
Well
of
Being

Childhood,
Subjectivity,
and Education

David Kennedy

STATE UNIVERSITY OF NEW YORK PRESS

Published by
State University of New York Press, Albany

For information, address State University of New York Press,
194 Washington Avenue, Suite 305, Albany, NY 12210-2384

Production by Diane Ganeles
Marketing by Susan M. Petrie

Library of Congress Cataloging in Publication Data

Kennedy, David, 1943-
  The well of being : childhood, subjectivity, and education / David
Kennedy.
      p. cm. — (SUNY series, early childhood education)
  Includes bibliographical references and index.
  ISBN-13: 978-0-7914-6825-8 (hardcover : alk. paper)
  ISBN-10: 0-7914-6825-9 (hardcover : alk. paper)
  ISBN-13: 978-0-7914-6826-5 (pbk. : alk. paper)
  ISBN-10: 0-7914-6826-7 (pbk. : alk. paper)
    1. Children. 2. Children and adults. 3. Education. 4. Postmodernism.
I. Title. II. Series.

HQ767.9.K453 2006
305.23—dc22

                                                                    2005025462

10 9 8 7 6 5 4 3 2 1

For my children—Irene, Sean, Anna and Joel—
in the form of a question

Contents

Preface   ix

1. Questioning Childhood   1
   Whose Child?   1
   Which Adult?   5
   The Western Construction of Childhood   8
   Theorizing Childhood   13
   Adult-Child Dialogue   14
   *The Child Before Us: Education, Parenting, and the
      Evolution of Subjectivity*   21

2. The Primordial Child   27
   The Divine Child   27
   The Romantic Child   44
   Romanticism, Education, and the New Humanity   56

3. The Invention of Adulthood   63
   Adultism and Models of the Self   63
   The Evolution of Adulthood/Childhood   75
   The Evolution of the Adult-Child Relationship   85

4. Childhood and the Intersubject   105
   Boundary Work   105
   The Ego Dethroned   116
   The Emergence of the Intersubject   120
   Psychogenic Theory of History and the Present Age   132

The Dialectics of Reason and Desire   136
The Privileged Stranger   142

5. Reimagining School   151
   The Purposes of Schooling   151
   The Space of Dialogue   158
   The School as Laboratory of the Third Way of Living 165
   The Dark and the Light   183

   Notes   187

   Bibliography   211

   Index   229

Preface

On How This Book Got Its Name

This book represents an attempt at a synthesis of the multiple realities and the discourses they spawn (or which spawn them), which have preoccupied me in one way or another for as long as I can remember. I began by putting the words "postmodern subjectivity" in the title, but decided that the new form of subjectivity, which I am at pains to tease out of the welter of postmodernity might sit very poorly with any number of self-professed postmoderns; that in fact they might find it, not just naïve, but dangerous in its implications, and even consider it premodern or another hopeless twist of modernity itself. So I determined to back off from any claims on postmodernity and to own the fundamental discourse that guides the work, and that in fact has provided for me a context of belief that has endured behind or underneath all the permutations of belief (or lack of it) that have characterized various periods of my life—Romanticism. I decided I would call the second half of the title "Childhood and Subjectivity in the Romantic Imagination."

But of course Romanticism is a name applied after the fact. Those who considered themselves "Romantics" during the Romantic period of roughly the first half of the nineteenth century might have held any number of beliefs about what it meant to "be" one, and by a principle that evokes the Cretan Liar Paradox, those who most firmly professed to be so were probably least so, and those who are now remembered as prime examples may, in their lifetimes, have either scorned or been ignorant of the term. In addition, the Romanticism with which I so deeply identify—as demonstrated by the scholar of Romantic literature M.H. Abrams, whose major work, *Natural Supernaturalism*, plays such an important role in this one—is a perennial one, to be found both in the past and the future of that particular epoch in the nineteenth century. It is found both in ancient religious and hermetic traditions, esoteric and exoteric philosophers, artistic and literary movements, depth psychologies and political philosophies from both before and after the period called "Romantic." As a case in point, probably the most important acknowledgment of a broad intellectual debt incurred in this work is, among several others, to Herbert Marcuse, the German-American philosopher who in his later work—in particularly *Eros and Civilization*—reclaims the Romantic vision of personal and cultural transformation on the other side of Marx and Freud. I consider this work—as closely reasoned as it is—to be an example, along with N.O. Brown's masterwork *Love's Body*, of High Romantic Genius. But given the scope and influence of Romanticism, the self-interested use I make of its arguments, and the extent to which my use is—in that it is interpretive and critical—already *post*-Romantic, I decided that to place the word in the title of this book would be pretentious.

This left me with what I began with—children, childhood, and the worlds constructed for children by adults, and in particular that primary site where children and adults meet in the modern world, school; a decidedly *un*-Romantic place, where so often, in the twentieth century Romantic poet Rilke's words, "Time . . . drags along with so much worry, and waiting, things so dumb and stupid."[1] To place the child and childhood, as they are conceived by Romantic theory, in the quintessentially dreary institutional environment of bells, loud speakers, drab colors, and fluorescent lights, permission slips for the toilet, endless worksheets decorated with mawkish cartoons, teachers with no particular intellectual, ethical, or aesthetic interests, many of them teetering on the edge of burnout as they deliver "teacher-proof" curricula to groups of children too large to handle except through threats of individual or collective punishment of one kind or another, in spaces too small and unimaginative for anything but seatwork, and those children themselves engaged in all manner of collaboration with or subversion of the bureaucratized, quasi-military authority, which sits like bad air in the lungs of teachers and children alike. . . . For the Romantic imagination, for which the perceptual and intentional structures of childhood are prophetic of the highest potentialities of human development, this form of schooling is utter travesty, and takes the greatest theoretical restraint not to interpret as a calculated act of social oppression.

If we consider Rousseau as the first, fitful exemplar of the Romantic imagination, then we can say that the primary business of this new impulse in the West was the reconstruction of education. His *Emile* of

1763 cleared the educational decks in a dramatic way for a vision of reconstruction of the adult-child relation, and the rhetorical energy of his reformulation traced a clear and increasingly articulate path through Pestalozzi, Froebel, and Montessori, arriving in the early twentieth century in Dewey shorn of obscurantism and covert adultism, and ready for dialogue with children. The problem is that the school that *Emile* deconstructs did not yet exist: universal compulsory public education arrived forty years after its publication, with the rise of the reactionary post-French revolutionary nationalistic states in Europe, of which Napoleon's was the first example—the culmination of the Revolution in a police state, and public schooling inaugurated as a national monopoly administered with an iron hand by the Grand Master of the Imperial University. Public schooling has either ignored, suppressed, or co-opted the Romantic reconstruction of schooling ever since. Even the practical force of Dewey's philosophical reconstruction, put to the test during the Progressive Education movement of the first three decades of the twentieth century, ended in mostly cosmetic change and, with the rise of the Cold War, reaction and repudiation.

But the impulse will not go away. It reemerges periodically, when the times allow it—often, we might hypothesize, in periods when the pressure for change from *within* culture and society is stronger than the pressures exerted by external forces. In the latter case, the fears and insecurities that those external forces inspire are manipulated by ideologues, demagogues, and cultural opportunists who implicitly—and, in times of "danger," explicitly—construct universal compulsory education as the first line of national defense and job security. This appears to be the case today. The only consolation for those who stubbornly hold to the possibilities that the institution of the school offers for personal self-actualization and social transformation is the testimony of history, which assures us that another moment of opportunity for reconstruction will emerge, and, further, that this opportunity will carry with it the resources developed in past periods of emergence.

This consolation is guaranteed, not by some law of history but by another sort of internal necessity that informs the first part of the title of this book. It is a phrase taken from Gaston Bachelard's extraordinary chapter, "Reveries toward Childhood," a sort of prose poem, both celebratory and strangely melancholic, an extended meditation on the Jungian "archetype" of childhood, which is explored here, in Chapter 2, from another, mythological and historical angle. For Bachelard, childhood—whatever the experience of one's particular childhood—"remains within us a principle of deep life, of life always in harmony with the possibilities of new beginnings." "We cannot," he says, "love water, fire, the tree without putting a love into them, a friendship which goes back to our childhood. We love them with childhood. When we love all these beauties of the world . . . we love them in a new found childhood, in a childhood reanimated with that childhood which is latent in each of us."[2]

Bachelard confirms for us that the childhood of the adult is an invention of sorts, but also the impossible memory of a perceptual condition, of a form of subject-world relation that we can observe in the actual children with whom we are in relation but never experience again, except perhaps in flashes. The adult-child relationship, even in such a socially and psychologically degraded atmosphere as the one so often produced by universal compulsory schooling, will always carry this complex relation between what we were and what they are, what they might become and what we might have become, what they are and what we might become, and what they might become and what the world might become as a result. This book is about the possibilities that inhabit the interstices of these relations and, finally, about the sort of school that would be capable of mining their depths.

1

Questioning Childhood

> I cannot reach it; and my striving eye
> Dazzles at it, as at eternity.
> —Henry Vaughan, from "Childe-hood"[1]

Whose Child?

It is now about one hundred years since the child became an official object of Western science. Child study was institutionalized in the universities, the media, and the government extension offices at the moment that the Darwinian explanatory paradigm was sweeping Western self-understanding, and the notion of Progress had not yet been fatally complicated by the Great War. Its birth coincides with the birth of the disciplines that have regulated its discursive space ever since—psychology, sociology, and pedagogy.

Child study is traditionally thought of as the domain of these three forms of discourse. The questions these discourses ask of the child are determined by their historical self-understanding as aspirants to "hard science," i.e., a science that can make the same universally verifiable knowledge claims as physics or biology say they can about the world and how it works. In order to bend the object of understanding to the method of understanding, the human sciences fall into the unavoidable trap of objectifying children in the same way that hard science must objectify its objects in order to know them. The object of the discipline is born with the discipline—in this case, the child as a natural kind, and the study of the child as an extension of the science of biology. The questions that get asked of children and of childhood are the same questions that get asked of any organism in its environment. And further, these questions get asked as if by one species—the adult—of another—the child.

This inquiry is not so much directly about the negative consequences of this view of the child and of childhood, of which there are several,[2] as about the questions of and to children and childhood that it leaves out. Those of us in search of a thicker, more dynamic view of the phenomenon of human childhood are regularly disappointed by the absence of any questions that cannot be answered in terms of the narrowed framework of the search for statistical norms, arrived at through standardized forms of research, leaving us with a child who has been—at the very moment we thought we had accessed the "thing itself"—neutralized by the techniques used to study him or her.

The problem is not just epistemological—not just about what adults can know about children and how—but political. Modern science is as hegemonic a knowledge framework as was the theocentric. Like the theocentric, it presumes to be an epistemological bottom line; in the end, all other knowledge claims must meet its criteria for legitimacy. When a big knowledge framework assumes that kind of self-importance, its fundamental beliefs become elements of perception itself, and are put beyond question. So enframed, we no longer feel the need for identification of and ongoing inquiry into the founding philosophical assumptions that undergird our knowledge claims—we no longer understand ourselves as interpreters, but as direct knowers.

In the case of child study, the interpretations that provide research frameworks for the "child" of normal science are, on the surface anyway, the result of the philosophical constructions of childhood of one or another massively seminal thinker—a Darwin, a Freud, or a Piaget. These thinkers—who are sometimes but not always more aware of their philosophical assumptions than their followers—provide normal science with the big picture for its local research agendas, which take decades to play out, hedged about as they are with self-contained, internally developed methodologies. Typically enough, all three of the giants mentioned above considered themselves scientists rather than philosophers, but the further we are from them in time, the more we see them to have been speaking in the context of ontological, epistemological, and anthropological assumptions that they never felt obliged to fully articulate or clarify. To put it bluntly, the "child" of the modern scientists is a culturally and historically mediated, philosophical construct disguised as the hard object of experimental science.

If one of the aims of this critique is to contribute to the deconstruction of the philosophical assumptions underlying any positivist "science" of childhood, it is only in the service of a richer, both more diverse and more complete view. Only by decentering from the standard normative account can we allow other perspectives to interplay, and find the discursive location from which to ask how and why children have meant, mean, and might mean for the world of adults. The questions that drive such an inquiry can only be described as philosophical, because no matter how many insights or even concrete solutions these questions may lead to, they are themselves ultimately unanswerable. There are questions to ask about and of children that are logically prior to any particular positive model we might hold to as to the nature and experience of childhood, the child's similarities and differences from adults, the structural dynamics of the developmental process, and even the mechanics of learning.

One such founding question is epistemological: what *can* adults know about children, and how? It is, after all, always as adults that we regard children and childhood. What we call "child" is first of all a child-for-an-adult, and as such, a construct. When we describe the child, we are in one very important sense not directly describing his or her nature, but one characteristic of the relation between the adult and the child. There is no such thing as a "child" apart from an "adult" to observe it. Children only begin to reflect on themselves as children when they are aware there is something called "adulthood," which they are not part of, and to that extent they have already reached beyond childhood. Childhood and adulthood are two terms of one bipolar concept. If all humans were either children or adults, both terms would lose their meaning.

This observation becomes more obvious once we step out of our own cultural or historical context. Then we find that the boundary between the two terms of this bipolar concept has been drawn differently in different historical epochs, and it is drawn variously along cultural and subcultural lines, and within each individual. All the human sciences—whether psychology, anthropology, sociology, or history—are, in this age of global intervisibility, increasingly aware that, as Kenneth Keniston so neatly put it, "the relationship between historical context and psychological development is far more intimate than we have heretofore suspected."[3] One culture may seem "childlike" to adult Western eyes. On the other hand, Western "adults" may seem curiously obsessive, overly serious, unidimensional beings to some non-Western adults, as well as to certain Western countercultures. In fact the boring, unimaginative "grown-up" has been a major motif in Western children's literature since the nineteenth century.

In classical Athens and in some aboriginal cultures, children were regarded as messengers of the gods—beings, as Pierre Erny says, "still full of emanations from the beyond."[4] The theme of the child as an opening to the divine is also invoked in the Romantic formulation of the "infant sensibility, great birthright of our being," a line from perhaps the most popular poem of the nineteenth century—Wordsworth's "Ode—Intimations of Immortality from Recollections of Early Childhood." Emerson also stated the theme in his proclamation of infancy as the "perpetual Messiah which comes into the arms of fallen men and pleads with them to return to paradise."[5] For Plato, children exemplified untamed appetite, the soul out of balance. Aristotle concurred. For him, children were incapable of happiness in his sense of the term, because they lacked judgment, or reason.[6] The modern state invokes children as "future citizens," which is often used as a code phrase for resources—much like oil reserves, or stands of future timber harvest—for the modern nation-state/economy, which shapes them to its purposes through universal, compulsory schooling. The cost of the state's educational system to its adult citizens is most typically justified on the assumption that, once fed through the mill of cultural and social reproduction, they will eventually become economically and politically "productive."

Each of these various ways of knowing children depends on a construction that emerges from a particular balance of the adult-child polarity. Each, in defining "child," defines "adult." Some historians of childhood suspect that medieval adults had no concept of "child," at least after the age of seven or so, because they themselves shared so many characteristics that today we would call "childlike" or "childish."[7] The Romantic view of the child as an original openness to being is based at least partly on adult memories of childhood; very often the memories are either selective, or shaped by a religious or cultural-historical discourse. The genre of adult autobiography called the "Childhood" arose in the West at the moment in which the massive social and cultural dislocations of the Industrial Revolution removed large segments of the population from the possibility of a "homeland," thus driving the latter to a homeland within, to a psychological rather than a geographical location.[8]

The notion of developmental stages itself is not just a biological, but a social construct as well—or a social construct that uses biology as its ruling metaphor. Freud's "latency" stage, for example, has been described as an invention of late-nineteenth-century educators and child psychologists under the influence of social, economic, and political pressures, which made it expedient to remove children from the workforce, and to suppress their sexuality.[9] A stage theory of childhood fits very nicely with the practice of modern schooling, which had its origins in a larger project of "discipline" of the marginalized—the poor, the insane, the native—in the interests of social control.[10] Conversely, during the early Industrial Revolution, as Max Wartofsky pointed out, "the sliding scale of what constitutes 'childhood' was adjusted to the political and economic realities of a rapacious factory system."[11]

Which Adult?

The concept *adult* is equally liable to historical and cultural deconstruction. As the historian John Boswell demonstrated, there were few "adults" in our sense of the term until relatively recently:

> During most of Western history only a minority of grown-ups ever achieved . . . independence: the rest of the population remained throughout their lives in a juridical status more comparable to "childhood," in the sense that they remained under someone else's control—a father, a lord, a husband, etc. . . . Words for "children" designate servile adults well into the High Middle Ages, and it is often impossible to be sure, without adequate context, whether the appellation is based on age, or status, or both.[12]

Boswell finds widely varying criteria for determining when adulthood began in ancient and medieval cultures—from biological considerations to legal responsibility, to attributions of a moral sense, to release from paternal authority, to a concept of psychological maturity. Most often, and befitting the shifting bipolarity of the concept "adult-child," adulthood represents an end to certain incapacities of children—as in Aristotle, their inability to acquire knowledge and to exercise sound judgment—that is, the overcoming of a deficit condition, whether cognitive, psychological, physical, moral, or legal. Norbert Elias confirms this judgment in his narration of the rise of the modern adult subject in the late Middle Ages and early Renaissance as an incremental process of instinctual and affective *separation* from the impulses and feelings of childhood, in the interests of a "private self," for whom a main concern is the development of clear, closely watched boundaries in relation to other private selves.[13]

It could be that the twenty-first century West is experiencing yet another historical shift in the adult-child balance. There are those who suggest that, as the child as we have know him or her "disappears," the classical modern adult—the one for whom "growing up" or "coming of age" meant leaving his naive, childlike medieval counterpart behind in order to brave the lonely Copernican universe—disappears as well. The most suggestive accounts single out as the prime variable in this shift a new postliterate electronic information environment, which tends to give rise to not only a child privy through the media to the mysteries and brutalities of sex and death, but what has been referred to as the "adult-child"—an adult whose emotional and discursive capacities approximate those of a thirteen year old.[14]

The ideal adult of the ancients is the "contemplative" man (sic) formulated by Aristotle and developed by the Stoics and Epicureans. The ideal adult of the early modern period and beyond is the "active" man, the one who acts from a firmly based individual perspective.[15] The late modern adult has acquired an "inner child," thus signaling a new concern with a revision of the boundaries of the contrastive pair.[16] And it is only since the 1960s that Western adulthood has been increasingly conceived as a period of potential psychological, vocational, and conjugal disruption and change, rendering grownups as liable as children to the risks, opportunities, and vicissitudes of "growth and development"—that is, more like children.

We also find historical and cultural variability, not just in the adult construal of children, but in the ways adults and children interact in real time and space—in the adult-child relation. Adults deal with two kinds of children—both the flesh-and-blood child, which the adult is called on to protect, nurture, and lead forth into adulthood; and the child the adult once was, whether interpreted as the child of memory or the child within. These two children are mutually determinative, in that the way adults relate to their own "child" strongly influences how they see children, and correlatively, their child-rearing attitudes, theories, and practices. But child-rearing attitudes and practices seem to be in a process of evolution: they change as medicine, religion, politics, technology, economics, and demographics change; whereas the adult's relation with the "child within" seems to persist in certain archetypal characteristics.

Perhaps as an outcome of the ambiguous relation between the historical child and the "child within," or mythic child, the concept "child" has a way of both attracting and continuously escaping adult projections, and this projective ambivalence makes for a wide variety of adult attitudes toward children, some of them perennial and some of them changing according to cultural fashion. In our time at least, some adults fawn over children; some treat them as if they were hardly there; some become strangely nervous and distant in their presence; some engage them with a naturalistic gusto they would never demonstrate with other adults; some feel obliged to quiz them on their status—how old are you? Where do you go to school? What grade are you in?—as if childhood were some prolonged military training episode. A historical gallery of child-rearing philosophies and practices would run the gamut from Locke's recommendations for cold baths in the morning, to the renowned distancing of the nineteenth-century British upper classes toward their offspring, to the radically child-centered parents of the contemporary USA, who attribute levels of cognitive and psychological maturity to their children that they can only maintain through a concentrated focus on their own "child within."

All of these examples point again to the extent to which the adult's construction of the child is at the same time his or her self-construction as an adult—whether through mechanisms of distancing children or attempting to relive, re-evoke, or exorcise his or her own childhood through them. This projective, involuntarily transgressive relation to the other may be true of interpersonal life in general, but it has particular poignancy and significance in the case of the adult-child relation, because the child is not just any other for the adult, but an exemplary one.

It is, for one thing, an asymmetrical situation: the child does not influence the adult with her projections as much as the adult does the child with hers—she is less powerful. And because of the child's *difference*—in height, weight, organ size and function, hormonal configuration, and neurological state, as well as, although in a weaker sense than the latter, cognitive, linguistic, affective, and motoric distinctives—she lends herself to being used as a screen for adult projections in the same way that, for white patriarchal civilization, women, "natives," the insane, animals, and the gods do. Her distance from adults makes of her a liminal figure, the representation of a limit condition of the human. Like those other liminal figures, she is easily subspeciated—whether divinized, bestialized, or demonized. She comes to represent a lost totality, a sense of *presence*—of the marriage of the for-itself and the in-itself that haunts adult consciousness, in which presence and absence are in inseparable interplay. She stands for what Derrida characterizes as a life "without differance," which adults both dread and long for: "Man calls himself man only by drawing limits excluding his other from the play of supplementarity: the purity of nature, of animality, primitivism, childhood, madness, divinity. The approach to these limits is at once feared as a threat of death, and desired as access to a life without differance."[17] But like those other liminal figures, she also represents an opening for psychological development. She is the other who finally cannot be gotten around: her radical alterity demands either violence or dialogue in response. We do not have to look far for the former; the latter, I will argue, offers an enormous promise for the possibilities of personal, social and cultural evolution.

The Western Construction of Childhood

In the realm of alterity and interhuman projection, the child typically serves adults as a sort of cipher, proof-text, or icon for their fundamental assumptions about human nature—or absence thereof—and for the politics of the human condition. Is the child a "person" from the beginning? If not, at what point, and through what processes, does he become so? What does children's pregenital, polymorphous sexuality tell us about our own? Are girls really born girls, and boys boys? Are children inherently good, or is there a root of evil, or at least of profound egocentrism, which shows itself undissimulated in children? Does humanity—starting with children—require violence, whether "the rod" or the electric chair, in order not to slip into personal and social chaos? Is psychological development a relatively organic, individually driven self-correcting process, or a form of social reproduction? Children draw visceral, involuntary projective answers from adults to these fundamental and unanswerable questions—they evoke them like lightning rods. Interestingly enough, the question, are children different across cultures? rarely evokes such responses. Adults tend to believe implicitly in the universality of childhood.

If we look at the history of those answers, we find a fault line of ambivalence running through the way childhood has been signified in Western classical and Judeo-Christian traditions. On the one hand, children get excluded from full personhood at the very start of the Western rationalist tradition. As has already been mentioned, for Plato and Aristotle children, although they have free will, lack the ability to choose, and are strongly associated with the "appetitive" nature. For Aristotle,

> . . . what desires the base and what grows wild needs to be "checked" or "pruned," and that is, above all, appetite and a child. For, like self-indulgent men, children live as their appetite directs them, and the desire for pleasure is especially strong in them. . . . For it is true that children and beasts are endowed with natural qualities or characteristics, but it is evi-

dent that without intelligence these are harmful. [The free
male, the slave, the female, and the child] all have the requisite
parts of the soul, but they have them in completely different
ways: the deliberative element is completely lacking in the
slave; the female has it but without authority; and the child
has it but in incomplete form.[18]

Plato also often associates children with slaves, women, and animals,
and both he and Aristotle group children with the "the sick, the drunk,
the insane, and the wicked."[19]

But even here—in the invocation of the human limit condition of
animals, the mad, the intoxicated—the positive side of the ambivalence
glimmers, for a perennial tradition identifies the drunk and the insane
with the "wisdom of the gods." "Drunkards and children tell the
truth," quotes the (drunken) Alcibiades proverbially in the *Symposium*
(then slyly blurts out—"drunkards anyway").[20] Children were indeed
associated in Greek mythic lore with nature and the gods, and played
parts in festivals and ceremonies to which this association gave them a
natural right. Like the gods themselves, children were marginal to the
adult world of the *polis*, and so could act as intercessors with beings
from other worlds. In Athens, a child was chosen each year to act as
intermediary between the initiates and the divine presence in the Mysteries of Eleusis.[21] The otherness of nature and the otherness of the
divine meet in the child archetype in art, myth, and ceremony—not just
in the ancient world, but in the medieval, modern, and postmodern,
under various tropes.

The ambivalent and even polarized iconic location of "child" both
evokes and locates the fault line running through the history of Western
subjectivity—between body and mind, flesh and spirit, instinctual
expression and repression, license and control, unconscious and conscious, profane and sacred. To the extent that children act as screens
for adults' projections of the first term of each of these contrastive
pairs—body, flesh, instinct, license, the unconscious, the profane—they
represent the dangerous otherness of the left hand, or "sinister" in the
Western discourses of self—the shadow, the unconscious, desire—with
which our rationalist tradition heroically struggles, wielding the
weapons of what Michel Foucault called "technologies of the self." As
representations of desire, their status—like the status of women, the
terminally nonrational (the mad), and the "primitive"—in Western
patriarchal culture is both marginal and prophetic. Traditionally, these
groups evoke both destructive chaos and the transformative potential
of desire. The child's location in this paradox of subjectivity will play

an important part later in this book, in a discussion of the role of the adult-child relation in the evolution of Western cultural values, and children's status as "privileged strangers" in the politics both of culture and of subjectivity.

The perennial ambivalence toward children travels forward in Western cultural history with greater point and focus in the Judeo-Christian formulation of childhood than in the ancient Greek. The Old Testament tradition is more or less the same as the latter; for both, "Foolishness is bound up in the heart of a child."[22] The Old Testament notion of child as "fool" in the negative sense—undisciplined, lacking in judgment, in need of strict and careful shaping—is carried into Christianity in Paul's Epistles, where we are admonished to "no longer to be children, tossed about by every wind of doctrine," and to "grow up to the mature man." But the Gospels take up the other side, thus building ambivalence toward children into the most universal founding text of the West. Jesus presented the child's epistemological difference as a spiritual advantage, and offered her as a model of receptivity to the Word. First, he alludes indirectly to the one evidence of the "left-hand" tradition in the Old Testament (Psalms) when he says, "I praise you father, Lord of heaven and earth, because you have hidden these things from the wise and learned and revealed them to infants."[23] Then, as if to make it clear that he is making more than a rhetorical gesture, ". . . he called a little child and had him stand among them. And he said, 'I tell you the truth, unless you change and become like little children, you will never enter the kingdom of heaven . . . See that you do not look down on one of these little ones . . .'"[24] Finally, when he enters the Temple, it is children who publicly identify him as the Messiah. In answering the shocked and angry adults, he then refers directly to the prophetic motif of child as knower that is present in their own sacred and immemorial tradition: "Do you hear what these children are saying?" they asked him. "Yes," replied Jesus, "have you never read, 'From the lips of children and infants you have ordained praise'?"[25]

Christianity, as Peter Fuller has pointed out, "exalted childhood and held it up as an exemplar for living . . . that a child should be put forward as an example is something quite new in the history of religions, and equally new in the history of cultures."[26] Yet the early church fathers seem to have followed Paul's view of the child as deficit and danger, and interpreted Jesus' injunction to become "as little children" in a strictly metaphorical way. The child as negative exemplar was perfected by the next greatest influence in early Christianity, Augustine, for whom—as he lamented his own jealousy, selfishness and deviancy even as an infant—she became the proof-text of original sin.

Jesus' evocation of the ancient tradition of child as unconscious master—already articulated by Lao Tzu five hundred years earlier, and present in world mythology—has had a much more gradual, more secret influence. In the real world of cultural politics, recognition of the personhood of children grew with Christianity—the Church was the first to take a consistent, articulated stand against infanticide—but it was not until the High Middles Ages, in Saint Francis, Bernard of Clairvoix, Anselm, and the increasing influence of the cult of Mary, that the radical dimension of these Jesus sayings started bearing cultural fruit. It is in the medieval mystical tradition that the child starts being mentioned as a model for positive understanding in the sphere of spiritual life and discipline, rather than just ignorance of evil.[27]

The Jesus sayings on childhood, while they can be placed in a more ancient wisdom-of-the-child tradition, also set another theme for Western self-understanding in terms of the child as exemplar of instinct, the unconscious, and desire. Christ embodies a number of mythic archetypes and motifs of the divine that had already been stated in the ancient world: the dying and rising god of ancient agricultural religions (Attis, Adonis), the god of miracle and intoxication, or the "new wine" (Dionysius), the childhood of the god (Hermes, Dionysius), the myth of the hero's descent to the underworld (Orpheus, Jonah). It is in his role as divine Fool, however—the ragged, holy wanderer with "no place to lay his head," whose involuntary, necessarily cryptic wisdom is misunderstood by the adults around him—that he identifies most closely with children. Both the Fool and the Divine Child effect a reversal of an established patriarchal wisdom tradition. Both assert the claims of a form of knowledge that comes from the margins, and therefore is paradoxical, enigmatic, even garbled, and spoken in a "prelapsarian tongue." This prelapsarian language is not conscious, but a secret language of the world that is expressed unconsciously in play. In *King Lear*, for example, only the Fool can speak the whole truth of the situation, but in riddles and nonsense, or he will lose his head. Augustine's conversion is triggered by the voice of a child chanting playfully on the other side of a garden wall. The Fool and the child differ in that one is post-adult and one pre-adult, but both point to the same thing—a transgressive wisdom, the wisdom of the liminal and the marginalized, of reversal and play and subversion of conventional norms and understanding.[28] This theme does not lack practical significance for the evolution of the adult-child relation in the West.

In addition to the fundamental ambivalence that runs through Western adults' construction of children and childhood, the child has also served as a screen for specific historical projections based on that ambivalence, none of which seem to have very much to do with the actual conditions of childhood, or adults' treatment of children. The high medieval period had its holy child; the Calvinist Reformation used the child to prove original sin, or "total depravity." For the Romantics, the child represented genius and the unity of being and knowing, or nature unconstrained. For Darwin and his followers, the child shows us the childhood of the race; for behaviorism, the child is proof-text for the *tabula rasa*, or blank slate, or drives-waiting-to-be-shaped. For Freud, childhood is present through the whole life cycle, for it is the moment of formation of a permanent style of relation between primary narcissism and the reality principle, and thus the point of origin of adult health or neurosis. For Piaget, the child demonstrates a structuralist account of the ontogenesis of rationality.[29] In all cases the child's difference makes of her a text that is just distant enough in time and experience for theory to not just appropriate, but to colonize.

Piaget, whose cognitive child was as influential in the second half of the twentieth century as Freud's affective child was in the first, also marks a clear set of preunderstandings about the fundamental issues for which children are proof-texts. Piaget's child is modeled on lower organisms engrossed in adaptive, evolutionary processes. Implicit in his developmental hierarchy is the assumption that, as Stephen Toulmin puts it, "the child's 'native capacities' are specifically pre-adapted to construct one and only one final conception of 'reality' and to reinvent the same concepts of causality, conservation, etc., in all situations—so recapitulating the cultural experience of the species."[30] Further, this "final conception of 'reality'" is, as the philosopher Charles Taylor points out, based on two directing ideas—decentration and reversibility—both of them elements of a particularly Western conception of objectivity.[31] We attain reversibility when we grasp our object as a coherent system of potential transformations, and hence as an ideally manipulable object, whose operations we therefore dominate, intellectually if not in act. For Piaget, cognitive objectivity is a result of normal development, and overcomes childhood's "egocentrism," just as for Freud the mature adult overcomes "the residues of childhood" through a "prolongation of education," that is, progressive rationalization.[32] Yet both of these analytic giants, although they maintained a deficit theory of childhood, opened the way for insights that have contradicted it, thus maintaining the tradition of ambivalence.

As a characteristic of an adult white male form of interpretation, the modern "science of childhood" tends consistently to represent the young child's own perceptions of and judgments about the world as *not* the adult's, and to distort them in the image of the bipolar adult projections sketched above—projections which remain, if not unconscious, at least suppressed. That the "child" of child psychology is as much a portrait of the adult observer as of the observed is a perfectly normal situation, were it recognized as such and explored bilaterally rather than unilaterally. The classical positivistic scientific model denies or ignores it. But the anterior unity of knower and known that the adult-child relation illustrates so well is actually paradigmatic for the human sciences, if not, as modern physics is making increasingly clear, for science in general.

Theorizing Childhood

As a form of interpretation of the other, modern scientific theory is structurally impositional and non-dialogical, since it associates truth with objectification. When it is applied to groups of exemplary others—children, women, "natives," etc.—such theory can become violent. Because it is philosophically unreflective, it is difficult to locate the divide between theory and the educational practices it legitimates, which are so constructed as to reinforce, in turn, the theory. Both theory and practice work in the service of an overarching ideology whose fundamental assumptions are more or less masked or unconscious. This is glaringly obvious in various historical racial and gender theories. The latter provide a legitimating discourse for the ideology of colonialism, which, as the postcolonial scholar Ashis Nandy has pointed out, is a close relative to what he calls the "ideology of adulthood."[33] The ideology of adulthood underlies mainstream theory and practice in education, child rearing, and children's law. Nandy's point is that the ideology of colonialism, like the ideology of adulthood, construes the "native" as "child"—immature, dependent, and incomplete. Children—if they are male and non-native—hold the promise of journeying out of this deficit condition into fully socialized adult human normality. Natives hold the promise of developing into Westerners.

The ideology of adulthood is reflected in the practices of state-mandated and provided universal schooling. Here theory works in the service of objectification and disempowerment of both children and their teachers in several ways. Theories of child development, which are characterized by a stage model, make it easy for a capitalist—a competitive, extrinsic-motivation—model of education to go unchallenged; if we already know where children are going and how, then we have arrived there before them, and can plan their journey for them. Theory also provides convenient labels—ADD, ADHD, ED, SLD, ODD, etc.—for childhood disorders that are exacerbated if not brought on by disempowering practices of traditional schooling itself. There is no dimension in impositional theory that allows for dialogue with children, so when it gets translated into educational practice, the result is not transformation through the dialectics of the theory-practice relation, but rigidification and stagnation of that relation, and intensification of habitual practices.

Like any ideology, the ideology of adulthood, which depends on and interacts with a theory of childhood, has its origins in larger issues than just those of education or child rearing. An ideology of adulthood implies a set of cultural norms that determine beliefs—and therefore institutions and behaviors—about the relationship between good and evil, autonomy and heteronomy, justice and injustice, individual and community, instinct and repression, freedom and control, the biological and the cultural, nature and supernature, a view of persons and of the nature of cosmos. If this is the case, then change in how adults see the deeper issues that inform ideology should lead to change in how they view themselves as adults, and therefore how they view children. This, in turn, should lead to change in the sort of theory that is applied to children, and to the forms of life of adults and children together, including the one we call "school." The question is whether this is a necessary causal chain. Could it work backward, or in some other combination of causes and effects? Could, for instance, a change in schooling follow from a dialogical rather than an impositional theory, leading to more widespread change in the adult-child relation, and thereby to ideological change? This direction places the burden on theory. My assumption is that the five variables just mentioned—how adults see the deeper issues, how they understand themselves, how they view children, which theory they apply to children, and adult-child forms of life—are in a relationship of mutual causality; any one or more can trigger any other or others. When theory becomes dialogical, prevailing ideology is challenged by new information, which leads to social and cultural transformation. When children are no longer reified, colonized subjects—when their voices are heard—the ideology of adulthood will change. As ideology changes, the theory of childhood and therefore the form of life of children will change, which will lead to changes in the form of life of adults. The issue is how to find a theory—that is, a form of interpretation—which allows children voice, which is where dialogue begins.

Adult-Child Dialogue

Adult-child dialogue is distinguished from adult-adult dialogue by a few complicating factors. All adults were children once, and this makes it easy for them to assume a kind of first-hand knowledge about child-hood and children—an attitude that tends to preclude dialogue, for the latter involves the bracketing of commonsense knowledge in the recognition of difference. Adults live with their own childhoods in an ambiguous state of memory and forgetting. Most experience what Freud called "childhood amnesia," the near total loss of memory of the events and the mental and emotional states of one's early years. The adult finds himself with few categories into which his early childhood experience, which seems to precede the development of conventional memory, can fit in order to be retained. Yet not only does he know he was a child once, but often still feels like a child—treated like a child, for example—or in a child's position of what Dieter Misgeld calls "having to start over"—even if he can't quite connect it with his own experience *as* a child. Misgeld says, ". . . being an adult, if treated as a matter to be achieved again and again, makes us take note that we, as adults, must sometimes think of ourselves as being *like* children in order for us to say that we are adults."[34] This creates a situation of both familiarity and strangeness that makes it easy for adults to use children as screens onto which they project their own unacknowledged psychological complexes. It sets the stage either for projective reactions to children, or for dialogue.

The child also lives ambiguously in the world of adults. She is born into and grows up in a world physically scaled to adults,[35] and scheduled, planned, ordered, and controlled by them. Until her capacities for categorization and inference are fully developed, she can only take it on faith that she will some day grow out of her childhood and into a world that fits her sense of growing autonomy and her hunger for mastery. As the adult is but is not a child, so she is but is not an adult. She herself is often impatient of, and sometimes in contempt of, her own childhood. Maurice Merleau-Ponty evokes this ambiguity: "It is true, both that adult functions are already represented in children, and that they don't mean in the same way as they do in adults."[36] Although she shares and participates in the adult's life world, that participation is not as straight-forward as it seems. Often she demonstrates a style of lived experience that differs significantly from adults'. Not only her physical vulnerability, but her emotional and behavioral lability make of her what Merleau-Ponty described as a "polymorph," neither "an absolute 'other'," nor "'the same' as us."[37] She is only discovering, or has just discovered death—first that of other living things, and in a slowly dawning way, the logical inevitability of her own. She is only just discovering murder, war, criminality and the police, theft, natural catastrophe, the intentionality of evil, human cruelty (including her own), and her own vulnerability to physical and emotional pain. She is only just acquiring the adult language games that interpret the limits of cause and effect, the definition of what is alive and what is not, the boundaries between self and other, and the metaphysics of the self-body relation.

Children's sense of time does not seem to be just the same as adults'—there is not the same balance that adults have struck between objectivized time and lived time. Children's strong drives to touch things, their intrinsically playful use of the physical environment, their sometimes startling attention to detail, their often dramatic emotional lability, their diffuse, or "polymorphous" form of sexuality—all of these and more start, as we give our attention to them, to show subtle differences, which add up to a form of life that is related yet different from adults. We recognize it, even find it within ourselves, yet also find it alien, sometimes even disturbing. Some of these differences have to do with organic factors like the neuronal environment of the brain, some with experience or lack of it, and some with culture and historical worldview. Culture and historical worldview can either play up the differences in biology and maturation between children and adults or minimize them, depending on where and how they draw the line between "child" and "adult." We gather, for example, that medieval adults shared more of the characteristics of children alluded to above than do modern adults.[38] But wherever the line is drawn, there are differences.

Whatever causal factors bring these differences about, and whether they are differences of kind or degree—or some of both—they are effective differences within the human lifeworld. They make for conflict, misunderstanding, delight, astonishment, awe, frustration, anger, attachment, etc. between adults and children, in somewhat the same way two similar cultures might have differences (e.g., Spanish and Italian) or two different cultures might have similarities (e.g., African-American and tribal African), and never really be able to distinguish what's quite the same and different. This ambiguity of difference and similarity between the lifeworlds of children and adults presents us squarely with what Alfred Schutz called the "dialectical difficulty" that arises in their attempts at mutual understanding. The passing from one "province of meaning" to the other can only be performed by what he describes as "a 'leap', . . . a specific shock, which compels us to break through the limits of this [adult] 'finite' province of meaning and to shift the accent of reality to another one."[39] This is complicated by the fact that the difference between the two provinces of meaning can vary across culture and historical period. In an epoch or a culture in which a significant distance has not opened up between children and adults—as we shall see is thought to have been the case in Europe until the early modern period—there was hardly a leap to be made. The factors contributing to the opening of this distance in the West—along with the implications for cultural development that this distance represents—will be taken up further along.

The "dialectical difficulty" that Schutz mentions is in fact the very difficulty that hermeneutics, or interpretation theory—which is a theory of dialogue—works to overcome. Hermeneutics was originally about reading texts, but it emerged from a situation analogous to the adult-child relation: people were seeking to understand texts written during one historical epoch that had become distant and even strange to another. In other words, the hermeneutical situation begins when we (adults) confront a text (child) from which we have become distant, thus creating a relation in which we encounter both familiarity and strangeness, and a certain level of alienation and misunderstanding.[40] If this were not the case, the whole interpretive process would not even be called for. "The aim of all hermeneutics," according to Paul Ricoeur, "is to struggle against cultural distance and historical alienation. Interpretation brings together, equalizes, renders contemporary and similar."[41] Like the Schutzian leap, interpretation has, as Hans-Georg Gadamer says, "to cross the abyss of historical consciousness."[42] As there is an abyss between us and our historical past, so there is a potential abyss between each individual and her childhood.

Forgetfulness is the pervasive context of our experience of finitude, and it is forgetfulness that works to create the distance between adult and child. Hermeneutics operates in a space of difference between, not only reader and text, but subject and object. It is dialogical in that the reader/subject places himself within that space of difference, in what Martin Buber called "actuality," that is "participation in a being that is neither merely a part of him nor merely outside of him,"[43] and takes it as his task to interrogate this "between." The hermeneutical relationship is particularly apposite to the adult-child relation because it denies in its very structure the possibility of the situation of objectivity that is exemplified by modernist theory. It represents a move beyond the Western objectivity-myth, in that, for interpretation-theory a science free from prejudice is impossible. There is always a set of preunderstandings—a historical-cultural horizon—from which we view the text-other. This is not only a historical-cultural horizon, but an ontological situation, which Ricoeur describes as "belonging." The "allegedly autonomous subject and the allegedly adverse object," he insists, are actually two terms of a "prior relation of inclusion" that encompasses

them both.[44] It is through the subject coming into dialogue with the
object rather than isolating it in theoretical constructs that understanding
emerges. As such, hermeneutics is theory as affinity and participation,
rather than as distance and domination. It resists the idea that through
subjecting nature—in this case in the form of the child—to mathemati-
cal/statistical construction nature can be known except partially.

It is central to the dialogical relation that the knower is changed by
the known in the act of knowing. Through opening oneself to the object
and its different meanings, one comes, not only to a new understanding
of the object, but to a new self-understanding. There is no overview that
would enable us to grasp in a single glance the whole of the object, or
even its complete context, but only the horizon of the play of our relation, and the discipline of the dialogue. "To understand," says Ricoeur,
"is not to project oneself into the text [read "child"] but to expose oneself to it; it is to receive a self enlarged by the appropriation of the pro-
posed worlds which interpretation unfolds":

> To appropriate is to make what was alien become one's own.
> What is appropriated is indeed the matter of the text. But the
> matter of the text becomes my own only if I disappropriate
> myself, in order to let the matter of the text be. So I exchange
> the me, master of itself, for the self, disciple of the text . . .
> This radical and final form of distanciation is the ruin of the
> ego's pretention to constitute itself as ultimate origin.[45]

The movement of distanciation and appropriation in encountering
texts is directly analogous to what occurs when the adult engages in
hermeneutical dialogue with children. The resulting "fusion of horizons"—to use Gadamer's well-known phrase—involves what he calls a
"moment of negativity" before another form of life, or manner of being
in the world.[46] This is equivalent to Ricoeur's notion of disappropriation of (adult) self in order to let the "matter of the text" of the child's
form of life be. It could also be described as the withdrawal of projection, in order to allow the phenomenon of the child's form of life to
appear. It is to enter the province of meaning of what Aristotle called
thaumazein, or "wonder," before the "text" of the young child. In
wonder, the stereotypic world of projection is stopped momentarily, and
things appear as if for the first time.

The appropriation of the child-text that follows the moment of
negativity is also a letting go: "It is in allowing itself to be carried off
towards the reference of the text that the ego divests itself of itself." [47]
For the adult in hermeneutical relationship to childhood, the latter has a

revelatory power. It involves a new self-understanding, which includes at the least an understanding of the child as a positive phenomenon—a real interlocutor, a full-fledged other. The adult self, thus enlarged by the appropriation of the form of life of the child, is a self to which childhood speaks more coherently from its place in the life cycle than before; correlatively, it is a self that has begun the process of re-appropriating its own childhood to some greater degree.

The adult appropriation of childhood is also the appropriation of a new or rediscovered form of knowledge. Through my dialogue with children and childhood, I am provided with a new pattern for reading experience. Gadamer associates this with the Platonic *anamnesis* or "recollection,"[48] in the sense that "what is known in the event of understanding is made present again, but not as a mere retrieval or a repetition of a past actuality."[49] Rather, it is an event into which we are continually being drawn, and which is never completely ascertained in some final understanding. The characteristic of the fusion of horizons between the adult and the child is, as in all dialectical relationships, that ultimately the "tension between the other and oneself is unsurpassable. . . . The first guiding insight is to admit of the endlessness of this task. . . . The very idea of a definitive interpretation seems to be intrinsically contradictory. Interpretation is always on the way."[50] The fusion of horizons is never complete.

The hermeneutics of the adult-child relation is a primary, archetypal example of the "belonging" between subject and object, and in fact calls into question the primacy of the individual subject. It acts to demystify the notion of the autonomous, separated adult consciousness, and of adulthood as an end state of development. It is also a hermeneutics of recollection—a restoration, or reappropriation of the meaning of childhood for the whole life cycle, and a "revelation of new modes of being"—new capacities for knowing oneself through exposing ourselves to the "text" of the child.

Even the notion of approaching the young child as a text, perhaps on the surface a most unlikely analogy, has confirmation in the modern understanding of not only myth and literature, but the unconscious itself as structured like language. This is particularly true of early childhood to the extent that its forms of life are relatively unreflective, involuntary, and spontaneous—that is, more direct expressions of unconscious structures. The form of life of early childhood can be understood as an inscription by existence itself, that is, a human text with certain universal characteristics that we find across history and culture. The young child, not yet fully aware that he is present to himself from some location beyond himself that keeps time and marks the spot, is caught up in his early childhood as in a dream. The years until six or seven are typically ones that, as Herbert Read said in his memoirs, "we seemed not so much to live as to be lived by forces outside of us, by the wind and the trees and moving clouds and all the mobile engines of our expanding world."[51] We may even loosely characterize early childhood as a universal, original form of life. Gaston Bachelard, in his epic meditation on childhood, referred to it as a "well of being"—"an anonymous childhood, a pure threshold of life, original life, original human life."[52]

The universal characteristics of the form of life of early childhood are perhaps expressed most dramatically in children's art and play, but are present to us more directly as linguistic, perceptual, cognitive, affective, and relational patterns. We sense the vulnerability and lability of this form of life, and both the beauty and the terror connected with it, as if to be a young child were often to be in a sort of fugue state. This poignant immediacy is captured by Rilke in the poem "Childhood," both in his evocation of "miraculous time," when "the streets are gleaming and ringing, all the fountains flash up from the squares," and the "senseless grief. . . dream . . . dread . . . bottomless abyss" of childhood anonymity. The young child, kneeling beside the "great gray pond," forced by something he doesn't yet recognize as himself to "have to think about the little pale face that shone up from the water, sinking," is alternately freed and imprisoned by the personal anonymity and universal humanity of childhood.[53]

The form of life of early childhood was of great interest to Merleau-Ponty, because it also represented for him an "original life," a life lived more closely in the subject-world unity founded in perception. He characterized this unity prior to reflection variously as the "tacit cogito," and *ouverture au monde* or "opening on the world," as a fundamental "intimacy between vision and the visible" and in his final formulation, "wild being." If, as he says, "the body belongs to the order of things as the world is universal flesh,"[54] the young child's perceptual, noetic, and affective modes are the text authored by this universal flesh, and it is this text we are concerned to read through our dialogue with the child's form of life. The task is to read it, not as a decipherment—as if it were a code for something that, through a formula of transformation, we could translate into adult perception, cognition, affect, or relation—nor reductively, as if it were the accidental human face of a nonhuman process of organismic development. Both of those readings are possible, and perhaps even necessary to approximate a complete account. Rather, we may read it like a narrative or poetic text—the representation of involuntary imaginative child life, which presents to me, the adult, what Ricoeur refers to as "new possibilities of being-in-the-world opened up within everyday reality." For me, the adult reader of childhood, the text of the child's form of knowledge is a redescription of reality, an "imaginative variation . . . on the [adult] real."[55]

The adult drive for reappropriation and imaginative variation is most often expressed in the play of art and literature, of myth, of religious symbolism and iconography. The hermeneutical movement of recollection is a long-standing theme, in the Western tradition at least, of adult psychological and spiritual development. The child is a central symbol for this theme, which in religion and psychoanalysis is the archetypal story of an original unity, followed by a necessary voyage into disunity or "fall," followed by the search for the recovery of that unity on a higher level. This story is a key paradigm, not just for adult development, but for the evolution of child rearing and educational practices as well, because through seeing optimal adult development as in some way a reappropriation of childhood, it links the process of adult development with our relations with the real child, the child before us, whether as son or daughter, student or friend.

The Child Before Us: Education, Parenting, and the Evolution of Subjectivity

Objectivism in whatever form is the appropriate and inevitable theoretical mode for education as mere cultural reproduction, because it remains strategically ignorant of its grounding beliefs—an ignorance made possible by an incalculable mixture of "common sense" and scientism. It is theory as force and as violence, whether that violence be personal or structural, and however it may be palliated by the presence of dialogical persons attempting naively to wield it, or simply to survive the instrumental structures it creates and maintains. It is a system that is structured according to the ideology of adulthood. We are all familiar with the force that permeates the structures of our world[56]—but to consider it inevitable in the world of education and child rearing is to foreclose on one of the most crucial possible contexts for transforming the world in the image of something other than force.

A hermeneutics of childhood calls for a form of education based on dialogue, in the notion of which is implicit the development and the "leading forth" (*educare*) of the adult as well as the child. What we have called "school" at least since the advent of universal, compulsory schooling, is in the vast majority of cases a locus of reproduction—a machine through which there is inscribed on the body and in the discourse of the child the codified violence of a society whose main engine is force. In the language of dialogical education, "school" is, on the contrary, an adult-child collective—a locus for the reshaping of adult habit and self-understanding through dialogue with the impulse life of the child as much as the shaping of the child's impulse life into habit associated with adulthood.[57] It is a place of mutual reconstruction through the forms of life of a community whose main preoccupation is the intergenerational reconstruction, through project and inquiry, of philosophy, art, science, and politics. Its overarching social goal is the formation of, not rationality but reason—in the sense that rationality is objectifying, monological, and impositional, while reason is based on reciprocity, intersubjectivity, dialogue, and negotiation.

Such a school implies understanding education as an ongoing social experiment, where child meets adult in the interests of mutual transformation. That exactly the opposite is generally the case—that the traditional school is a place where the law is inscribed on the flesh, where possibility is curbed and curtailed in the interests of efficiency and "fit" to existing norms and patterns—is no reason to commit the genetic fallacy, as the majority of practicing educators do, and assume that because it is that way it ought to be that way, or that it can be no other way. Education is not the only Western institution that toils in the service of larger structures of domination that continually betray its possibilities. We have comparatively few models of education as social experiment in the intentional community of an adult-child collective, and many of them, because they are "excluded others" to the educational establishment, are boundary cases.

The ideology of adulthood—if we follow the psychohistorian Lloyd deMause's account of the evolution of Western child-rearing modes in the direction of the "empathic"[58]—is already under deconstruction, and perhaps has been since Jean-Jacques Rousseau was moved to write *Emile*, if not before among the British upper middle classes of the late seventeenth century.[59] The fact that schools have not been in the vanguard of this evolution suggests that they were founded in the early modern period to function as mechanisms of social reproduction and state control[60]—a suspicion amply confirmed in Michel Foucault's analysis of the rise of "discipline" during the late eighteenth and early nineteenth centuries[61]—and will only change under the influence of much larger changes from outside of them. Although it would be naive to seek a model of profound social change that depends on anything but multiple influences in reciprocal interaction, the fissure that has been opened in adult self-understanding in the postmodern West is perhaps the most promising—and the most volatile—of the five variables

involved in major change mentioned above (p. 14) for the deconstruction of the ideology of adulthood and the decolonization of education.
For it is how adults understand themselves and the structure, limits and
possibilities of their own subjectivity that determines how they understand children and childhood.

Postmodern adult subjectivity is laboring under a number of influences that act to deconstruct the ideology of adulthood. The original
template for the Western notion of the adult subject, stated clearly by
Plato in his utopian treatise *Republic*, not only excludes childhood
altogether—which Plato seems to have implicitly understood as a kind
of deformity of self—but is founded upon relations of internal hierarchy and domination. His seminal characterization described the self as
composed of three elements or dimensions—appetite, volition or will,
and reason—which in order to function optimally, require the domination of the first two elements by the last and smallest. Appetite must
come under the rulership of will, and will of reason, or the consequence is personal and social chaos.[62] Plato's conception is a static,
hierarchical one—at least from our position in the history of subjectivity—which defines optimal adulthood (i.e., the successful self) as a
nested structure of domination, directly analogous to the traditional
Indo-European tripartite class structure of royalty, military, and peas-
ant.[63] This model of self traveled into the modern West through Stoic
and Christian traditions, and was rendered into a radical dualistic
ontology in early modernism in Descartes' *res cogitans* and *res extensa*.
Not only is it a coercive notion of self-formation, but from Plato until
now it forces children—whom it characterizes as naturally dominated
by appetite and self-will—in the position of chaotic, even monstrous
beings, in need of specific discipline to bring the dimensions of the self
into successful balance.

Perhaps the most influential Western model of subjectivity after
Plato's—Freud's—deconstructs this hierarchy, and places the elements
of the self not just in a more complex, but in a dialogical and even
dialectical, relationship.[64] There is still an internal politics of self in
Freud, but it is a politics in which ambiguity and mutual influence and
even interpenetration of contradictory elements predominate. Relationships of hierarchy are reinterpreted as relations of repression, displacement and sublimation—none of which presuppose conscious mastery of
one element by another, but rather fluid negotiations—and the possibility is at least acknowledged[65] of cultural influences that can minimize
repression. Most importantly for child rearing and education, Freud's
model leads to the redefinition of the human life cycle as multi- rather
than unilinear: all the phases of the cycle are represented in each one,

whether—as Erik Erikson has shown us—in prefiguration or recon-struction.[66] This shift indicates that childhood is now understood as a permanent or perennial aspect of adulthood, a dimension of subjectivity with which the adult is in continual, lifelong dialogue.

It is this dialogue within adult subjectivity that distinguishes the parent or teacher as "hermeneut" from the one for whom childhood still represents a buried or undiscovered aspect of self. In the semiotics of intersubjectivity, the character of my relations with the child before me is linked with the character of my relations with the child I still am, with whom other dimensions of my selfhood are in a continual process of dialectical reconstruction. As a subject-in-process, for whom change and development are the very conditions of subjectivity, and who has no developmental terminus beyond a continuously receding horizon of ulti-mate integration, the child I still am comes to represent the promise of a self that is a permeable structure, open to dialectical transformation and less liable to the habituated ruts of adult subjectivity. The vertiginous character of this shift from self as closed to open structure in the post-modern West is lost neither on its advocates nor its conservative critics. The politics of subjectivity is the deep undercurrent of the culture wars of our time, and the school has become a strategic field of battle—per-haps even, for now, more strategic than the family, for it is here that children are initiated into the forms of intersubjectivity of the culture as a whole.

Questioning childhood means questioning adulthood, and ques-tioning adulthood means reconsidering the goals, processes, and funda-mental values of the life cycle—which means, in turn, reconsidering our mutual relationships, both individual and collective, whether economic, political, or sexual. Childhood represents one point of convergence of these reconsiderations, and signifies the ever-recurring possibility for social and cultural transformation. To repress that possibility is to repress our own possibilities as a species and its capacity for reconstruc-tion. The chapters that follow take up that possibility along multiple lines of inquiry—historical, mythological, artistic, literary, psychoana-lytic and, finally, educational. What emerges from their interplay is, simply put, a sketch for cultural evolution based on the evolving adult-child relationship. On a biological level, the phenomenon of neoteny—the prolonged childhood of the human species—could be considered to be the key ingredient in that evolution, for it represents the plasticity of the species. My argument revolves around the assumption that the lived world of childhood is the open space in the human experience for cul-tural transformation; and that as children are progressively accorded the status of full-fledged interlocutors with adults, that space will bloom in ways that have been characteristically suppressed until now, and the human experience will, however slowly, change to allow—as the Romantic poet and philosopher Samuel Taylor Coleridge put it at the moment of the discovery of childhood in the modern West—each of us to "carry the feelings of childhood into the powers of manhood."[67]

2

The Primordial Child

"Comment vivre, sinon édeniquement?"
—Eugene Ionesco[1]

The Divine Child

The passage from childhood to adulthood is one of the grand narratives of the modern West. Its subplots are various and complex, and can be traced in the history of manners, in the transition to universal literacy, in colonialism and all its hidden and explicit assumptions, in the ideology of evolutionary theory, in the eternal politics of what is knowable and what is not, in forms of spirituality, in attitudes toward the body and the natural world, and in the ongoing reconstruction of subjectivity. The story Enlightened Westerners tell each other about themselves is about "growing up," about leaving childhood behind. Paradoxically enough, but in keeping with the hermeneutical relation sketched in Chapter 1, it is also about discovering (or inventing) childhood, to which the designation of the twentieth century as the "century of the child" attests. This apparent contradiction seems to indicate some sort of dialectical movement.

The modern West received its original command to "grow up" from the same tradition—Christianity—which heaped honors on childhood in its own right by connecting it with divinity. Both can be seen as psychocultural messages that traveled from the ancient into the modern world through their formulation in Judaic and Christian scriptures and Stoic philosophies. St. Paul's injunction to "put away childish things," and his emphasis on watchfulness and self-control carry forward the classical Greek and Roman disdain for, even impatience with, childhood. Paul's adult as not-child became a subjective template for Christian adulthood that did not reach full effect until the rise of the modern world in Protestantism, the centralized state, "Enlightenment," universal education, capitalism, and the emergence of a form of subjectivity characterized by different self-other and self-world boundaries.

On the other hand, God came as an infant in Jesus, thereby exemplifying the archetype of the *puer aeternus*, or primordial child—that recurrent motif of myth, scripture, dream, and fairy tale—as an infant or young child, often of divine origin, usually an orphan or a foundling, who, in C.G. Jung's formulation, is a "paradoxical union of lowest and highest."[2] The adult Jesus also identified himself clearly with the poor and the marginalized—among whom he counted children, who were characteristically minor, lesser, not worthy of full adult attention. This unequivocal identification with the underclass, in a world in which only freeborn Greek or Roman men were recognized as full persons, was revolutionary, and may be understood as a legacy that the West is still struggling to appropriate. Certainly it problematized childhood, which could no longer be seen as a state—like the animal's—without reason. In fact Jesus' famous saying "for the kingdom of heaven belongs to such as these,"[3] suggests a higher reason—something akin to the Platonic *intellectus*, which is beyond *ratio*, or mere reasoning. The form of knowledge that Jesus associates with young children is taken up again by Paul in *1 Corinthians*, where he develops the inversion further in the notion that the wisdom of God is "hidden," and "spoken in a mystery," and that it is "foolishness" to the Greek rationalist tradition. Paul calls on the one who "thinks he is wise by the standards of this age, to become a 'fool' so that he may become wise."[4] Thus in the life and practice and teaching of Christ, the child and the fool—both of whom subvert adult models of knowledge and conduct—become models of spiritual knowledge and development. This particular epistemological tradition of an other, subversive knowledge, held by those who seem to be least in the adult world, is not only perennial in the West—where it has taken philosophical as well as theological forms—but is found in cultures throughout history.[5]

Like the tendency to view children either as quasi-animals or little adults, that tradition which sees childhood—and in particular early childhood—as either embodying, or as prophetic of, a form of knowledge that is qualitatively different from that of adults, is also based on experience, although perhaps of a less common variety. The tradition of the young child as knower of an expanded world that shrinks and fragments in adulthood is typically associated with religious or spiritual traditions, whether expressed in scriptures, gnomic sayings, folkloric and mythological motifs, psychoanalytic data, various wisdom traditions, literature, art, or mystical experience. It even insinuates itself into the confessions of the man who contributed most to the association of the child with original sin: Augustine's (354–430) famous conversion experience in the garden has all the characteristics of this tradition of the child as unconscious spiritual master:

> I was asking myself these questions, weeping all the while with the most bitter sorrow in my heart, when all at once I heard the sing-song voice of a child in a nearby house. Whether it was the voice of a boy or a girl I cannot say, but again and again it repeated the refrain "Take it and read, take it and read." At this I looked up, thinking hard whether there was any kind of game in which children used to chant words like these, but I could not remember ever hearing them before. I stemmed my flood of tears and stood up, telling myself that this could only be a divine command to open my book of Scripture and read the first passage on which my eyes should fall.[6]

This incident strongly conveys one of the characteristic marks of the tradition that understands the child as expressing a form of knowledge lost or mostly unavailable to adults. What distinguishes "infant" from adult is her inability to speak (*in*="not", *fari*="speak")—that is to make sense, to reason, to frame discourse. Like the wise beast in the fairy tale, the *infans* is the unconscious guide of the adult mind cut off from its own intuitive ground by the inherent limitations of its own discursive framework. The same figure operates in the classic Western Fool, whose babbling riddles conceal true knowledge. The child's very marginality to rational discourse is a form of discourse itself—the discourse of nature before the Fall, of a being directly in touch with its source and ground. The child is so profoundly and unconsciously grounded in her own existence and free of the tyranny of speech and reason, that truth proceeds from her every word and action as from an oracle. This archetypal knowledge theme assumes a connection between innocence and wisdom; the child represents Edenic consciousness, a state of psychic equilibrium such that even—and especially—her apparently nonsensical play expresses a sort of knowledge that shows forth the essence of things, and reveals us to ourselves.

The "primordial child," "child god," or "divine child"—found in religion, myth, literature, film, and dreamwork is a symbolic expression of this kind of knowledge. Because of the way it symbolizes, Jung added it to his taxonomy of the archetypes of the collective unconscious. The motif is characterized in mythic narrative as an infant or young child, often of divine origin, and usually an orphan or foundling—thus a "paradoxical union of lowest and highest, weakest and strongest"— who survives abandonment, trial, and persecution through extraordinary, elemental sorts of powers, representative of the powers of the unconscious. The mythologem of the child god is usually hermaphroditic or androgynous (note Augustine's "whether it was the voice of a boy or a girl I cannot say"), a primary being: its elemental origins make of it a representation of "a state of being not yet separated from notbeing, yet still being,"[7] a form of psychic nondifferentiation that manifests as a numinous form of integration.

In the infant god or hero, the mythologem of the *puer aeternus* or "eternal child" expresses a form of intentional consciousness characterized by psychological wholeness and integration of which the adult is aware as a memory and a potentiality, but perceives himself as not possessing. The figure appeared to Jung's patients both in dreams and through his therapeutic technique called "active imagination." Jung understood this "bisexual, primordial being" as "a symbol of the unity of personality, a symbol of self, where the war of opposites finds peace. In this way the primordial being becomes the distant goal of man's self-development, having been from the very beginning a projection of his unconscious wholeness. Wholeness consists in the union of the conscious and unconscious personality."[8] Often it manifested as the Christ child; but it also emerged from earlier, altogether non-Christian levels— out of chthonic animals such as crocodiles, dragons, serpents, or monkeys. Sometimes the child appears in the cup of a flower, or out of a golden egg, or as the center of a mandala. In dreams it often appears as the dreamer's son or daughter or as a boy, youth, or young girl; for white Westerners, it occasionally seems to be of exotic origin—Indian or Chinese—with dusky skin; or, appearing more cosmically, it is surrounded by stars or wearing a starry coronet. Sometimes it appears as the king's son or the witch's child with daemonic attributes.[9] Jung interpreted the appearance of the archetype in dreams and psychotherapy as a herald, "smaller than small and bigger than big," which appears in anticipation of future psychological development, initiating the individuation process—an emergent synthesis of unconscious and conscious elements of the personality that Jung refers to as the Self. As such this symbolic child is also a mediator and a healing figure, representing a form of psychic energy that unites the opposites and thereby makes whole.

The apparent insignificance and powerlessness of the mythic child figure—its characteristic history of abandonment, exposure, and danger—testifies, not only to a world where, well into the eighteenth century, child abandonment was routine, but on another (and perhaps analogous) level, to the precariousness and difficulty of the self's attempt at wholeness and integrity. But as in the mythic narratives nature itself cradles the abandoned child hero—as, for example, the infant Dionysius was hidden and protected from an infanticidal Zeus by the nymph Leuca—so our instinctual life secretly nourishes this "inner child," which represents the ineluctable drive in each being to realize itself, however small and vulnerable its origins. "Child" also recognizes an original psychological—and to a certain extent cognitive—state of indissociation between subject and object, knower and known, an unconscious identity of self and universe that is inscribed in perception itself.

The original wholeness out of which human development cuts a limited, if functional field of action and meaning through processes of separation, distinction, hierarchization, and typification, is for the adult both a pre- and a postconscious condition—a place of origin and a terminal state. As such, it represents the unity of consciousness implicit in the drive for self-realization. One emerges from and returns to childhood. "Child" must always accompany "adult" as its contrastive pair. So for depth psychology, "child" is what is too small to see emerging—a form of knowledge lost through the vicissitudes of development but always in the process of being regained dialectically through further development, which is the key to the integrity, or wholeness, of the self.

The child archetype found its most universal and compelling Western historical statement in representations of the infant Jesus with his mother; but that infant-mother dyad, which became a major theme in the medieval and Renaissance epochs, and which stated the archetype in a definitive way, is a confluence of several themes that were already present in the ancient pre-Christian world. The idea of the humanation of God in an infant is found, if in a relatively confused and idiosyncratic form, in the infancy of Dionysius, and the Jesus/Mary pair is already foreshadowed in goddess/child pairs from at least 2000 BCE in Cycladic idols, in Mycenean statuary, and classical representations of Aphrodite/Eros, Isis/Horus, and even Demeter/Triptymelos. Although early Egyptian, Greek, and Roman representations are usually idealized portraits of children as parts of families, the divine child is a psychological icon, a sacred character—anonymous, numinous, and universal.[10]

The naked *eroti* who flooded the Hellenistic world of art are the primordial child multiplied and genericized—the iterative, fractalized body of Eros, or Love, who in ancient myth unites heaven and earth. Their trademark is an innocent sensuality that was later reappropriated in the *putti*, or "cupids" of Renaissance art, where they find their way into both pagan and Christian themes. There they accompany both Aphrodite in her *amours*, and the Holy Child and his mother—and even God the Father, or the adult Jesus as he comes from heaven to carry off a dying or enraptured saint. Often they appear in legion, filling the sky. In their representation in pagan themes, these naked, playful super-toddlers are often depicted in contact with the elemental forces of nature— wrestling playfully with a swan, riding a dolphin, or even riding rams, panthers, lions, officiating serenely over preliminaries to the act of love or accompanying the dead to the underworld. Some are winged. Josef Kunstmann connects them with "daemons," or intermediaries between heaven and earth, creatures who connect the above and the below, the holy and the profane. The naked toddler, in his uninhibited play, releases and secures the connection between the sensual and the sacred. Like their original prototype Eros, who was first represented as an adolescent, the *eroti*, according to Kunstmann, "combine the most unlikely contrasts and hold together body and soul, heaven, earth, and the underworld."[11]

The Orphic sect worshipped Eros as the creator of the world. For Plato he represented the desire to create in beauty—he who evokes in the soul the memory of the primal Ideas. But there is also, from the beginning, a curious ambivalence about this naked youth. The mythic tradition identified both a lofty (Uranios) and a base (Pandemos) Eros, matching the dual aspects of his mother Aphrodite. Boethius (480–524) said of the god whom Homer ignored, he is "the most beautiful of the immortal gods, who loosens the limbs and restrains the temper of all men and gods, but who also overthrows wise counsel."[12] The *eroti* represent both the fleshly nature of the spiritual and the spiritual nature of the fleshly—opposites that, when not promoting ecstatic unity, tempt excess and bad judgment.

But in fact they were appropriated by Christian art—if not with the gusto of their pagan counterparts—quite early. They are found on early Christian graves and sarcophagi playing with hoops and balls (symbols of the soul), or placing wreaths on the heads of husband and wife. They are identified with the guardian spirits of early Christianity, but retain their erotic function as the element that knits things up in love and makes them flow, while their demonic element—the possibility for "pandemonium"—is muted or elided. They appear to have no symbolic connection with the child Jesus—who first appears in late Hellenistic times as well—but in this case with his mother, nursing, in a second-century fresco in the catacomb of Priscilla.[13] The representation of the nursing mother was already present in the worship of the Egyptian Isis, who is generally represented nursing Horus; in fact the form of icon called Virgo Lactans appears to have traveled to Byzantium and the West from the Egyptian church.

Thus, both the toddler-eros and the mother-child pair existed before Christianity. The former dropped out of Christian art in the late fifth and early sixth century[14]; the mother-child pair was consolidated in Byzantine Christian iconography, where the divine pair assumed the stiff, formal, hieretic posture that we associate with early Christian art. Until the end of the twelfth century, the divine child of the Byzantine icon is much closer to a *puer senex*, an "old man child," than an *eros*. This is not surprising, given that the purpose of Byzantine iconography is to represent an ideal of adulthood—the Divine Wisdom, the Word (and by implication, Reason) Incarnate. This child, seated on his mother the God-bearer as on a throne, one hand extended in blessing, is the timeless adult Person of the Christ, and his expression is very similar to that of the equally popular icon of the Christ Pantocrator or "all powerful," which represents Jesus as manly hero. To argue that the Byzantine Christ child is a "little adult," as some historians of childhood have done, is to at least partially misread the icons.[15] However, they do seem to indicate that for patristic Christianity, the identification between the infant Jesus and either real children or the primordial child had been muted.

It is commonly accepted that it was in the transition from the Romanesque to the Gothic period in the late eleventh and twelfth centuries that the stiff, hieretic mother and child pair began to soften, and their humanization began. Actually it was a process with its roots deep in earlier centuries. Representations of the Virgo Lactans in which the infant Jesus was represented with sensitive realism can be found at least from the ninth century on.[16] These images of Jesus as an actual infant, done with observant subtlety, were both the first representations of an emerging naturalism in Western art, and a restatement of the association between early childhood and spirituality so strongly marked in the Gospels. Truth had already been represented as an infant during the Carolingian Renaissance, and the soul is also typically represented as a child in medieval art—often shown as a tiny, naked infant emerging from the mouth of a dying person.[17] But the association of Jesus with real human infancy signals the activation of the child archetype as a spiritual and developmental ideal in Western psychohistory.

The growing emphasis on the "appealing humanity" of the divine pair which started in the twelfth century is both a cultural reappropriation of the Jesus sayings about children and their natural spirituality, and the fruit of attention to real children. The increased prevalence of oblation—the giving over of children to monasteries to be raised up for the Church, at least from the fifth century on[18]—led to increased sensitivity to their characteristics. St. Anselm (1033–1109) was particularly sympathetic toward children, and Bernard (1090–1153), founder of the Cistercian Order, based his teachings on the connection between the real, human infancy of Jesus, and adults' needs to "become as little children" and be converted.[19] The revolutionary spirituality of St. Francis (1182–1226), which exploded on the world in the early 1200s, summarized the medieval tradition of the "holy innocent," and the Christian identification of the young child with *homo religiosis*. The Franciscan movement was a powerful, summative statement of the medieval (i.e., Christian and Platonic) epistemology of the sacred: in a world turned upside down, where *doxa* (opinion) and *ratio* (mere reason) ruled, the higher knowledge (*intellectus, noesis*), apprehended nondiscursively, becomes a subversive knowledge, the domain of the Fool and other marginalized ones.[20] Francis encouraged a childlike spontaneity and lack of decorum in his Christian practice that combined the notion of a "foolishness for Christ's sake" with that of the simple faith and dependency on God of a little child on its parent. The knowledge of the Fool for Christ was dangerous, in that it was anarchic, existentially charged, and threatened established practices.

The end of the Middle Ages and the emergence of the early modern world in Renaissance art and thought saw the reemergence of the toddler-*eros*—a result both of an ever-increasing naturalism in Western art, and of the Renaissance rediscovery of antiquity. In the Renaissance, this figure appeared again both in the image of the traditional classic *eroti*—who were now found crowding the borders of paintings, or hovering in clouds of infant flesh—and also in depictions of the Christ Child as infant or toddler with his mother. In fact it is instructive to follow the artistic representations of the Christian Mother and Child through this period, because it shows, as if in a photographic time-lapse, a process of naturalization of the divine child culminating in the High Renaissance, which then moved on, in Mannerism and the Baroque, to a sort of reversal, through which the natural child was in turn divinized, thus forming one iconographic basis for the nineteenth-century Romantic image of the young child.

The early Renaissance representations of the divine pair, true to the model provided by the Byzantine icon, present mother and child as both looking gravely outward at the viewer, as befits the divine Word and its human matrix, the Mother. The first softening and naturalization of the image appears when the child turns to his mother, and they gaze at each other. This motif is actually first suggested in the Byzantine *Eleousa* or "mercy" icon type, in which their cheeks are pressed poignantly together. But the motif, along with the Virgo Lactans (the mother nursing the child) and the Hodegetria (the mother carrying the child, who is seated on one arm), traveled to Italy in the twelfth and early thirteenth centuries, where its gradual naturalization began the trend that finished in the Mother and Child portraits of Raphael and Michaelangelo. In the Italian painting of the Dugento and Trecento, the *Eleousa* throws off, in the words of art historian Victor Lasareff, its "Byzantine austerity and abstractness."[21] For example, in the Lorenzetto altarpiece in Pieve, Arezzo, 1320, mother and child gaze at each other in intense mutual regard. In Fra Filippo Lippi's *Madonna and Child* of 1455 (Uffizi Gallery, Florence), the child is shown reaching for his mother with outstretched arms. In Hans Holbein the Elder's Madonna and Christ Child of 1510 (Kunsthistorisches Museum, Vienna), the child is seen holding or reaching for a ball, symbol of the universe. And gradually, in a steady, traceable progression, the child is represented with fewer and fewer clothes: in Fra Angelico's *Madonna of the Star* (c. 1430, San Marco, Florence), the child is in royal dress; in Lippi's *Madonna of Tarquinia* of 1465 (Barberini Gallery, Rome), the child is clothed only from the waist down; in Quentin Massay's *Madonna with Cherries* of 1490 (Flemish, Ringling Museum of Art, Sarasota), the child wears only a wispy loincloth; in Raphael's Cowper *Madonna* of 1505 (National Gallery of Art, Washington), the child is completely naked.

As the Renaissance progresses, the familiar postures and gestures of the real child became increasingly recognizable in the Holy Infant. Here he is reaching for an object or for the breast, there grasping the mother's breast and looking up into her eyes as if in the first or last moments of nursing, or pressing into the mother's body in a cuddling motion, or stretching away from the mother while in her arms, often with his arm out as if indicating something. The Divine Child appears with a finger in his mouth, or with the recognizable alert smile of the six-month-old infant, or demonstrating the startle reflex, or involuntarily mimicking the mother's expression, as infants do. The child grasps the mother's neck with one hand, as if to kiss her or rub cheeks, or reaches to touch her mouth, in typical infant fashion. Offered a gift by the Magi, the child reaches forward very realistically to grasp it with both hands. A close reading of the iconography shows increasingly detailed and sympathetic observation of infant behavior and affect by the painters of the divine pair. All that is lacking, curiously enough, in this gradual naturalization, is a realistic representation of the proportionate size of head to body among infants, which is different from that of adults. Even in the

High Renaissance, painters still represented the head-to-whole body proportion as the adult ratio (1:8) rather than the larger ratio of infants and toddlers (1:4 and 1:5). The adult head-to-body proportion is the last vestige of the Word of God as *homunculus*—of the Infant Christ as an adult in a child's body.

This movement of increasing realism, corresponding to the gradual secularization associated with modernity, reached, in the High Renaissance depiction of the Mother and Child, a balance between the natural and the divine which stated the archetype of the divine child with a power and immediacy that is still profoundly influential in Western mythic iconography. In its early sixteenth-century formulation, the archetype is completely humanized, but expresses none of the sentimentalism or sensuality that accompanied its further naturalization from the mid-sixteenth century on. Its power as an image is a reflection of the fact that in the emergent Christian incarnational theology of the Renaissance, the *infans*, rather than the Christ Pantocrator or the Christ Crucified, became the primary icon and psychological symbol of self. This is accomplished, as is characteristic of the period, through a synthesis of Christian and pagan themes: the child has the sensual beauty and playfulness of the ancient *eroti*, and the Queen of Heaven has the qualities of Aphrodite Urania, goddess of celestial love. Thus the pair evokes, as striking a note evokes a harmonic, the pagan through the Christian pair, and summarizes thousands of years of images of the archetypal dyad.

The naked child god is, for a Christianity reencountering the Hermetic tradition, an alchemical philosopher's stone. He is spiritual flesh and fleshly spirit, and so represents the *coniunctio oppositorum* of both Christian and pagan spirituality. As Jesus is the second Adam, the "Messiah of Nature,"[22] the naked infant Savior is the first icon of the cosmology of Renaissance incarnational theology: "a world restored to admirable perfection."[23] The Incarnation announces a rectification and sanctification of the created order, which implies the restoration of the Adamic body in its original, sexual glory, made in the image of the glory of God.

In his polymorphic love-play with his mother, the child also evokes Eros—both the licentious Eros of the Olympians in the arms of his mother-consort Aphrodite, and the Eros of the Sixth Book of Plotinus' *Enneads*, whose beauty lures Psyche (the soul) back toward the One and the "true life."[24] So in some representations, Christ the Infant Spouse reaches to cup the chin of the mother with his palm—a conventional erotic gesture in ancient iconography.[25] As an evocation of both Amor and Psyche and Eros and Aphrodite, the naked child in amorous interaction with his goddess mother is central to the Renaissance attempt at a synthesis of Christian and pagan themes. Christian neo-Platonism set about to find the hidden Christian prefigurations in the pagan mysteries, and the pagan elements expressed in the Christian, and one of its main vehicles in this search was art. As Leo Steinberg has suggested, "What the Christian art of the Renaissance took from pagan antiquity was the license to plumb its own mythic depths."[26] The visual symbol became of prime importance to this search, for it was assumed to have the capacity to reveal realities that are not expressible in discursive speech. In the Renaissance, this principle of church iconography began to be applied beyond the church, leading, as the historian of art Erich Gombrich has said, to "the opening up, to secular art, of emotional spheres which had hitherto been the preserve of religious worship."[27]

Marcilio Ficino (1433–1499), a major voice in the Renaissance synthesis, adopted the Platonic idea that the highest knowledge is not properly described as cognition, but as love, which "embraces" cognition.[28] He wrote: "Since the good is far superior to the intellect, and its fruition is hence not correctly named intelligence, it appears that it also should not be called cognition: for it is more natural and more desirable than cognition." What distinguished Ficino's use of the Platonic *noesis*, or direct intuitive knowledge of the whole, was his characterization of it as a kind of "frenzy," a being taken beyond oneself, a form of joyful experience strictly analogous to the "joy of the senses," or *voluptas*. On this account, the rigor of spiritual will or *voluntas* actually becomes *voluptas* when it expands from finite to infinite. This is only in keeping with the thought of his master Plotinus himself, who, according to Edgar Wind, "repeatedly advised his disciples to model their expectation of spiritual joy on what they knew of the delusive joys of the senses."[29] The drive for spiritual knowledge is appetitive, and based on a love and a desire for the beauty of the world that is sacramental. What the Christian neo-Platonism of the Renaissance sought was a revelation of the fundamental connection between *eros* and *agape*, the two forms of love that had been separated in the Christian tradition. And the vehicle for this revelation of knowledge as appetite, will and reason integrated became the child, who, as the divine child, is sacramental flesh, the resolution of Plato's tripartite self without resort to internal hierarchy and domination.

In the history of the Western dialogue between reason and desire, the divine child and the Queen of Heaven communicate this ecstatic balancing of pagan *eros* and Christian *agape* through representing the divine archetypes in increasingly realistic form. The process of the secularization of the mother-child icon during the Renaissance reflects a psychohistorical internalization of the archetypes. Instead of being worshipped "out there" in a statue or icon, the gods and goddesses—including the divine child—are discovered within, as both individual and cultural possibilities. They are recognized as archetypal patternings of the unconscious—thematic elements in the process of psychological and spiritual development that Jung called "individuation," whereby conscious and unconscious dimensions of the self are brought into ever-further integration, with a corresponding decentering of the executive function, or ego.

The child-mother icon of Renaissance incarnationalism communicates its fundamental meaning "in a flash"—not through a direct one-to-one correspondence, laboriously unpacked, or within a doctrinal framework, but given all at once. Nor does it have only one identifiable meaning, but carries, as Gombrich described such symbols, multiple meanings, apprehended nondiscursively in the interaction with the symbol itself. It is what he called an "open sign," which "penetrates to new and unexpected categories of experience," and has a magical quality that derives from its character as an intermediary in a cosmos of correspondences and sympathies, where microcosm and macrocosm are understood as a "series of concentric circles surrounding the ineffable unity in an ever widening distance." Through the mediation of the analogies between these levels of being, the archetypal symbol has, according to Gombrich, the power to "impart to the image something of the power of the spiritual essence which it embodies."[30]

Beyond—if implicit in—the Christian and hermetic motifs that overflow in the luminous naked child archetype, the image represents for the psychology of persons a total, unashamed world-openness, a form of being in which the self-consciousness that characterizes the adult is overcome—in which "inside" and "outside" are one. The naked child evokes self revealed in a unity, an integrity that is regained for consciousness only through the long and arduous journey into the division of adulthood and beyond. And if we understand—as is common in dream analysis—child and mother as aspects of one person, together they comprise the primal unity of the androgyn—the "bisexual primal being" that characterizes the divine pair Aphrodite and Eros.[31] Philosophically, the pair represents the unity of knowledge and being, of mind and nature; psychologically, the "primary narcissism" that Freud characterized as the infant state, which for the adult is a lost paradise. Phenomenologically, it evokes the form of knowledge of the child, which is immediate and nondiscursive, and not dependent on the stereotypifications of language and cognitive schemas. Each of these evocations is central to the nineteenth-century Romantic formulation of childhood and its importance in the life cycle, which will be taken up below.

When the naked child is not in amorous interaction with the mother, but held among other adults—particularly in depictions of the Adoration of the Magi, and the paintings of the Madonna and Child with the saints, another symbolic aspect emerges. Nothing could better communicate the stunning glory of the flesh revealed in its restoration than setting it off against a surrounding group of fully clothed, intensely concentrating adults. All the bodies of the adults, in various stages of age and experience, are hidden, but stand in astonishment and grave wonder before the insouciant, gleaming nakedness of Desire. If, for purposes of analysis, we bracket out the narrative of this child as God-King of the universe—or even keep the narrative but assign to it a psychological and archetypal rather than a purely historical or theological emphasis—the extent to which the divine child is the "inner child" of all the observing adults becomes more insistent. On the psychological level, these scenes are object lessons in the developmental command of the Western wisdom tradition that calls on each adult to be "born again," and "become like a little child."

Finally, the divine child of the Renaissance reemerges, as we have already seen, in the *eroti* of the earlier Hellenistic period, now become cupid-angels, who reassert their function as mediators between flesh and spirit, earth and sky. We find them particularly in paintings where heaven opens up, and they are seated, hovering, or flying just on the boundary between earth and heaven. In his analysis of Raphael's widely reproduced Sistine Madonna (1514, Royal Picture Gallery, Dresden), Kunstmann compares the two *eroti* posted on the picture plane to "sentries" at the transition point between the real and the visionary worlds, mediators between time and eternity, inner and outer space.[32] They are expressions of the elemental sympathy by which the whole cosmos is held together in the divine love, the "impossible" union between *eros* and *agape*. Nor have they lost the ambivalence that they had in Hellenism, for they are also present wherever erotic pandemonium suggests itself—as in the effulgent Venuses of Titian, or the woodland revels of Silenus and his entourage.

The direction of the representation of the divine child from the Gothic onward was one of ever increasing realism and naturalism. Although "real" children were depicted relatively infrequently and usually as marginal figures in Renaissance art, the trend toward realism was part of an emergent secularism in a West "coming of age" in early modernism, which understood itself as no longer preoccupied with mere "myths." Yet at its point of balance in the High Renaissance, the new realism was used in the service of the mythic—to justify the faith in the divinity of Christ, and to summarize the archetype of the divine child with a new, not just theological, but psychological immediacy. In its struggle to integrate pagan and Christian spirituality, Renaissance art found that the more realistic the body and behavior of the divine child, the more the mystery of the "humanation of the divine" is revealed, and the better incarnational Christian theory makes its point. The more the child acts and looks like a child, the more astonishing and significant his divinity appears, and the more we recognize in his own psychological unity the goal—set before us rather than in our past—of our own development as adults. The "little child" that the paintings instruct us wordlessly to become is here represented, not as a limitation or even a return, but as a further synthesis, beyond the necessary fall into the division of adulthood. The child announces the unification of the opposites—flesh and spirit, mind and heart—which is the goal of human development. And it is of particular dialectical significance that it was here, at the onset of an epoch in which "adult" became a cultural, psychological, and epistemological ideal, that the child archetype took on this personal, psychological interest for adult development, and that God—the primary image of wholeness—was stated not as an adult but as a naked, playing infant.

In keeping with the growth of a naturalistic ideal in modernism, the mythic elements of the child archetype experienced a subtle but increasing obscuration as the art of the Renaissance reached its apogee and was transformed along with the world it was representing. This was already reflected in the legendary psychological accuracy of Leonardo's (1452–1519) work, whereby even the figures of the holy family, while presented in a fully traditional manner, show with an almost uncanny immediacy their individual, idiosyncratic personalities, which tend to deemphasize the mythic and archetypal elements. In Michaelangelo (1475–1564), the brooding interiority of the *human* began to make earlier painters like Raphael (1483–1520) look psychologically naive.

This more radical naturalism of the High Renaissance increased steadily through Mannerism and the Baroque. In the sixteenth and seventeenth centuries, painters like Caravaggio (1573–1610), Parmigianino (1503–1540), and Rubens (1577–1640) created transitional forms between the iconography of the humanation of the divine and a naturalistic iconography from which the divine seems to have withdrawn. In Parmigianino's *Madonna with the Long Neck* (c. 1540, Florence, Uffizi

Gallery) the flesh of the divine pair itself is numinous, rather than evoking or expressing the *noumenon*. Ostensibly, it assumes the iconographic tradition of Renaissance incarnational theology, but there is a not-so-subtle change toward the glory of the carnal in and for itself, rather than the glory of redeemed or redeeming carnality. A spiritualization of pure immanence begins to replace the naturalization of the spiritual that incarnation implies. Rather than the divine taking on body, the body in itself comes to be seen as divine—or, if not as divine, as complete in its immanence, represented in its erotic beauty, through which it comes to reference only itself, rather than to point beyond itself. When the sensuality of the *eros-agape* union is portrayed in this increasingly naturalistic style, it becomes—for example in the *Madonna with the Long Neck*—sexually provocative. Heaven has drawn away from the divine pair, leaving them as direct, unequivocal objects of desire.

In sixteenth- and seventeenth-century European art, the infant Christ-Eros, although he by no means disappeared, began to lose his symbolic power, and to become—as for example in Jose Ribera's *The Holy Family with Saint Catherine* (1648, Metropolitan Museum, New York)—merely the youngest member of a rather mundane-looking holy family, now portrayed as a unit, in idealization of Europe's emerging middle class nuclear family. In Northern Europe, children began to appear in family portraits, which, for the Protestant bourgeoisie became a new sort of icon. The golden age of seventeenth-century Dutch art reveals the modern, newly "invented" child of the middle classes, typically portrayed with her mother, as in de Hooch's (1629–1684) portraits of domestic life, or dressed up for a family portrait. These portraits, which at first glance seem to portray children as "little adults"—an impression created by the fact that they wear the same clothes as adults—when given close attention, show a sensitivity to the nature of children—their gaze, their posture—which is in continuity with Renaissance naturalism, but which has escaped the melodramatic sensuality of mannerism. The archetype of the divine child is muted, if only in the fact that the child is portrayed as a part of a larger group, or when with her mother, in a mundane activity setting. When the divine child motif does appear, particularly among the French and English aristocracy, it is either as an occasion for a refined prurience or as a legitimation of royal power; it has become an iconographic marker in the politics of class.

The rise and ascendency of the bourgeoisie made of the painter a social observer rather than a theologian. The Dutch child dressed in his father's clothes is no less a child, but his new, more prominent but also more strictly controlled role in the adult world is what the paintings convey. This child is the subject of much more attention—she has entered history. She now carries the clear marker "child," with the corollary assumption of one who is being socialized, with the help of child-rearing manuals and schools, into adulthood. Children have become important to parents in a new way, as necessary actors in a new social project—whether Protestant pietism, early capitalism, or some combination of the two. The Reformed vision of piety emphasizes the priesthood of the believer, the home as spiritual locus, and the necessity (given the now universal availability of the Bible, and its importance) of literacy, and therefore of education, for proper development. All of these factors place the child in a new position, both of fond attention and of a new constraint.

The direct, unequivocal expression of the divine child would not appear again in Western art—and then with a quite different sort of emphasis—until the English aristocratic portraiture of the late eighteenth century that heralded Romanticism. In these completely secular portraits of the children of the aristocracy, the archetype is still present as a certain *otherness*, signified in the paintings of a Reynolds (1723–1792), a Gainsborough (1727–1788) or John Hoppner (1758–1810) by paradisiacal or haunted woodland settings, full or partial nudity, and dreamy or exalted facial expressions—for example in Hoppner's portrait of his own children (The National Gallery, Washington). Shrouded as it is in the new meanings of childhood that had by then been imposed on children for about a century, the representation of the archetype moves toward, not the proclamation of a goal of adulthood, but a melancholy critique of the rationalized Enlightenment adulthood of the late eighteenth century—a form of adulthood that feels itself increasingly to be cut off from its own childhood. This critique would become a major theme of early-nineteenth-century Romanticism, and a trigger for a movement that reinstated the divine child as a prophet of psychological integration.

Child alienation in a newly adultocentric world already haunts Velasquez's late seveenth- and early eighteenth-century paintings of Spanish royalty. Although Velasquez was used as a propagandist for the court, his paintings aspire to tell the truth. Among others, the great psychological painting *Las Meninas* (*The Maids of Honor,* 1656, El Prado, Madrid) captures with dreamlike precision the felt world of the child placed in this new cosmos. Here the Infanta Dona Margarita is both the central figure of the painting and an outsider to her own childhood. She provides a prophetic glimpse of the final production of modernism—the Freudian child. Her parents' appearance in the mirror behind her (and the absent presences at whom she is looking) suggest they are introjected images, and her retinue, so both slavishly and indifferently attentive (including a faithful animal) can, by a slight displacement of the imagination, be seen both as the real people they are, and as creatures of her imagination, dream-figures in the tortuous narrative landscape of childhood.

Las Meninas can also be understood as a first statement of a modern twist on the divine child—the "enigmatic child," the child who has become a mystery to the adult, who is too removed from childhood to experience it as anything but an ambiguous message from another world.[33] The Infanta's watchful, removed facial expression, her stiff, adult dress, her gaze fixed on an absent presence, her encirclement by a troupe of retainers who, given her overwhelming centrality, appear almost as other aspects of herself, reflect that different sort of wonder that, from the mid-nineteenth century on, surround fictional and poetic representations of children. This too is a divine child—an enigmatic symbol of intimate otherness—but it is a symbol of alienation, akin to madness and animality, both of which are also "divine," rather than unity. It reflects a new distance between adulthood and childhood, rather than a recognition of the psychological centrality of childhood throughout the life cycle. Thus, the ever-emerging iconography of modernism finally closed around the mythological theme of the divine child, and expressed it negatively rather than positively.

The periodic neoclassicisms of the modern world, when they do invoke the ancient themes, do so with either a sentimentality or a self-conscious eroticism that is a mockery of the power of Renaissance symbolism. The "cute" erotic child of the world of advertising[34] may be said to be yet another image of this child, in which the spiritual evocation of divine carnality, or "innocent flesh" has become all flesh, and the Eden to which she points an Eden of soaps, diapers, and baby foods. But the divine child also appears periodically in spontaneous images, for example in William Zorach's *Affection* which evokes the Hellenistic putti riding dolphins, or wrestling with geese. And Phillip Evergood's *Lilly and the Sparrows* (1939, Whitney Museum, New York) portrays the edenic unity in a tenement window. There is no longer a tradition like the Christ Child to carry the archetype, but it emerges spontaneously in images that are, as they were in the High Renaissance, also the most phenemonologically accurate, in that they tend to express characteristics of the young child's lived experience which we recognize from our observations and interactions with children themselves.

The Romantic Child

The primordial child is an image of our own forgotten, monumental, half-remembered and half-projected childhood,[35] of the child that the adult still is, and on another symbolic level—the level of the archetype—of all new beginnings, of the promise of future wholeness, a condition of psychological integration that many adults experience as both a lost and an emerging continent. The *mythos* is a cultural and historical construct, based on a fundamental Western theme of the human life cycle as a fall into fragmentation and a restoration to unity—death and rebirth, the loss and recovery of a primary unity. It is a mythos that in fact has broken into historical, cultural time during certain periods, and shaped the thinking of artists, poets, and a few philosophers. Since its banalization in the Victorian middle-class construction of childhood, it has lived a sort of half-life in popular sentimental art and advertising, where its revolutionary implications are captured and tamed, and it is used as yet another instrument of the colonization of childhood, and of the legitimation of class and gender stereotypes.

The Romantic child of the modern West does not, as is commonly thought, appear for the first time in the late eighteenth and early nineteenth century, but in the seventeenth. In fact we can locate three periods in the history of the West during which the child became a subject of special interest among adults: the fourteenth century as expressed in St. Francis and his Order; seventeenth-century Anglican England as expressed in certain of its poets; and in the Romantic tradition of the early nineteenth century.[36] Like the late eighteenth and early nineteenth centuries on the continent, seventeenth century England was a time and place of violent, often incoherent change and cultural conflict. A preoccupation with childhood has in fact been identified with periods of rapid, unsettling change, and explained as an urge to regress to a happier, more stable time. This may be true; in fact modernism itself, in its deepest character, is identified with rapid, transformative change. It is also true that the modern preoccupation with childhood is continuous with a long tradition of formulations of the archetype.

It was the major Anglican poets of seventeenth century England—specifically Henry Vaughan, Richard Crashaw, Thomas Traherne, Andrew Marvell, George Herbert, and Robert Herrick—who first explored the archetype as a modern theme, which is to say from the point of view of self-conscious adulthood. The themes that emerged in strength in nineteenth-century Romanticism are first expressed here: childhood as a lost paradise, childhood as a form of knowledge no longer accessible to adults, "growing up" as a diminution of a native world-openness, and the unbridgeable distance between childhood and adulthood. These poets undertook the first important exploration of the lost paradise of childhood from the perspective of the adult separated from his childhood in a new way, and hence a first example of the modern hermeneutics of childhood.

Except for Andrew Marvell, all of them approached childhood within the framework of the Christian exhortation to "become as a little child," but with a new sense of discontinuity from childhood that was not present in its medieval expression—whether in Francis, Anselm, or Bernard. Crashaw (1613–1649) revels in images of a return to the mother's breast, and understands salvation as a divine play before God. For Vaughan (1622–1695), as Leah Marcus, in her study of the seventeenth century English poets of childhood has pointed out, "childhood and adulthood are separated by a tremendous gulf." The poet knows himself only as one cut off from his source in the "white designs" of childhood, and thereby separated from the sacred as well. Childhood is for Vaughan an "age of mysteries, which he must live twice that would God's face see." But the poet, whose "soul with too much stay is drunk, and staggers in the way," searches in vain to feel again "through all this fleshly dress bright shoots of everlastingness," which he identifies with childhood.[37]

This new sense of the spiritual isolation of the adult, to whom the child becomes an often enigmatic messenger from a lost realm of universal connectedness (which, as the "enigmatic child," could sometimes be a universal pathology), is taken up with a precociously modern irony in Marvell (1621–1678), in his exploration of how growing up is also a losing of one's "home" in the natural world. The adult's is a fallen world—a world of time, decay, death, and the alienation and psychological division introduced by sexual experience. The adult's "double Heart" makes of him a creature divided against himself, and every attempt to regain singleness and unity of self through sexual passion simply increases the sense of division. As a counterpoint to this newly alienated adult, the child is a figure and an expression of the Adamic, androgynous person, in whom body and soul, heart and mind, are still in harmony. But to contemplate the unity of consciousness of the child is in itself ironic, because of the adult's knowledge that it passes, and that any attempt on his part to reenter this world is doomed. This new melancholy understanding comes to self-conscious expression a century later in Thomas Gray's "Ode on a Distant Prospect of Eton College" (1742), where adulthood is understood as a metaphor of a doomed state, a fallen condition, but a necessary one. The poet is trapped in a paradox, in that to be an adult, he must accept the painful knowledge of the loss of a richer world; while to remain a child is to renege on the possibilities for growth.[38]

Thus is first heard the theme, prevalent in the West thereafter, of adulthood as a condition of being "outcast from Paradise," and of childhood, as Robert Pattison has put it, as a "medium through which the poet can look to gain perspective on man's fallen place in a fallen world."[39] For the poet Thomas Traherne (1637–1674) on the other hand, the unity of consciousness represented by early childhood is not merely one stage in the life cycle, passed through and forever lost, but a form of knowledge obscured in "coming of age," and is in fact the goal of spiritual development. Traherne re-evokes the Christian notion—which finds secular expression roughly a century later in Wordsworth—that the childhood "paradise" is not just one stage of the life cycle, but an ever-present psychological reality capable of informing every stage of our lives, and which in fact is the origin of the poetic imagination.[40] As for the exemplary Romantic William Blake the poetic genius, or "Imagination," is the essence of our spiritual nature, so in Traherne what he calls "Glory"—the goal of psychological development—is a condition in which subject and object, perceiver and perceived, form a unity in which the distinction between real and imagined becomes meaningless, with the result that the world is seen and understood as the paradise it is.

Traherne's view of the child stands between the Gospel tradition, which associates childhood with religious conversion ("I must becom a Child again,"[41]), and Romanticism, which understands the imagination as the power through which we unify experience, and the child as paradigmatic of the "innocent eye," in whose unity of vision all objects take on the paradisiacal meaning and beauty of first creation. Traherne's child is both exemplar and first citizen of the living, personalistic cosmos that was falling in ruins during his lifetime, a "naked, simple, pure Intelligence,"[42] whose primal, visionary "Infant-Ey" perceives in direct immediacy the lineaments of a spiritual universe of which nature itself is a luminous expression. Each human infant repeats Adam's experience in Paradise: his union with the world, before his fall into the sinful condition of human custom, is so complete that "every sense/Was in me like to som Intelligence." For the infant Traherne,

> The World resembled his *Eternitie*,
> In which my soul did walk;
> And every thing that I did see
> Did with me talk. . . .
> My naked simple Life was I. . . .

The Sense its self was I. . . .
This made me present evermore
With whatsoere I saw.
An Object, if it were before
Mine Ey, was by Dame Nature's Law
Within my Soul: Her Store
Was all at once within me; all her Treasures
Were my Imediat and Internal Pleasures, ...[43]

At first glance, Traherne appears to be presenting an idealized vision of childhood. A closer look suggests that in fact the subject-world interpenetration he is describing in this passage and in many more is a commonplace in the twentieth-century psychological interpretive tradition of infancy and early childhood. Melanie Klein described the fundamental movement of the Infant-Ey as "introjection," J.M. Baldwin as adualism or indissociation, Freud as "primary narcissism," Heinz Werner as "fusion," D.W. Winnicott as "transitional" or "potential" space; and in the phenomenological tradition, Merleau-Ponty evoked it when he spoke of that primary coexistence or reversibility of body-subject and world that he called chiasm, or "wild being." Traherne also neatly characterizes young children's animistic world view, their qualitatively different mode of temporalization, and what Piaget characterized as epistemological "egocentrism":

The East was once my Joy; and so the Skies
And Stars at first I thought; the West was mine:
Then Praises from the Mountains did arise,
As well as Vapors: Evry Vine
Did bear me Fruit; the Fields my Gardens were;
My larger Store-house all the Hemisphere.[44]

Whereas for Piaget "egocentrism" is an index of cognitive deficit, later to be overcome in the development of the capacity to "decenter" and entertain multiple perspectives, Traherne's infant egocentrism does not exclude others, but is in fact a form of boundarilessness—an acentrism or "infinity," which lives in compelling immediacy the fluid, relational unity of the subject-object field. It recognizes itself in the world and the world in itself. This is a central element of what Ernst Cassirer called "mythical thought," in which, as he describes it, ". . . the rigid limit between 'inside' and 'outside', the 'subjective' and the 'objective' does not subsist as such, but begins, as it were, to grow fluid. The inward and outward do not stand side by side, each as a separate province; each, rather, is reflected in the other, and only in this reciprocal relation does each disclose its own meaning."[45]

What in fact Traherne is projecting in his work is an image of the lived experience of early childhood as a form of knowledge that could be called "sacramental," in that it operates in a participatory mode, and grasps its object through a unifying act of the imagination, rather than through the division implicit in analytic knowledge. It is this form of knowledge that Romanticism, in reaction to the objectifying epistemology of modern science, undertook to explore more than a century after Traherne, and which reemerged in psychoanalytic theory yet another century later in Winnicott's notion of transitional space. Traherne's is a preliminary statement of Romantic epistemological themes, and a bridge between their religious and psychological expressions. And the uses he makes of infant awareness—to see it as both a founding, original state and as a goal of adult development, is a first psychological interpretation of Jesus' command to "become as a little child."

Traherne also stated other major themes that later preoccupied certain Romantics.[46] One was the loss of continuity between childhood and adulthood, and the sense that they represented two separate manifestations of the self. The adult not only must attempt to explain the relationship between that self and this one, but to explain how they could be so different. For the modern adult, childhood is a lost world; for the poets of childhood of the seventeenth century, a lost paradise. To regain it was not a matter, as it may have been with Crashaw or Vaughan, of a regression, but of a dialectical reappropriation, involving the journey out of what Traherne called Innocence, through the stages of Sin and Grace, and on to Glory, which recovered the original openness to the world that was given in childhood. So Traherne could say, "I perceived that we were to live the life of God when we lived the true life of nature according to knowledge: and that by blindness and corruption we had strayed from it."[47]

The way was prepared for the Romantic theme of finding the lost connection by the decline, at the end of the eighteenth century, of the literary genre called Pastoral and the rise during that same period of the childhood autobiography, or Childhood.[48] Both genres deal with an original innocence, destroyed by a fall. In the earlier Pastoral, a primary world in which nature and society are in perfect harmony—Arcady—is interrupted. In the Childhood, the arcadian world has long since receded beyond the view of social possibility and all that remains of it is one's childhood. The process of memory and the project of reappropriation occurs, not—as in the Pastoral—in the mythic history of the race, but in the history of the individual, and it happens in real time and place, in the story of each individual's passage out of childhood. This primitivist myth is associated in turn with the grand narrative of the dialectical cultural evolution of the species, stated in Christian myth as the expulsion from Eden—followed, after much travail, by a restoration in Christ, the "second Adam." For this tradition the fall is a necessary moment of development, and hence in retrospect a "happy fall." The original unity must be broken in order for development to take place: the fall into division is part of a process analogous to the one identified in modern organismic developmental theory of differentiation in the service of the articulation and reorganization of parts in "higher"— meaning in this case more adequate to the environment—unities.[49]

This guiding myth of development took on increasing poignancy and power with the social, economic, and psychological dislocations— and the resultant new aspirations—which reached a new intensity in connection with the French and the Industrial Revolutions. Before that time, childhood was considered unworthy of any but the most cursory mention by memoirists. The disclaimer by the mid-eighteenth-century French writer, Antoine Bret, is representative: "I shall pass," he writes, "rapidly over my first years of life. There is nothing in them savory enough for the curiosity of readers; almost all childhoods are alike."[50] Later in the same century, that attitude was changing under the influence of what Lawrence Stone termed a new "affective individualism," which he identifies with the rising middle classes. This, in turn, was connected with two other related aspects of modernism—a growing concern with personal identity, and a pervasive sense of religious crisis. If the roots of identity were no longer to be found in kinship, a tight-knit social structure, or, for an increasingly mobile population, geographical stability, it meant a crisis for the individual, who now sought his or her personal resources within the nuclear family—of which children were an essential part. The new interest in the child that emerged in the eighteenth century was related to all those forms of middle-class life that we recognize as characteristically modern: an emphasis on personal privacy, on warmer affective relations between husband and wife and parents and children, an increasing separation of the nuclear family from the surrounding community, and thus an increasing separation between public and private life.[51]

The search for self undertaken by the progressively deracinated adult led him or her back to childhood, which now represented the possibility of finding a sense of identity independent of the fugal character of the secularized life cycle. The search for identity became an obsessive theme in modern literature, and the search for one's own childhood in the memoir a primary exercise in self-recovery. This is already present in Traherne, for whom the Infant is, if not the higher, truer self, then the originary, prophetic manifestation of that true self, to be recovered through adult spiritual discipline. As the poet Georges Bernanos said, "The deadest of the dead is the little boy I used to be. And yet, when the time comes, it is he who will resume his place at the head of my life."[52]

The religious crisis that was symptomatic of the Western middle classes in the ages both of Enlightenment and Romance, made of childhood the Eden from which the adolescent, experiencing the loss of faith in Church and creed, was expelled. It is significant that childhood came to represent religious experience, because such experience, given the young child's place before religious discourse, is necessarily not one that can be described in terms of confessional doctrine. So, as in Traherne's account, the spiritual experience lost in leaving early childhood is the existential experience of the numinosity of the natural world—the "glory" of wildflowers and grains of sand. It is a condition of perception rather than an exercise of the will, as Christianity more typically was for the adult. Traherne says:

> Everything was at rest, free and immortal . . . The corn was orient and immortal wheat, which never should be reaped, nor was ever sown. I thought it had stood from everlasting to everlasting. The dust and stones of the street were as precious as gold: the gates were at first the end of the world. The green trees when I saw them first through one of the gates transported and ravished me, their sweetness and unusual beauty made my heart to leap, almost mad with ecstasy, they were such strange and wonderful things. The Men! O what vulnerable and reverent creatures did the aged seem! Immortal Cherubims! And young men glittering and sparkling Angels, and maids strange seraphic pieces of life and beauty! Boys and girls tumbling in the street, and playing, were moving jewels. I knew not that they were born or should die; but all things abided eternally as they were in their proper places. Eternity was manifest in the Light of Day, and something infinite behind everything appeared.[53]

The spirituality of early childhood identified by the Childhood is just that unity with the world that the adult can hardly remember, but which is offered as a state to be reattained. So Traherne said, "I knew by intuition those things which since my Apostasy I collected again by the highest reason." To mistake this spirituality for an other-worldli-ness, as in the Victorian popularization of the "cult of childhood," is to misunderstand the fundamental intuition of Romanticism, and what Romantics saw in early childhood. In probably the clearest statement of the significance of childhood for Romantic thought, the German drama-tist, historian and first philosopher of childhood Friedrich von Schiller identified children directly with "nature," by which he understood the existence of things "in accordance with their own immutable laws," and which he associated with "genius." We love in the elements of nature—under which he includes children—"the serene spontaneity of their activity . . . the inner necessity, the eternal unity with themselves." We recognize that, like other elements of nature, they are creatures of necessity, whereas we (adults) are "free," and so we do not envy them, but we "see eternally that which escapes us, but for which we are chal-lenged to strive, and which, even if we never attain to it, we may still hope to approach in endless progress." Schiller clearly articulates the reversal that characterizes the hermeneutics of childhood: childhood comes to lie, not only behind the adult, but in his future, as something to be reappropriated. "The child," he says, "is therefore a lively repre-sentation to us of the ideal, not indeed as it is fulfilled, but as it is enjoined."[54]

This is the case because, in the crisis of modern Western subjectiv-ity, the adult is almost by definition denatured. This is both an ontolog-ical and a historical situation. For Schiller, "We"—Western Faustian moderns—"impetuously fled abroad in the arrogance of our freedom" into a form of civilization that has become our prison. "Nature in us has disappeared from humanity," we "are not at one with ourselves"[55]; "the essential bond of human nature was torn apart, and a ruinous con-flict sets its harmonious powers at variance." The child assumes great importance for the implications of this fall, because "our childhood is the only undisfigured nature that we still encounter in civilized mankind."[56]

This sense of a being stranded outside nature—feeling for nature "like the feeling of an invalid for health"[57]—is not represented by Schiller as a falling into corruption, or decadence, or the straying away from an original innocence to which we can return by a simple reversal, but as a necessary self-alienation associated with the life cycle, that is, a developmental phenomenon. The "sensuous harmony" of the child—the "correspondence between his feeling and thought that in his first condition actually took place, exists now only *ideally*; it is no longer within him, but outside of him, as an idea still to be realized, no longer

as a fact in his life." In fact in the Romantics the limitations of childhood as "nature" are fully realized and accounted for. It is the developmental calling of humans, both the individual and the species, to
abandon nature and undergo division. The hidden agenda associated
with the conflict between "sense and reason, passive and active faculties,"[58] is the reunification of mind and nature, which can be attained in
no other way. Mind must abandon nature in order to recognize its own
individuality, its autonomy, its infinite, unconditioned character in order
finally to be reconciled to nature in freedom and the moral order. It is a
tragic calling, in the sense that we give up a limited perfection, undergoing a "dismemberment of . . . being,"[59] in order to strive for a perfection that we understand to be an infinitely receding goal. "The goal to
which man in civilization strives is infinitely preferable to that which he
attains in nature. For the one obtains its value by the absolute achievement of a finite, the other by approximation to an infinite greatness."[60]

Like Traherne, Schiller reformulated the child archetype in psychological terms. If more ironically than Traherne, and with a new secularism, he re-included the child in the life cycle—not as an absence, a
deficit, or even just a lost paradise, but as an original statement of a
form of knowledge that it is the goal of the human journey to reappropriate. The final goal—if infinitely receding—of the adult is in fact a
state of "innocence" that is characteristic of children, but which in
Romanticism is stated as both an individual and a social condition. It is
a secular restatement of Christian millenialism, the idea of, not a return,
but a progression to paradise. The gates of the original paradise of
infancy are barred by the angel with a flaming sword: the Eden of childhood is broken by the self-consciousness, the double-mindedness represented by the tree of knowledge. The goal of human development is
reunification.

Schiller is critical of Rousseau, whom he accuses of "preferring to
restore man to the spiritless uniformity of his first state in order simply
to be rid of the conflict within him, rather than to look for the termina-
tion of that conflict in the spiritual harmony of a completely fulfilled
education." Speaking of the modern poet, who in Romanticism replaces
the mystic or the saint as the hero of psychological and social development, Schiller says, "Let him not lead us backwards into our childhood
. . . but rather lead us forward into our maturity in order to permit us
to perceive that higher harmony." Humanity, which cannot now go
back to Arcady, must be led "forward to Elysium."[61]

For the Romantic imagination, the second unity is a revolution of
consciousness whose final goal Schiller states succinctly as a reconcilia-

tion of the opposition between "actuality and the ideal"—that is, an actualization of the ideal and an idealization of the actual, a condition towards which Hegel, the grand philosopher of Romanticism, saw all historical time as ultimately moving.[62] The child stands for this end state, and signifies it in a number of ways. The young child, for example, is premoral, and free from fixed social roles. She lives the ideal in the actual in the sense that the boundaries between the time and space of the unconscious and the time and space of the self-aware ego are still permeable and interactive. As has already been pointed out, the child psychoanalyst D.W. Winnicott referred to the psychological space between self and world in early childhood as "transitional" or "potential"; it occupies a psychological terrain that is "outside the individual, but . . . is not the external world." It is a space into which "the child gathers objects or phenomena from external reality and uses . . . in the service of . . . inner or personal reality."[63] Correspondingly, in the recovered psychological Eden of the Romantic imagination, the opposition between "inner" and "outer" has been entered, fully experienced, and overcome. This ideal was carried for centuries by Christian millenialism; in the Enlightenment, it was posited politically and socially— by Reason rather than by God—and in Romanticism it became a psychological and cultural developmental ideal. As a social and psychological vision, it is equivalent to the end of history. As Reinhard Kuhn characterized it in his discussion of the Surrealist movement of the early twentieth century, "a triumphant childhood will be the model for life" in a society "based on the transparence of its inhabitants and the subsequent perfection of their inter-relationships."[64]

The Romantic ideal, at whose heart the "Infant-Ey" dwells as a sort of talisman, is put in more concrete if no less ambitious psychological terms by William Wordsworth, whose adult, upon leaving a childhood balanced perfectly between the "elemental polarity of mind and nature" discovers nature as an alien reality, severed from mind. Their reintegration, which is the goal of the life cycle, is equivalent to a marital union between the two. Through this union, nature, which was a victim of the ontology of death of Western philosophical materialism, is reanimated, and becomes again as it was in the universe of childhood, where in "all things I saw one life, and felt that it was joy." Wordsworth's marriage is not a step outside of time, but the outcome of human process, temporally determined. In the union, "Paradise, and groves Elysian" are experienced as "a simple produce of the common day." The redeemed world is the ordinary world of life's everyday appearances, in which perception itself is renovated, and the seeing and feeling eye itself, "wedded to this goodly universe in love and holy passion," experiences the joy of unconditioned existence, and thereby finds the world transformed.[65]

The reanimation of the perceptual universe characteristic of Wordsworth's vision is a reappropriation of the panvital cosmos of the premoderns, based on a psychological rather than a theological rationale, although it certainly could have theological implications. Perception transformed in joy now "reads" the book of nature—the ancient Christian *liber naturae*—and finds "all things there look[ed] immortality, revolving life, and greatness still revolving, infinite." This renewal of mind in nature through the imagination results, in turn, in a society of persons that "is here a true Community, a genuine frame of many into one incorporate. . . . One household, under God, for high and low."[66]

Like many of his generation, Wordsworth was in his youth a passionate supporter of the ideals and goals of the French Revolution. His desire for social transformation was not secondary to his thought, but was deeply influenced by the failure of that most crucial of social experiments. Having experienced the end of Enlightenment in the Terror, he rejected the possibility of a planned utopia based on social engineering, and henceforth assumed that the inner transformation of the individual can be the only basis for a society redeemed from endemic structural evil—which is nothing more (or less) than the principle of radical separation. Romanticism is the Revolution internalized, a transformation of consciousness in each adult, prefigured for each adult in his own childhood, which points to the infinite task of the formation of a human society in which, as in early childhood, the distinction between public and private self is abolished, we "live and feel in the present," and live a "unitary, undivided existence." The polarities that make for the "dividedness, alienation, and inner deadness of modernity"—polarities between spirit and matter, mind and nature, desire and contingency—are overcome, leading, in Schiller's words, to "a conflict fully reconciled not only in the individual, but in society, . . . a free uniting of inclination with the law, of a nature illuminated by the highest moral dignity, briefly, none other than the ideal of beauty applied to actual life."[67]

The developmental goal of the Romantic adult is also profoundly informed by childhood through its relationship to play, which is the *modus operandi* of children. For Schiller, the human ontolological vocation is to build—in a dialectical overcoming of the polarization of spirit and matter, of reason and the sensuous—a "third joyous kingdom of play and of semblance, in which man is released from all that might be called constraint, whether physical or moral." The "aesthetic state" is the form of consciousness of a "'new age' in which mankind will achieve on earth the fullness of freedom, community, joy, and intellect."[68] In fact Winnicott calls the form of subjectivity characterized by transitional or potential space the "third area of cultural experience" or "third way of living," "sacred to the individual," which he opposed to the subject in an instrumental relationship with an external world in which the object is a fixed reality; or, conversely, in which the subject is a "unit self," characterized by the "limiting membrane" of discrete boundaries. He founds this intermediate area of experience in the mother-infant relationship, and describes it, as we have seen, as a form of subjectivity in which the inner and the outer are still in a fluid relation, a "potential" space "between the subjective and that which is objectively perceived." Winnicott associates the "third way of living," not just with the experience of infancy and early childhood, but with culture and creativity, and with art, religion and philosophy in adult life.[69]

Both Schiller and Winnicott described the primary dimension of this form of subjectivity as play. Play, in the words of the former, describes "everything that is neither subjectively not objectively contingent, and yet imposes neither outward nor inward necessity."[70] As a form of knowledge it is paradigmatic of the active universe of Wordsworth's "first poetic spirit of our human life," a mind that "creates, creator and receiver both, working but in alliance with the works which it beholds"[71]—that is, a form of dialogue between knower and known, and thus a radical constructivism. This first poetic spirit is given (or, according to Winnicott, not given, depending on the mother's capacity to provide a "good enough" environment for its development) in the first relationship—in "mute dialogues with my Mother's heart," in the experience of a form of communion with the world in which "all knowledge is delight"[72]—which is to say, the primary narcissism that is our first condition, and to which all experience is implicitly compared thereafter.

Play most perfectly represents the balanced, interactive unity of self and world in which the internal division of the inner person has been reconstructed as a higher, more articulated subjective equilibrium. The adult will reach again her complete humanity when she has reincorporated the "infant sensibility . . . great birthright of our being,"[73] in which intentionality will again become structured as play. Historically, Westerners have, according to Schiller, "surrendered the wholeness of their being to pursue truth along separate roads." But this very surrender was in the interests of a higher state of development that is manifested in the realm of play, for "in every condition of humanity it is precisely play, and play alone, that makes man complete and displays at once his twofold nature."[74] The play impulse exemplifies the union of mind and nature that was Wordsworth's ideal, and which made of the young child, for him, a symbol of greatest significance for an inquiry into subjectivity, and thereby the basis of a philosophy of human nature.[75] Once it is understood, as Eugen Fink put it, that "Being in its totality functions like play,"[76] then play becomes an ontological framework for our understanding of the subject-world relation, and an individual and cultural ideal.

Romanticism, Education, and the New Humanity

The Romantic uses of childhood involved not only its emblematic character as prophetic of a psychological and sociocultural goal, but, more practically, the actual historical work of the creation of that goal—the "third joyous kingdom" or "third way of living"—and the social construction of a style of human subjectivity which makes it possible. The history of the Romantic period in Europe and even the U.S. is filled with extraordinary social experiments—experiments that extend to the level of the reconstruction, not just of economy, but of family and sexuality. The communist impulse and aspiration was in no way created by Marx, but he provided it with a grand theory of history. The two socialist visionaries Saint-Simon and Fourier were spiritually affiliated with Wordsworth and Schiller to the extent that they understood the fundamental reconstruction of social forms as in mutual causal relationship with the reconstruction of subjectivity.

The efficient cause of Romantic social and political theory was the social nemesis of rapid industrialization, the accumulation of capital in the hands of the few, and aggressive centralized state control of populations. Universal compulsory education, which emerged during the early nineteenth century, was fueled, not by a concern for a marriage of mind and nature, but by the ambition of the increasingly hegemonic and reactionary nation-state and its dominant elites to shape the world to their political, social and economic interests. The reproductive goals of state and economy and the technological ambitions of the Industrial Revolution made early and increasingly binding alliance: the "factory model" of schooling is virtually synonymous with universal education in the West. Seen dialectically, this harnessing of education to individual and social repression and economic exploitation may have been necessary in order to create a society with enough economic surplus to allow for the leisure necessary for the universal emergence of the "third way." If this is the case, the West is now in a prolonged and difficult transition, for the circular problem that plagues this hope is that the economic justice necessary to distribute the surplus in a way that is necessary for the transition is not possible except as a result of the transition itself.

Romanticism was the first revolt against the society of what Herbert Marcuse called "surplus-repression," which he defined as the "modification of the instincts" required by the particular "reality principle" of the modern Western social and economic system, which is characterized by the unequal distribution of resources and economic and political and class domination by particular groups or individuals, resulting in dramatic economic inequalities and a large proportion of alienated labor. As he puts it:

> . . . while any form of the reality principle demands a considerable degree and scope of repressive control over the instincts, the specific historical institutions of the reality principle and the specific interests of domination introduce *additional* controls over and above those indispensable for civilized human association. These additional controls arising from the specific institutions of domination are what we denote as *surplus-repression.*[77]

Marcuse refers to the prevailing form of the reality principle in Western civilization as the "performance principle," which he associates with a specific, unequal organization of scarcity, the existential attitude this organization requires, and the domination by privileged groups necessary to keep this particular reality principle in place. Under the performance principle, both body and mind are transformed into instruments of alienated labor, and they can function in this way only if they renounce the "freedom of the libidinal subject-object" that is the fundamental characteristic of the human organism.[78] The signs of surplus-repression and the performance principle have hung over state-mandated, universal compulsory schooling from the moment of its emergence. As such public, universal state-mandated and/or provided education must be understood as an instrument of repression in the hands of the specific interests of domination. The institution of the school is the site where the body and mind of the child are subjected to the existential attitudes and dispositions—most specifically in the relation between work and play, and analogously, reason and desire—necessary for the maintenance of those interests.

The Romantic vision of social reconstruction, in which, as Schiller said, "conflict [is] fully reconciled not only in the individual, but in society, . . . a free uniting of inclination with the law," may seem hopelessly utopian, but in fact it represents a dialectical response to a form of life, emergent in capitalist industrialist economies in the early nineteenth century, of growing social dystopia in the onset of an instinctual economy characterized by surplus-repression, splitting, and alienation. As early as the publication of Rousseau's *Emile* in 1764, the subjugated "citizen," or "mass man," had already been counterpoised against the "man"—the individual in whom mind and nature, law and freedom, reason and desire are in creative, transformative relation. In his classic statement, "We must choose between making a man and making a citizen. We cannot make both,"[79] Rousseau prophesied humanity colonized by the state, the subjected, "docile body" of the individual domesticated by the technologies of that new form of the distribution of power that Foucault later called "discipline." Discipline inscribes the culture of surplus-repression deeply in all human institutions, then represents them as embodiments of liberated rationality.

What is significant about Rousseau's prophecy of mass man in *Emile* is his implicit claim that any culture in which the experience of childhood is not allowed its place will be a culture in which the developmental possibilities of adulthood will be stunted. His educational anti-theory, which swept the British and European intelligentsia at the moment of the Revolution, has nothing to do with curriculum or pedagogy. The point of transformation for him is the adult-child relation. The effective teacher is the one who legitimates childhood as a life phase and empowers children through allowing their forms of knowledge full play in the world. "Childhood has its place in the scheme of human life. We must view the man as a man, and the child as a child. . . . Nature wants children to be children before they are men,"[80] he insisted; and Friedrich Froebel—who carried Romantic thought directly forward into educational theory—added "the boy has not become a boy, nor has the youth become a youth, by reaching a certain age, but only by having lived through childhood, and, further on, through boyhood, true to the requirements of his mind, his feelings, and his body; similarly, adult man has not become an adult man by reaching a certain age, but only by faithfully satisfying the requirements of his childhood, boyhood, and youth."[81] A form of education is necessary that allows the child to "live through"—only in this way will an adult emerge who is able to reappropriate the "third joyous kingdom" through the dialectics of the lifelong developmental process.

For Romantic thought, the ideal education would then reestablish the continuity between childhood and adulthood that was felt to have been lost, and make it possible for the feelings and perceptual modalities of early childhood—now obscured in amnesia because they are so radically different from adult modalities[82]—to be retained into adult-

hood. This is a first statement of that reevaluation of the role of childhood in the life cycle that, two centuries later, the influence of Freud has
turned into a normative assumption, and which has the greatest significance not only for the future of child rearing and education, but for the
evolution of adulthood as well. The Freudian revolution in human self-
understanding has convinced us that childhood and adulthood are in
fact not two distinct periods of the life cycle, destined to supplant each
other, but parts of a continuum that is both diachronic and synchronic.
Each is always present to the other within the whole, and it is the
dialectical relation between the two that drives development.[83] To the
extent that Freud suggests a form of human subjectivity whose dimensions are in interactive, dialogical relation rather than in relations of
hierarchical domination, so the question of childhood becomes essential
to an understanding of adult subjectivity; and the question of education
becomes essential to the historical problematics of this understanding.

If we reconceive the life cycle as no longer only sequential and
diachronous, but as a process of dialectical, developmental change
among dimensions that are always present in some form,[84] childhood is
indeed emblematic and exemplary for the reconstruction of adult subjectivity, for the child is caught up in rapid and continuous change, as
much biologically as experientially. It makes sense that a cosmos that is
now being reinterpreted in terms of growth and transformation, takes
as its new representative the stage of life in which explosive, breathtak-
ing growth is the most manifest. The goal of this process is neither to
remain a child nor to return to childhood, but to grow into an adult
whose childhood is still active within her and available to her, and this
adult is represented for Romanticism in the artist, or "genius."[85]
Genius, as Baudelaire claimed, is "childhood recovered at will ("*retrou-
vée a volunté*").[86] In the artist, the child's freshness of sensation survives
in the powers of the adult, and manifests itself in the perception of nov-
elty in old and familiar appearances. The genius, like the child, enjoys
the power to take a lively interest in all things, even those that seem to
be the most trivial. The Romantic notion of genius represents, not so
much the extraordinary gift as, in modern terms, self-actualization; and
"artist" signifies the artist of one's own life. In this sense, the genius is
the fulfillment of childhood, a realization of its prophetic world-openness. This new ideal adult is in fact, according to Novalis, the "highest
synthetic degree of the child,"[87] for he or she incorporates an original
simplicity into a higher harmony, reached through a process of development that involves continual self-reconstruction.

Genius as self-actualization is generic and universal—Marx's
"species being"—and represents the entrance (or rather the ongoing

process of entering) a new subject-object relation. Like the young child, the genius lives the universal in the concrete, through work on the boundaries between the inner world of the imagination and the actual conditions of the world. The "third way of living" is, as Wordsworth claimed, the "great birthright of our being" if only because it is the characteristic noetic style of infancy. N.O. Brown, that other (with Marcuse) post-Freudian Romantic, characterizes it as the fundamental unconscious goal of the human to live in what he calls "the erotic mode of activity," play—activity "governed by the pleasure principle": "Our indestructible unconscious desire for a return to childhood, our deep childhood-fixation," he claims, "is a desire for a return to the pleasure principle, for a recovery of the body from which culture alienates us, and for play instead of work."[88]

The third joyous kingdom of play is the realm, not just of art, religion, and philosophy in the service of recovery of the body, but of social and cultural reconstruction, because the subject who retains the capacity for deep play into adulthood is in active, transformative relation with the world. The playing child encounters external phenomena in the service of the dream. The play space is a sacred one to the individual, because it is here that she encounters the subject-object relation as a form of creativity—here subjectivity is understood as creativity per se. And for this very reason it implies a social vision—the boundary phenomenon of a society having reached the condition of collective and institutional life lived and shaped and reshaped within the transitional space of creative play. The social vision implied by the individual's creative relation to the world is an ever-receding horizon of human collective possibility, but the phenomenon of transitional space from which it springs is a human birthright. It does not imply a repudiation of the reality principle—a world of objects which, in Winnicott's words, "the individual has decided to recognize (with whatever difficulty and even pain) as truly external"[89]—but a reconstruction of the reality principle through a transformation of instinctual structure, that is, the dialectical relation between repression and instinct, reason and desire. The "erotic mode of activity" is in fact such a reorganizational mode—a move beyond the fixed form of genital sexuality, which we usually identify as a terminal form in adults, to a further stage. This stage, which Marcuse, following Freud, identified as pregenital and polymorphous eroticism— that is, a whole-body sexuality—is a dialectical reappropriation of infant sexuality. It is represented in the iconography of the Divine Child as an original bisexuality. Brown describes it as "the pursuit of pleasure obtained through the activity of any and all organs of the human body. . . . delight in the active life of all the human body."[90] It is the deconstruction of the "tyranny" of genital organization and the erotization of the whole body that makes possible what we will encounter later in Marcuse's thought as "non-repressive sublimation." The latter refers to a form of the reality principle which has moved beyond surplus-repression and the performance principle—and thereby implicitly beyond domination.

In summary, the goal of the recovery of the primordial child is expressed in the human vocation of continual reconstruction of the subject-world relation—a vocation associated with art and play—in order to render the external (or nature) internal (or thought), and vice versa. Play is exemplary of the transitional nature of the subject-world relation, and the recognition that the boundaries between the two are fluid, historically, culturally, and individually mediated, and productive of plural forms both of subjective, social, and even physical reality. For Romantic educators since Froebel, and for those who, like John Dewey, were deeply influenced by its anthropological convictions, the intentional community of children and adults we call "school" assumes major importance for the hope of the transformation of adulthood in the image of the transitional subject-world relation, and the possibility of nonrepressive sublimation as a characteristic style of subjectivity. As a community of dialogue and negotiation, purposeful project, celebration and the practice of justice between adult and child, it is the location where the diachronic and synchronic dimensions of the life-cycles interplay—a place set apart for the meeting of the two, in a context marked by the creative imperative. In the school reconstructed in the image of the "third way of living," children undertake transformative action on the world through art, science, and philosophy—forms of inquiry that are already implicit and formative in their early play. They are both initiated into these adult cultural institutions (which, in turn, are continually formed and reformed through adult transitional play)—and influence these institutions through their own capacities for constructive play and inquiry.[92] The school is an institution that has generally so far been used to the most limited purposes to which civilization could put it—for the "normalization" of human subjectivity in the service of a repressive system that requires low-grade alienation in order to function. For those who recognize the role of childhood and—as will be seen in the next chapter—of the adult-child relation in cultural evolution, the school becomes an institution of the greatest significance for individual and social change.

In its current condition, the school might be described as a machine of the state and the economy for writing the "law" on the flesh of its future operative units. It could never be put to those purposes unless the adults who worked there thought that children could or should be thus sacrificed—that they were expendable, or that they had nothing more to offer than to be shaped by such a system. Such adults either don't recognize the primordial child—themselves or the child before them—or consider the "third way of living" to be a narcissistic, decadent ideal, impractical, hubristic ("spoiled"), dangerous, and better expunged through mechanical habituation. This returns us to the questions posed in the first chapter concerning the characteristics, causes, and implications of the ideology of adulthood, or "adultism," which lies at the heart of the stubborn and pervasive mediocrity of the theory and practices of traditional schooling.

To get a sense of the range and depth of this particular and near universal—however sentimentalized—form of the adult-child relation, it is necessary to at least look into the history of adulthood, particularly in the area of adult self-understanding. If "adult-child" is an inseparable, contrastive pair, then any adult construction of subjectivity will imply a construction of the child subject—both within me ("inner child") and outside of me (the child before me). If the child is colonized in the modern Western structures of schooling, she is colonized within the subjective structure of the adults who are her caretakers. And if the adult-child relation is changing, then a different adult-child balance or economy is being created within modal adult subjectivity, and adult subjectivity is changing. The next chapter is dedicated to exploring further both that chiasmic structure adult-child, and its implications for individual, cultural, and social transformation.

3

The Invention of Adulthood

> Have I ever been a child
> I who know how to speak of childhood
> As I speak of death
> —Paul Eluard[1]

Adultism and Models of the Self

It has already been suggested that early modernism was the historical moment at which there began an increasing social separation between adult and child through age-graded institutions, economic and domestic isolation, and, over centuries, psychological theories of childhood that acted to objectify children as a separate class. One could go further and claim that, just as Philippe Aries, in his seminal study of the history of childhood[2] made the phrase "invention of childhood" famous, so this moment in Western history was also the moment of the invention of adulthood, or at least the form of adulthood of our age.

The history of adulthood in the West—in the privileged, patriarchal West anyway, which is mostly what we have a record of—is characterized by an attitude toward childhood and children that I have called "adultism." Like racism, ethnocentrism, and sexism, adultism is based on what appear to be empirical differences—in anatomy, neural development, ego-structure, psychoculture, size, and physical strength. These "real" differences very often lead to "subspeciation," or the tendency to regard and to treat certain human others implicitly as if they were members of a separate species. As a psychological phenomenon, subspeciation is projective, which means that the subspeciator—the one with the power—attributes his or her unconscious, unresolved sexual and aggressive material to the subspeciated. The projection is typically bipolar, in that the subspeciated receives both the dark and the light side of the subspeciator's unconscious material—hence the divine child/deficit child, the goddess/whore, and the noble/bestial "savage."

Subspeciation is a form of psychological colonization that acts in a vicious circle with social, sexual, political, and economic colonization. The subspeciated status of the child is slightly more complicated than that of either women or the "savage," since the child is, relative to the full-grown member of the human species, an undeveloped being. Aristotle, as we have seen, fudges the question of whether children represent a congenital or a developmental difference from free male adults. The child, he claims, has the deliberative element of the soul—which is what makes one an adult—but in incomplete and therefore nonfunctional, virtually useless form. But if the child is a woman, she will never have it with "authority," and if a slave never have it at all. The categorical confusion that this formulation demonstrates mirrors the existential confusion of adultism, which experiences the child as difference, deviation, deficit, the unformed, and unshaped. For adultism, the child may not quite represent a difference in kind as does "woman" and "slave," but she still lacks the requisite part of the soul—the one that makes us adult; so whether the difference is of degree or of kind becomes moot. The child is not just an incomplete, but an imperfect form of subjectivity.

Aristotle's theory of the nutritive (plant), sensitive (animal), and intellective (human) hierarchy of the parts of the soul,[3] however compelling, formalizes another common adultist perspective that influenced the science of child study from the advent of Darwinian evolutionism to approximately the mid-twentieth century. This is summarized in the theory that the journey through childhood to adulthood recapitulates the journey of the species from its nonhuman origins to civilized humanity. So the child in the womb is analogous to the fish, the infant to the primate, the young child to the monkey, the teenager to the primitive hunter-gatherer.[4] Each individual human history is a recapitulation of the history of the race. It follows that a good way to understand—and to treat—a five year old would be as one does a monkey.[5]

Analogously to this evolutionary model, Aristotle's child is somewhere on the continuum between sensitive and intellective soul, and thus is something more than an animal and something less than a human. She lacks the faculty of *prohairesis*—choice or resolve or purpose—and thus cannot be "happy" in Aristotle's deep, morally infused sense of that term. Choice would appear to be a necessary aspect of reasoning, or the power of deliberation, which is the essential aspect of the intellective soul. Aristotle would probably grant that children—at least male children—possess it *in potentia*, but in a "confused" state.

> For we do not say that a child acts, or a brute either; only someone who is already doing things from reasoning. . . . [T]he really pleasant things are not those pleasant to children and animals, but those pleasant to the adult. . . . And as a child or animal stands to an adult human being, so the bad and foolish man stands to the good and wise man.[6]

A child is a transitional being, and as such a sort of monster, in the sense that a monster is a mixture, or amalgam. Nor, though we can give and receiven "affection" from her, can we call a child "friend": "It would be absurd for a man to be the friend of a child."[7]

Aristotle's three levels of soul of *de Anima* are roughly analogous to Plato's tripartite soul of the *Republic*, at least in the sense that both trade on a hierarchy of form and function. Plato seems to hold that, in the child, the balance between the three dimensions of self—appetite, will or "the spirited element," and reason—is ontogenetically out of balance. The child lacks reason, or reason is represented so minimally that it amounts to the same thing. So Plato considered children to be exemplars of the "untamed appetite and the uncontrolled will." They are liable—along with women, slaves, and the "inferior multitude"—to the "great mass of multifarious appetites and pleasures and pains" of the naturally immoderate. "They are full of passionate feelings from their very birth." The "boy, . . . just because he more than any other has a fount of intelligence in him which has not yet 'run clear', . . . is the craftiest, most mischievous, and unruliest of brutes. So the creature must be held in check . . ."[8] Children's only virtue appears to be that they are "easily molded," that is, they are capable of being *made* into adults. This calls for a certain form of education as a personal and social necessity—so the *Republic* is the first Western educational tract.

In keeping with the principle that "child-adult" is a contrastive pair, there is implicit in this first reasoned view of the child that we have from the ancients, a theory of the adult. For Plato (as, later, for Piaget[9]), although only free men can become adults, even they can fail of this developmental goal. Plato's—and by analogy Aristotle's—tripartite self is a structural community of functions for which the attainment of adulthood is represented by the three parts coming into a normative balance. Development toward adulthood means bringing, in Plato's words, the three "elements into tune with one another by adjusting the tension of each to the right pitch," which he most often expresses as a situation of internal hierarchy. The child of Western patriarchal rationalism represents the ambiguity and ambivalence of what is given as the human at the beginning of the life cycle, and the possibility of the construction of an ideal self in which "each part of his nature is exercising its proper function, of ruling or of being ruled."[10] The disciplinary construction of the Platonic self is carried on into adult life in the history of Western subjectivity in what Foucault has called "the technologies of the [male adult] self."[11] Unity of self is accomplished only through the eternal vigilance of reason over appetite and will, a product of constant self-examination and readjustment through self-discipline. This system of internal relations of domination was replicated macrocosmically, not just in the utopia of Plato's *Republic*, but in the very real Indo-European social political class system as a whole, where kings (reason) controlled warriors (emotions, spirited will), who in turn ruled over the agricultural classes (appetite).[12] Once this domination model is internalized as an ideal of intrasubjective power relations—an internalization that has its first statement in the *Republic*—a technology becomes necessary in order to accomplish adulthood. This technology is education, which Aristotle defines as being "brought up in a particular way from our very youth, as Plato says, so as both to delight in and to be pained by the things that we ought; for this is the right education."[13] Education as habituation by adults then presents itself as a ritual of force and inscription, and an absolute cultural necessity.

Those who speak of the "invention" of childhood in the Renaissance and early modern period might more safely use the term "reinvention," for children have always been as much imagined as experienced by adults. And the post-medieval reinvention of childhood is necessarily an aspect of the reinvention of adulthood, in this case with similarities to the adult of Greco-Roman antiquity, albeit in a dramatically different cultural context, and with a different form of adult self-explanation. The attitudes and behaviors Foucault describes as the "cultivation of the self," common among Stoics and Epicureans in the first two centuries CE, have much in common with the psychosocial set of emergent middle-class values of adulthood in early modern Europe. In both cases there is a new emphasis on the individual as a discrete and separated subjectivity, on impulse control, on self-examination, or—as befits the new, print-based information environment of modernity—"reading" oneself.

Foucault described the first two centuries CE in the Hellenistic world as "the summit of a curve: a kind of golden age in the cultivation of the self—it being understood, of course, that this phenomenon concerned only the social groups, very limited in number, that were bearers of culture and for whose members a *techne tou biou* [technology or craft of life] could have a meaning and a reality."[14] Care of the self as an ideal of subjectivity is present in the Greek tradition at least since Socrates' injunction to "know" oneself, and has deeper if less individualistic roots in the wisdom traditions of earlier Mesopotamian civilizations. It appears to be associated with religious or philosophical monotheism. A pagan or polytheistic model of subjectivity would seem, as Julien Jaynes' speculation on the structure of the Homeric psyche suggests, to involve an internal pluralism, of which the pantheon of gods and goddesses is a projection onto an outer world that is not yet fully distinguished from the inner.[15] Read in this way, Plato's (which is not quite Socrates', who still had his *daemon*) rejection of the gods through reinterpreting them into "myth" represents a unification of subjectivity in Hellenic psychohistory equivalent to the advent of Hebrew monotheism in the history of religion.

If the first two centuries CE were the first golden age of the monotheistic self, the decline of Rome was the moment in which this ideal of privileged male-adult subjectivity was passed on into Christianity, where, as the story goes, it survived in monasteries and ecclesiastical centers of power as the church militant moved north to win the polytheistic psychocultures of the Celts and the Saxons to monotheism. If we stick to this account, the middle ages represent a dialectical moment of negation, in which the monotheistic, unified self-ideal of the classical era buried itself in the soil of northern "native" culture, a seed that emerged as a distinctively European culture in the High Middle Ages, and—in Renaissance, Reformation, and the rise of the centralized state—reached back to reappropriate its classical elements.

This in fact is the story Westerners tell themselves. One of its chief narrative themes is the idea that the Western middle-class notion of the successful adult as maintaining a relationship of ego-mastery within his own internal psychological economy—as balancing the self through mental force, with reason as a dominant element over recalcitrant and rebellious "lower" functions—is one of our millennial themes. And if this is the case, it would seem that adultism, which is associated with a view of self that trades on rejecting and excluding child-subjectivity, has always been present in Western culture. To say this is not to claim that, because this model places child-subjectivity under erasure, any model that does not do so will not be adultist. One can also not recognize children because one is too much like them. In fact it is the broad argument of this chapter that any general improvements in the adult-child

relationship made in the West are the result of a dialectical process—
that it is the recognition of differences between adults and children as
much as similarities, which eventually leads to adult-child dialogue, for
dialogue is impossible between either identical or fused interlocutors.
Dialogue is always with an other.

The adult who was reinvented in the early- modern period appears
to have had a different developmental goal than the adult of antiquity.
One basic model for modern adult subjectivity is derived from Christian
teaching and practice, for which desire—the emotional and the appetitive—represents a different kind of problem than it did for the Greeks.
It may be fair to say that for the Greeks, whose anthropology was based
on a more polytheistic sense of the whole, the problematic was not
"moral" in the sense we now understand it. Inderdiction of sexual acts,
for example, was not based on the fear of eternal torment by a right-
eous king-god, but was a local strategy in the service of life as art—as
an aesthetic whole that required mastery in order to construct.[16] The
Christian problematic, on the other hand, has to do with subordination
of desire not just to a practical form of reason (or *phronesis*) but to
Reason in the person of the Logos, the Word of God—indeed, to the
Law. On this model, alignment of the parts of the self is in the interest
of a total transparency before a w(holy) Other who is also one's father-
judge.

Successful Christian adulthood, accomplished through the same
techniques as the Stoic and Epicurean—careful and continuous self-
examination and acetic regimen (with the addition of meditative
prayer)—seeks to shift the locus of visibility toward the Father, toward
a subjectivity outside of oneself that includes oneself—understood as
the origin and ground of one's own subjectivity, and as knowing one
better than one knows oneself. In the case of the Greco-Christian ideal,
the all-encompassing gaze of the Father represents an exaltation of
reason to the point where reason is no longer simply the helmsman, as
in a more polytheistic model of self, but "all in all," a light of consciousness with no admixture of darkness, "no shadow of turning."[17]
This grandiose ideal has had an extraordinary effect on Western subjectivity. It might be said to have acted as a goad for consciousness, as creating the highly personalized form of objectivity that has brought the
West to its present ethical both crisis and opportunity—that is, to where
its concern for individual autonomy and self-determination is matched
only by its concern for social justice and equity. But its neurotic intoler-
ance of pluralism and multiplicity—both inter- and intrasubjective—and
its commandeering of instinct and emotion in the interest of a higher
Truth has left us in a cultural situation of polarization, where a sterile

rationalism is confronted by the "return of the repressed." At least from one point of view, Christianity may be said to have betrayed Christ—if we conceive Christ as the archetype of a form of self-unification beyond internal and external relations of domination, and as the integration of conscious and unconscious elements of the personality rather than the mastery of the latter by the former.

Whatever its religious or philosophical discourses, the monotheistic model of selfhood understands the child as danger and deficit, and has historically embraced a model of education as necessary coercion—as either forcible construction of a product (adult) from an inchoate, unshaped, unregulated material (child), or else, as in Calvinist anthropology, the forcible *re*-construction of an ontogenetically "fallen" nature. Correspondingly, the child has always offered—as has the "native" or "wild man," as has woman, as has the madman or madwoman—an alternate model of subjectivity, but one marked for oblivion (or at best nostalgia) in patriarchal self-understanding. It is only in the last two centuries that the cultured classes have experienced—slowly during the nineteenth, and with increasing, almost dizzying intensity during the twentieth—a loss of confidence in the hierarchical, domination-model of self. Those models that emerged with the advent of psychology as a systematic inquiry at the end of the nineteenth century—in particular the Freudian—have gradually replaced an ideal of internal mastery by one of internal dialogue.

The historical deconstruction of the Platonic tripartite model of subjectivity represents, at its worst—as the conservative Western imagination would understand it—a decline, a cultural corruption, a failure of nerve. A mastery model must always fear decline, insurrection, regicide, internal and external chaos, because it is a model in which light must drive out its own necessary shadow rather than live with it—in which reason, or *logos*, aspires to the shadowless. The drive for totality that is symbolized, embodied, and expressed in Western monotheisms, must do away with the partial, the developing, the regressive, the ambiguous, and the ambivalent with an ontology of being rather than becoming. The model matches, as we have seen, ancient Indo-European social and mythological structure, and also is in analogical relation with the tripartite structure of the human brain—where reason, or cerebral cortex, must rule limbic system or emotion, and brain stem, or appetite. It is also characteristic of colonial social and political structures, in which the "native" or the lower classes are understood as children, leading, as Nandy has said, to "the frequent use of childhood as a design of cultural and political immaturity or, it comes to the same thing, inferiority."[18]

Adultism, like colonialism, classism, racism, sexism, and homophobia, is a relation with an other that is dominated by projection. The ambivalent, the ambiguous, the liminal, the unresolved, the negative, the undeveloped aspects of subjectivity—what Jung characterized as the "shadow"[19]—are projected onto an other. The shadow is most easily projected onto an other who is different in obvious and consistent ways, whether physically, culturally, or sexually. In the case of adultism, the shadow projection on children is reified in theory by Plato and Aristotle, who ground it ontologically and epistemologically, and thereby implicitly create the child as a bearer of volitional deficit and dangerous instinct. In thus excluding the child from full personhood and in the exclusion from the ethics of dialogue that implies, the adult succeeds (but never succeeds completely) in splitting off the shadow and colonizing it in childhood. The sentimentalization of childhood that we usually associate with Victorianism is not an alternative to but a variation of adultism. The child understood as everything good, pure, and innocent is as much a deficit model, and as unproductive of dialogue with the real child, for it still aspires to the shadowless. Its only association with the primordial child is as a distancing through cooption, and it disempowers real children as much as does the shadow projection.

Jung's theory of the process of adult individuation—which involves the ongoing reconstruction of subjectivity through the integration of conscious and unconscious elements of the psyche and the repositioning of the ego (or reason) in the whole constellation of the self—holds that the first stage of the work is confronting the shadow.[20] Once the shadow is recognized and owned, the first archetype of the unconscious to emerge is the child archetype, or primordial child. The latter is a symbol of unification and the promise of psychic wholeness; it announces a process whereby, in Jungian psychologist Erich Neumann's words, "the centre of the personality is gradually shifted away from the ego and the conscious mind towards the Self and the phenomenon of the wholeness of the psyche."[21] It is this process that informs the gradual deconstruction of adultism (and all other forms of marginalization of the other through projective mechanisms), and assures the emergence of the healthy, evolving adult-child relation.

A form of adult self-understanding that evades the polarization and consequent marginalization of the child as a projected element of the adult unconscious cannot emerge until—as it is said in psychoanalytic parlance—there is a "withdrawal of the projection." This is something of an unfortunate term, for the dynamics of perception itself are projective, so the notion of a projection-free consciousness is nonsensical. There is, finally, no "objective" other waiting for the withdrawal of the projection to be seen as he, she, or it really is—only, as the philosopher Emmanuel Levinas put it, "an alterity which is always on the verge of presence but never comes to presence."[22] One might better speak of the cultivation of the ability to "dodge" the projection, or to "bracket" it—to hold it at bay, to remain in an attitude of suspicion toward it. The major element in the process is that one becomes aware of it—that one realizes it is there and at work, even if one can never experience it directly, for it always appears as the actual appearance of the other. To recognize and acknowledge the shadow in oneself is, for the ego, "to step down from its pedestal and realize the state of individual, constitutional and historical imperfection which is its appointed fate."[23] Through the ego's new position of self-reflection and growing self-awareness, the personality is able to work toward reintegrating those split-off and contradictory dimensions of subjectivity, and to regain, through an ongoing structural reorganization, its implicate wholeness.

The outcome of the withdrawal of projection is not the objectifying gaze—that too is a projection—but rather *dialogue*, which means that the field of interrogation and judgment and reflection vis a vis the other has opened to include myself. Any dyadic relationship is a structure in which there are no ultimately clear genetic distinctions between self and other, subject and object, here and there. What psychoanalysis refers to as transference and counter-transference are normative aspects of interpersonal structure. Projection can be discerned and challenged only in the "between," the field of dialogue. All of these principles of relationship apply just as much to the child-other as to the adult-other.

The adult-child relationship is a unique interpersonal structure, certainly as powerful—and as much a challenge to commonsense notions of the structure and dynamics of subjectivity—as the erotic. Levinas considered it to be the one human relationship that clearly disproves the common assumption of the Platonic and Cartesian ideal of the unity of personal identity, or the "identical subject." He put it this way:

> In a situation such as paternity [sic] the return of the I to the self, which is set forth in the monist concept of the identical subject, is found to be completely modified. The son [sic] is not only my work, like a poem or an object, nor is he my property. Neither the categories of power nor those of knowledge describe my relation with the child. . . . I do not have my child; I *am* my child. Paternity is a relation with a stranger Who while being Other *is* me, a relation of the self with a self which is yet not me. In this "I am" being is no longer Eleatic unity. In existing itself there is a multiplicity

and a transcendence. In this transcendence the I is not swept away, since the son is not me; and yet I *am* my son. The fecundity of the I is its very transcendence. [24]

The adult-child relationship is the relationship that first, like the sexual relationship but in a different way, offers the adult the existential experience of the multiplicity of selfhood *across* rather than within personal boundaries. This seems to be what Levinas means by "multiplicity and transcendence." This experience of alterity has the effect of initiating what he calls the "rupture of the egoist *I*," and its "reconditioning in the face of the Other, the re-orientation despite-itself of the for-itself to the for-the-other."[25] The rupture and reconditioning provide the context for the psychological development of the adult through her relationship with the child—a development based on the experience of dialogue.

The result of this development is an adult who is in touch with the child-dimension of her own subjectivity—its forms of feeling, intentionality, and cognitive style. Being more in touch with myself as a child means being more in touch with the child before me; being more in touch with the child before me allows me to make child rearing and educational decisions that are both the instigators and the consequences of dialogue—that is, of the skills and dispositions of painstakingly careful listening to the other, of considering the other's perspective, of recognizing my interconnectedness with the other, of arriving at values and decisions that take myself and the other into account equally, in short of the "re-orientation . . . to the for-the-other."

Adultism—like sexism, racism, and homophobia, all of them forms of marginalization and colonization—is held in place in self-understanding by an implicit theory of subjectivity and the *inter*subjective relations that theory implies. It is in the transitional spaces across the boundaries of the subject, in the realm of "multiplicity and transcendence," where the projective mechanisms that lead to subspeciation operate. The deconstruction of adultism requires a normative form of adult subjectivity that is aware both of its own shadow—all that is abject, needy, grasping, solipsistic, over-sexualized, out of the control of the ego—and, as a result of that awareness, is capable of moving beyond it, into the common intersubjective space of dialogue. The subject who recognizes her shadow and withdraws its projection onto the other has entered into another, permanently transitional form of subjectivity, based on a value of world-openness that assumes an ontological potential for ongoing personal—and by implication social—transformation, the basis for what Neumann called "a new ethic."

Social transformation—by which may be understood the ethical transformation of collectives in the postmodern West—promises to emerge in a culture in which the modal personality, that is, the normative style of subjectivity of the epoch, understands itself as an open, developmental structure, as a subject-in-process rather than a presumptive finality or a static tension produced by an internal zero sum game. Such a structure, which works from a sensed implicit wholeness toward which one is always moving rather than a self-imposed totality, is the only one capable of that "re-orientation despite-itself of the for-itself to the for-the-other" that for Levinas is the main axis of the ethical, and which overcomes adultism. The preoccupation with childhood that began with the Romantic revolt against the Platonic and Cartesian self two centuries ago implicitly puts the question: are we in a position to accomplish this new self-understanding, which is always promised in and through child rearing and education, as a cultural reality? Just what would have to be in place for the emergence of a form of personal and collective life in which the transformative influence on adult subjectivity of a new sort of adult-child relation—a relation based on dialogue—was generally as powerful as it is among a relative few today?

That there has been if not an evolution at least a change in the cultural construction of the adult-child relation over Western historical time seems incontestable. My assumption is that an alternative theory of childhood, and—since they are mutually determinative—of adulthood, will have two major cultural and social implications. Dialogue with that first and closest other, the child, promises to result, first, in a change in the implicit historically mediated normative model of subjectivity—one that finds a different sort of dynamic between Plato's three elements of the soul; second, in practical changes in child rearing and education that act to generate and reproduce that different sort of dynamic. This returns us to the questions posed earlier related to the problem of causality in processes involving broad cultural change. Does it take a different form of child rearing to produce a different style of subjectivity? But wouldn't a different style of subjectivity need to be in place in order to be produced through child rearing?

This vicious circle is based on a linear and reductionist view of causality in the social world. In fact historical inquiry indicates an intricate network of an indeterminable number of mutually determinative causal factors contributing to changes in how childhood and adulthood are understood by adults. Social and cultural change, and its long and short-term effects on individuals, including children, emerges from a host of structural variables: economic, religious, political, cultural, demographic, epidemiological, technological, class and gender related and relative to family structure, not to speak of historical events and epochs like migration, war, epidemic, cataclysm, climatic fluctuation, famine or moments of unprecedented economic prosperity or depression, etc. Together, these form a matrix of variables whose chaotic interactions bring forth new cultural and personal styles, new balances between order and disorder, instinct and repression, freedom and constraint, individual and collective identity. And if there is an "evolution," as deMause has claimed, of child-rearing modes that evolution depends as much on the "sport"—Rousseau for example—who through his or her own vision and intelligence and/or neurosis, presents an alternative for the culture to consider. We could even imagine an evolutionary collective "sport"—for example an intentional commune with an innovative child-rearing style—which represents a further evolutionary form that is too different to survive, but does provide the normative culture with precursors of future transformation. To confront this myriad of variables in search of the sources and crucial junctures of change is perhaps the task of a speculative historiography informed by chaostheory.[26] What I am concerned to do here is to sketch in broad outline a narrative theory of just one aspect of these changes that is not in contradiction with whatever facts and relations between facts we have, and to identify a further direction of change that might be implicit in those experienced so far.

If the only issue here were the effects that relations with children sometimes have on the psychological development of the adults involved in those relations, an inquiry into the possibility of broad psychohistorical change would be quite a bit simpler. We could then speculate that when people "grow up," many tend to become adultist—that is, they tend to think of children as the dangerous or deficit other—but that when they have children themselves, the influence of child rearing "reconditions" them "in the face of the other," leading to a more dialogical personality. We could in fact make this hypothesis about a fairly significant number of people who become parents. It is not, however, a significant enough number to protect children from child abuse, from abandonment in various forms, and, most significantly, from an educational system that historically suppresses the developmental potential, and stymies the motivation for growth and personal transformation of vast numbers of young people, and thereby of adults. The evidence of twentieth-century psychology would suggest that, although there are many factors contributing to what kinds of adults children turn out to be, the most important causal factor in the production of adults with enough both autonomy and sense of interdependence to be capable of dialogue with their own children is the extent to which their own parents and teachers were in dialogue with them when they were children.

The present Western historical moment contains—like any historical moment—a number of contradictions: an educational system that still largely colonizes childhood; a growing culture of adults who believe in and practice dialogue with their children and expect the educational system to do so as well; either increasing incidences of or increasing disclosure of incidences of sexual abuse of children; the cultural phenomenon of the "disappearance of childhood"—that is, the putative breaking down of "the dividing line" between adulthood and childhood—and an emergent reformulation of adult subjectivity, goaded forward by a myriad of influences, the most obvious of which is a new individual and cultural intervisibility made possible by an increasingly global, interconnected electronic information environment. In the search for a narrative capable of recognizing and including all of these phenomena, I want first to circle back yet again, in a closer approach, to the historical accounts we do have of the adult-child relation in the West, and search for their logic in a narrative that combines the accounts we have both of the history of childhood and of adulthood. I want to try to show what I have already suggested—a dialectical movement leading to the present situation, which assumes the necessity of each previous moment to the one succeeding it.

This dialectical narrative is symmetrical with the hermeneutical theory presented in Chapter 1, which is a narrative about the conditions and possibilities of dialogue per se. I want to consider adult-child dialogue both as a possibility within each cultural epoch of history, and as the metadialogue represented by the interrelations between succeeding cultural epochs—their themes, their emphases, and the dialectical logic of their transformations. What motivates this consideration is the search for an understanding that can guide a normative inquiry into the *praxis*, not just of child rearing and education, but of the cultural and social and political transformation that optimal child rearing and education always promise.

The Evolution of Adulthood/Childhood

As we have seen, the ancient world already had "grown-ups" who remind us very much of our own normative notions of maturity, but there were, it appears, fewer of them than today. Practically speaking, unless one were both free born and male, one could not become an adult in the modern sense of the term—an independent, autonomous individual. If one was a child, one shared what Boswell called the "general similarity between the status of children and slaves in ancient and medieval Europe." Just as in modern racist, sexist, and colonialist discourse, so in the ancient world the terms for child, boy, and girl were also regularly employed to mean slave or servant. The fact that a majority of people remained what we would today consider "children" in terms of rights and status, was balanced by the fact that in other ways people left what the modern middle classes think of as the marked-off world of childhood much earlier than they do in the contemporary West. Anglo-Saxon law, for example, considered males to be adults at ten, at least in terms of responsibility for their actions. The age of seven, the start of the period following what the Middle Ages called "infancy" (0–7 years), was considered by some to be the earliest age of consent to marriage. Custom, opinion, and level of consensus varied, of course, all over the ancient and medieval world, by period, culture, class, and gender; but we can probably draw the general conclusion that, if social and legal and economic "childhood" never ended for all but the small ruling class, then childhood as a lifeworld distinct from and protected from the adult lifeworld, ended quite a bit sooner than it does now.[27]

Philippe Aries' influential historical formulation of the medieval world of childhood confirms this picture of a life cycle in which, at around age seven, the child "went straight into the community of men, sharing in the work and play of their companions, old and young alike."[28] Aries' work has been used to legitimate the historical constructivist slogan "the invention of childhood," with its implication that childhood did not exist in the medieval world, and emerged as a result of religious Reformation and the rise of the bourgeoisie, the centralized state and the nuclear family. In fact it might be more accurate to reverse the wording of this formulation, and characterize the medieval world as a world of near-universal childhood, followed by the emergence in the modern world of near-universal adulthood, resulting in turn in children being separated off from adults, and placed in a class by themselves. Childhood as we now understand it could only have come into existence when adulthood had been separated from childhood, so there was something to compare it to. On the basis of the scholarly research of Aries, Johann Huizinga, and Norbert Elias,[29] we can infer that until the Renaissance and Reformation in Europe, adults and children had more of an existential world in common. What are now fairy tales for children were heard and appreciated by all ages; what are now children's games and dances were indulged in by the whole community. Physical privacy and modesty, whether in sleeping arrangements, eating, elimination and bathing behaviors, or attitudes about exposure of the body, were characteristically "childlike," that is, unselfconscious. If we are to believe Elias, the same was true for sexual expression and the expression of affect.

Elias bases his research on the etiquette manuals that began appearing in the late Middle Ages and early Renaissance, advising readers on socially acceptable ways to perform natural functions—manuals that only became necessary with a new self-consciousness about manners, or *civilité*. Prior to the end of the medieval world and the rise of the modern, "the degree of instinctual restraint and control expected by adults of each other was not much greater than that imposed on children. The distance between adults and children, measured by that of today, was slight."[30] Beginning in the sixteenth century, and coterminous with the onset of the new reality principle of capitalism and radical Protestanism, rising middle-class adults began imposing restraints on instinctual expression, involving new standards of shame and self-consciousness, new "thresholds of repugnance" which, through gradual social change, became part of normative adult self-awareness. The new regulation or molding of instinctual urges acted to separate adults—who (forgetting their own childhood) saw themselves as having grown naturally into these levels of repression of bodily instinct and impulse—from children, who had to be trained into them. With increasing levels of "social proscription of many impulses, and their repression from the surface both of social life and of consciousness, the distance between the personality structure and behavior of adults and children is necessarily increased." This, in turn, led to the necessity for greater attention to education and to the raising up of children. Gradually it came about that "the children have in the space of a few years to attain the advanced level of shame and revulsion that has developed over many centuries. Their instinctual life must be rapidly subjected to the strict control and specific molding that gives our societies their stamp, and which developed very slowly over centuries."[31]

Elias understands there to have been a major turn among certain classes in the early modern West toward a modal personality characterized by higher levels of self-restraint and personal shame, increased self-consciousness, and greater control of affect. This new, rationalized form of subjectivity was demanded by new economic realities—the division of labor, growing economic opportunities, competition, and an increasing tolerance of the forms of discipline necessary to capitalist economies—and represents the regulation and restraint of drives necessary for modern "work," which was assuming a new identity apart from play. Elias is in fact identifying a pattern of affect-control associated with the emergence of a capitalist-engendered and engendering reality principle, based on the performance principle and the cultural and social imperatives of surplus-repression, and associated in turn with domination by new groups of individuals interested in maintaining or gaining privilege. Surplus-repression describes the instinctual economy—or what Elias called "the interplay between drives and drive controls, between conscious and unconscious levels of the personality"[32]—characteristic of the new middle classes, which at this moment were engaged in challenging the social, political, and economic hegemony of the aristocracy in an atmosphere of an increasing centralization of political power, the rise of the nation state, and the emergence of capitalism fueled by expanding colonization. It is characterized by relatively high impulse control, a strict separation of work and play, the almost compulsive control and regulation of emotions, stricter habits of hygiene, and an emphasis on a newly "mannered" form of public interaction, which is both created by and creates what Elias called "the wall between people, the reserve, the emotional barrier erected by conditioning between one body and another."[33] The affect control, the repression of bodily impulses and pleasures, and the creation of barriers between individuals that prevent the flow of affect, are reified in an understanding of self as an individual ego in its "locked case," separated by an invisible wall, an "inside" facing an "outside." This new normative subjectivity was in turn reified in scientific, philosophical, and psychological formulations—whether the new empiricism in science, the Cartesian *cogito*, the Lockean self for whom memory is the only guarantee of personal identity, the Kantian subject who knows the world only through the implicitly theoretical toolkit of the categories, the Humean subject afloat in an empirical universe with no provable causal connections, all of them enframed in the revolutionary Newtonian cosmos of strict mathematical determinism. From the point of view of a dialectical theory of psychological development, this new self-construction represents the height of the ego's drive for perfection and central control of the personality, which involves an emphasis on conscious over unconscious elements of the self, and a repression of the latter, whereby, as we have seen, they are projected onto others, and especially marginalized others. This in fact is the central characteristic of the Western European colonialist personality.

The emergent modal personality of the modern West accompanied the cosmological change triggered by scientific discovery and technological development. Elias identifies in particular "the development of the idea that the earth circles round the sun in a purely mechanical way in accordance with natural laws"[34] as another key element in the new ideal of self-consciousness and restraint. Self-detachment was necessary in a universe of which one was no longer the center, and that now seemed to possess no intrinsic meaning traceable either to humans or gods. The ancient and medieval worldview was constructed as a holistic web of interconnections based on analogical relations between all its elements, and driven by sympathies and antipathies writ both large and small throughout.[35] Such a system of micro and macrososmic relations of mutual influence assumed an animate universe, moved by principles that today we might characterize, in comparison to the mechanical universe of modernism, as psychological rather than physical. But the ancient and medieval worlds drew the lines between "psychological" and "physical" differently. It took repression of the involuntary meaning-making of the body, and of the intrinsically projective, chiasmic nature of perception itself—a form of knowledge that has begun to be excavated in this century by gestalt and phenomenological psychology—for people to be able, as Elias points out, to "conceive of [physical] processes as an autonomous sphere operating without intention or purpose or destiny in a purely mechanical or causal way, and having a meaning or purpose for themselves only if they are in a position, through objective knowledge, to control it and thereby give it a meaning and a purpose."[36] The rise of modern adult modal subjectivity is associated with the rise of cosmic and psychological mechanistic theory.

The ancient and medieval cosmos was characterized by what the philosopher Hans Jonas termed an "ontology of life," according to which "soul flooded the whole of existence and encountered itself in all things."[37] The concept of "dead" matter was unknown. Panpsychism, or the idea that life is everywhere and pervades everything, made the problem of the ancients one of explaining, not that there is life in the universe, but that there is death. This living cosmos was childlike, not so much in the sense of being naive or foolish, as in the sense that it was an oral/aural world—a speaking world in which participation and mutual influence was the felt reality. The primary information environment was the spoken word, and writing was still considered a limited and limiting form of communication, appropriate for runes and sacred texts, but not for the discourse of the natural world. The ideal man was not the scribe but the rhetorician, the one who spoke rather than wrote his mind. Formal teaching was built on a question-and-answer format, on dialectic rather than propositional discourse. In this interlocutive, sounded cosmos, neutral mathematical space had not yet been fully developed, or the modern notion of "objectivity," or the extreme emphasis on the privacy of thought that can create pseudo-problems like the "problem of other minds." Like the cosmos of the young child, the oral/aural cosmos was "egocentric" in the sense that, as the historian of culture Walter Ong has pointed out, a speaking and hearing world "situates man in the middle of actuality and in simultaneity," and does not even entertain the notion of a knowledge that is separated from the deepest sort of personal commitment. In this psychoworld, knowledge *is* communication, an active principle within things—communicating from their life rather than from an understanding of covering laws, or principles outside of the things they regulate or describe. This world is whole and self-communicating and for this kind of understanding, being is event—hence personal and interactive—rather than something neutral, impersonal, or simply "there."[38]

The invention of moveable print came in 1450, fifty years before Erasmus' etiquette manual—the text upon which Elias bases his analysis of the transformation of adult subjectivity—became the first best seller (after the Bible), in an information environment that had been transformed, relatively speaking, as rapidly as the computer transformed the late twentieth century's. The argument for the critical effect of information environment on the construction of modal personality is based on the assumption that, as Ong puts it, "intelligence is relentlessly reflexive, so that even the external tools that it uses to implement its workings become 'internalized', that is, part of its own reflexive process."[39] With the rapid growth of the printing press, the external tool of not just the written, but the mechanically printed (i.e., standardized, universally distributed) word was fully internalized by Western culture. This internalization led, according to Ong, to a widespread reorganization of the "sensorium,"[40] whereby the primacy of the oral/aural sense axis was replaced by that of the visual, with a corresponding shift in the value and even function of the senses in knowledge-construction.

What Ong has referred to as the "psychodynamics of orality"—the psychological characteristics or style of subjectivity of oral as opposed to literate cultures—bear an interesting resemblance to the psychodynamics of young children. Primary oral culture's emphasis on the magical, illocutionary aspects of language, its emphasis on communication, on formulaic expression, its tendency to "totalize," its closeness to the human lifeworld, its empathetic and participatory mode of apprehending the world, its concrete, contextual, complexive forms of categorization, the mythic and agonistic qualities of its characteristic narrative, its "conservative holism" toward persons and situations, its form of temporalization[41]—all of these modes are familiar to students of the young child. By contrast, the psychodynamics of literacy that swept sixteenth-century Europe evoke the modal subjectivity of the modern, egosyntonic adult: removal of self from the existential present; attention to symbols, propositions, and representations rather than things; reflection (since texts are stopped in time and can be returned to again and again in different ways); individualism and a new privacy (since in silent reading, which gradually replaced the transitional phase of reading aloud, one must of necessity read alone, and withdraw from others in order to do so); an emphasis on logical and propositional thought (since writing follows an "argument" in a sequential direction, and can be evaluated logically more easily than speech, since it is exactly the same every time it is returned to); abstraction (since written symbols have no necessary correspondences to nature); decontextualization (e.g., sitting in New York City reading a book about daily life in ancient Egypt); separation of the knower from the known (since in writing, words are translated into digital symbols, and reconstructed in the reader's mind through complicated processes).[42] The change in subjectivity associated with literate culture corresponded with as dramatic a change in worldview: the end of the organic, personalistic, oral cosmos of the ancient and medieval worlds, and the rise of a cosmos rationalized by a new sense of space, time and causality, and concerned with the new sort of objectivity that issued from a new subject-world relationship. The "new science," according to Ong, amounted to a "campaign for a visually conceived cognitive enterprise."[43]

The visual cosmos is silent. One stands before it rather than in it. It has become an object, and the things and people within it have become objects, things—whether living or dead—thrown up against me (*ob*=toward, against, in the way of; *iacere*=throw). In this cosmos, knowledge is accomplished through separation rather than participation. The modern, empiricist notion of objectivity makes the assumption that something can be known in and of itself only through the systematic withdrawal of affective, psychological, and even perceptual projection by the knower. Everything tacit, everything transitional, every trace of the "between"—the body itself, which represents, in fact *is* the unconscious—must be expurgated or, at least bracketed. This kind of knowledge is accomplished through empirical *theory*, which is different from the ancient and medieval, Aristotelian notion of theory as contemplation (from the Greek *theoria*, "to behold").[44] Empiricism, which is most closely associated with the new, decentered Copernican self-world relation, is a way of controlling, formalizing, and standardizing the human projection through depersonalization. The hope of modern theory is that slowly, through successive attempts at application, and a purgative process of falsification, it is emptied of personal, affective, projective elements, and eventually describes the world with an exactitude that is confirmed by our ability to manipulate the thing thus described by predicting what will happen to it using the theory. Hence the connection between modernist theory and technology: the strategy of complete absence of felt identification with the object—whether animate or inanimate—is associated with mastery and control of that object. The Baconian project of "leading nature by the apron strings" requires a form of subjectivity associated with separation and objectification. Read through twentieth-century feminist psychoanalytic theory, it appears as a form of subjectivity modeled on the male relationship with mother/nature—for the male child must define himself through separation, not identification with the mother[45]—and is therefore based on a culturally valorized reification of the natural developmental phenomenon of splitting and projection of psychic elements. In other terms, this is a cultural reification of a subject-object relation in which the experience of transitional space—the "between" of subject and object—has entered a new era of repression.

The modern, silent "reader," removed from his "text," must repress the instinctual and affective ties with the object of his vision in order to know it as it "really" is. He approaches the cosmos from the point of view of what Jonas called an "ontology of death," or the assumption of "panmechanism." For panmechanism the universe, including its animate elements, is composed of combinations of inanimate elements, and so the task is not to explain death, for matter is by definition lifeless. Now "the problem posed to thought," according to Jonas, is "that there is life at all, and how such a thing is possible in a world of mere matter."[46] Mind becomes Descartes' *res cogitans*, a ghost, depending for its ontological status on a God who is outside matter. The thinking subject is placed outside the universe as well. The result is what Jonas called "split-personality theorizing": the theorizer reduces all phenomena to instances and parts of nature, determined by causal laws, except, necessarily himself, "while he assumes and exercises his freedom of inquiry and his openness to reason, evidence, and truth." Soul, once a universal principle of life—and thus of action—once both ground and expression of everything, is now isolated in persons, and becomes a principle of pure subjectivity. "Life" is reduced to "a fact of physics alone . . . a particular corporeal behavior following from a particular corporeal structure which distinguishes a class of objects in nature, viz., the natural automata."[47] Thus modernism performs an ontological reduction of nature, through which it becomes, no longer his filial interlocutor, but his cryptic text, his radical other, which he must learn to read with the controlled projection of mechanistic theory.

The child—particularly the young child—in that her orality is genetic rather than cultural, was necessarily left out of this shift in the Western sensorium and the correlative ontological reduction of nature. The result was that children no longer shared "world" with adults, and were assigned an increasingly different role in a Western culture "come of age." Young children stayed behind, in the cosmos abandoned by philosophers and scientists during the 1600's. Both the young child's world picture and premodern cosmology are marked by anthropocentrism, animism, and laws of correspondence between micro and macrocosm. Both inhabit an organic, teleological cosmos in which there is a magical, dynamic participation between its elements.[48] If this is the case, then the young child was much more at home in the world of the adult (and vice versa) before the Copernican revolution and the rise of panmechanism, and the demise of oral culture meant a new outsider status for the child. From now on the child must be inducted into the new cosmos through a process of training and education. She must be instructed in the form of subjectivity that allows, justifies, and maintains the new ontological convictions—the distances between persons demanded by the new adulthood, and its taboos on certain language and behavior. The child is also instructed, if through the subtlest of language games, about the new adult beliefs—about what is living and what is not, about the nature of, and especially the limits of causal relationships, about the degree of goal or purpose inherent in the life cycles of individuals or of nature itself, about how things came to be in the first place, about the nature of self and of persons in general, and above all about the ego's relations with the unconscious, and the "necessary" relation between instinct and reason.

Because subjectivity is in great part about boundaries and limits—within self, between self and other, and by extension, between self and world—and because boundaries and limits are the topological coordinates of morality, the instruction that children received in the new form of subjectivity was couched in moral terms. And, because adults have so completely internalized their own training in the new social principle marked as *civilité*, their anxiety is aroused when the now-involuntary shame limits are breached, even by children. As Elias put it:

> The more "natural" the standard of delicacy and shame appears to adults and the more the civilized restraint of instinctual urges is taken for granted, the more incomprehensible it becomes to adults that children do not have this delicacy and shame by "nature." The children necessarily touch again and again on the adult threshold of delicacy, and—since they

are not yet adapted—they infringe the taboos of society, cross
the adult shame frontier, and penetrate emotional danger
zones which the adult himself can only control with difficulty.
. . . And the peculiarly emotional undertone so often associated with moral demands, the aggressive and threatening
severity with which they are frequently upheld, reflects the
danger in which any breach of the prohibitions places the
unstable balance of all those for whom the standard behavior
of society has become more or less "second nature."[49]

Given the new atmosphere of the possibility of transgression and
moral danger between adults and children, there arose a need to separate children from the public world of adults. In a social world where
there is strict control of affect and instinctual expression in public, children are too natural for comfort, and they offend against the unspoken
rules of surplus-repression. Thus they were increasingly relegated to the
status of a separate class and isolated in the institutions of the new, private middle-class home, and the school. The separation between adults
and children among the middle classes was happening even as those
same middle classes moved to colonize the mad in asylums, aboriginals
on reservations, and, it could be argued, women in the home. The social
technologies that Foucault identifies as "discipline"—"normalization,"
the "examination" of one sort or another through which the "normal"
is defined, and hierarchical observation—are, as he argued, forms of
"subjection," or technologies for the production of a certain form of
individual subjectivity: a "docile body" that "may be subjected, used,
transformed and improved," a "body . . . in the grip of very strict
powers, which imposed on it constraints, prohibitions or obligations."[50]
The subjection of the child through the machinery of power of the institution of the school was—and remains—a project for constructing a
universal, standardized form of subjectivity suitable for the purposes of
an increasingly hegemonic centralized state and economy. This project
shaped the goals and methodologies of state-administered universal
compulsory education from its most obvious debut in post-revolutionary Napoleonic France, and throughout its growth and entrenchment
during the nineteenth century.[51] The child had become a new kind of
"native" for modern adult subjectivity, and one of the most dangerous
sort, for it came from one's own ranks.
   If the effective cause of the increasingly universal isolation of children in schools was the set of exigencies of the new information environment, the formal cause was state colonization. In a nonliterate world
there is little need to distinguish between children and adults or to treat

them that differently, whereas in a world in which information travels through print, there is a split between those who can read and those who cannot. Since children cannot read, in a literate world, they must undergo a qualitative shift in order to become adults, a shift that involves labor and discipline. In addition, the silent, removed world of print, inaccessible to children, creates what Neil Postman called a "non-observed, abstract world of knowledge"—a world apart from the common world that adults and children once shared. The split led to what he described as the "re-invention of the school" in Europe.[52] Universal schooling, combined with the separation of home and workplace effected by the Industrial Revolution, completed the separation of the worlds of children and adults. The movement was coterminous with the movement among the middle classes to isolate women in the home, removing them as well from a male world in which instrumentalism and separative individualism became the ideal. Like children's, women's ways of knowing were split off from the normative ideal, which Ashis Nandy has described as "the adult male as the ultimate in God's creation and as the this-worldly end-state for everyone [which] was endorsed by the new salience of the productivity principle and Promethean activism"[53] of modernism.

By the end of the nineteenth century, the traditional, commonsense view of childhood as a preliminary state to adulthood, and the unreflective understanding of childhood as a lesser, deficit-ridden condition, a period of excess and obscurity—that is, adultism—had thus been worked out historically and enshrined, not only in the modern institution of the school, but in the forms of life of modern middle-class culture. Children were no longer just functionally but psychologically and discursively marginalized. Dominant Western male genetic epistemologies had split off the child (and the woman) both internally and externally, and no longer recognized the child's form of knowledge except as sentimentality, superstition, or naivete. For the modern adult, inhabiting a silenced cosmos—its organic, unitary, elemental relations replaced by mechanistic, atomized ones—the child, who represented the old, participatory cosmos, became problematic, a stranger, another representation of danger, from within and from below, to the new instinctual economy of surplus-repression in the service of the performance principle.

The Evolution of the Adult-Child Relationship

And now another story, an even grander narrative, which claims that the adult-child relation has in fact been evolving over Western cultural time, and that each stage in this evolution represents a closer approach between the two. The direction of this evolution has—seen from the psychohistorical perspective just presented—been toward separation. Seen from a dialectical perspective, this separation is understood as a moment implicitly oriented toward overcoming separation in a more highly developed unity, or unity-in-difference. This is the story of adulthood separating from, then journeying toward a reencounter with childhood on another level. It is based on an understanding of both collective and individual development as beginning in undifferentiated fusion, followed by splitting and separation of elements, and leading through periods of growth and crisis to a reintegration of those elements as a differentiated, articulated unity. In psychoanalytic parlance, they are reconstellated under what Jung called a "transcendent function," a dialectical third that "resolves the tension—of energy and content—existing between the ego stability of consciousness and the contrary tendency of the unconscious to overwhelm it."[54] The story leads to the hypothesis—to be taken up in the next chapter—that the West is currently a century or two into a historical moment in which adultism is being overcome in those same middle classes in which it arose, and that there is emerging, not only a new form of adult-child relation, but a new form of adult subjectivity that results from this relation, since it is based on the adult's relationship with his own childhood, which is to say a new relationship between the elements of his or her own subjective structure.

In antiquity, as this story—developed by Lloyd deMause[55]—goes, adults were fused with their children to such an extent that they not only projected their shadow contents onto them, but acted upon those projections, and commonly battered and even murdered them as a result. According to deMause, infanticide was common in the ancient world, and what we would call child abuse—both physical and sexual—was a norm. The child was the "toilet lap" for the unresolved sexual and aggressive contents of adults. Children who expressed instinctual needs or aggression evoked those same poorly contained contents in adults, leading to murderous reaction, or—what is virtually the same thing—to considering them as scarcely human, accepted into life at the discretion of the head of the family (*pater potestias*). This was the "Infanticidal Mode" of the adult-child relation, which prevailed well into the first millenium.

The second mode, Abandonment, represented a partial withdrawal or containment of the projective reaction of adults to children. Now, especially under the influence of Christianity, infanticide was no longer socially acceptable. Adults were emotionally separated enough from their children that they dealt with their projective reactions through abandonment instead of battering or murder. This pattern was related—as was the first—to the dramatic fluctuations in the food supply to which whole populations were constantly liable, but whether this chronic instability caused or allowed the psychodynamics of infanticide and abandonment is moot. The abandoning parent distances his child—in our times often through television, day-care centers, nannies, or boarding schools—for the level of instinctual need the child evokes and surfaces in him or her is too dangerous, and the ethics of relation that the child's very presence calls for is too much self-work.

The ninth century saw the rise of the Ambivalent Mode. Parental love and tolerance of children was now a more accepted social value. The psychodynamics of selfhood were such in this period that the adult began to experience the projective reaction as the felt need to "discipline" his own projected contents—to "drive them out of" the child. Here are the roots of what came to ideological fruition in Calvinism: the conviction that human nature is inherently depraved, and that without the saving discipline of a higher power—the parent as a stand-in for God—we are condemned to our own selfishness and evil. Human subjectivity is here understood as permanently—unless dramatically converted—under the sign of the shadow, and children are its proof-text. One need only look at the nature of children—who don't conceal as adults do their cupidity, their egocentrism, their aggression, and the ease with which they are corrupted, whether by servants, pedophile priests, or peers—to see what human beings are really like. This was the age of the myth of the "changeling," a look-alike infant demon that the devil and his minions substitute, under cover of night, for the infant in his crib.

In the Ambivalent Mode the adult's shadow-projection is barely contained, but in fact it is contained, and translated into at least the beginnings of a strategic program of forceful transformation of the child through, if not education, at least discipline and punishment. Perhaps this was a first general recognition, if in (for us) a distorted and perverse form, of the malleability of human nature through child rearing and education. Erasmus, although he tended to represent later modes, strikes the tone when, in his best-selling child-rearing manual of 1530, he characterized the child as a "natural void," and asked "So what are we to expect of man? He will most certainly turn out to be an unproductive brute unless at once and without delay he is subjected to a process of intensive instruction."[56] In this stage the adult still sees only the shadow projection in the needy child, but it doesn't trigger extreme violence or abandonment; in fact Christian and in particular Calvinist anthropology could even be seen as a first stage in owning the shadow. Being able to recognize it in himself, and even attribute it to human nature in general, is a step beyond projecting it onto the other in the form of child, slave, woman, "native" or "barbarian." It is separated and well-enough contained within the adult that he begins to attribute it, not just to infantile, but to human nature in general.

With the Intrusive Mode, which was more or less coterminous with Renaissance, Reformation, and the gradual emergence of capitalism and the middle classes—that is, the rise of the modern reality principle—we rejoin the narrative of the invention of adulthood. Here the adult has separated himself from the child to the extent that he sees the possibility of a methodical process of eradication of the child "nature" (thereby securing again and vindicating the eradication of his own "fallen nature") through technologies of child rearing and education. The shadow contents are still split off within the adult and projected onto the paradigmatic other—the child, that "stranger who while being Other is me"—but the instinctual danger that the child represents is recognized as within all of us. The responsible parent must "reach inside the child and rearrange her very insides."[57] Now mental punishment is preferred over physical punishment, although the latter is sometimes necessary. Thus at the height of Reformational notions of innate sinfulness, Protestant religious and psychological individualism opens the door to the possibility of overcoming this sinfulness through technologies of the self; and the primary technology of the self, applied to the other, is education, training, and methodical, systematic planned action upon the infant body—in short, "discipline." As a German child-rearing manual of 1748 assures us, "If willfulness and wickedness are not driven out, it is impossible to give a child a good education. The moment these flaws appear in a child, it is high time to resist this evil so that it does not become ingrained through habit and the children do not become thoroughly depraved." And the author adds a rationale that evokes in a few sentences the level of splitting, fragmentation, and denial of the unconscious required by the new instinctual economy:

> One of the advantages of these early years is that then force and compulsion can be used. Over the years, children forget everything that ever happened to them in early childhood. If their wills can be broken at this time, they will never remember afterwards that they had a will, and for this very reason the severity that is required will not have any serious consequences.[58]

As ominous as this statement may seem to twenty-first century ears, this planned assault upon the soul and body of the child represented the moment in the evolution of the child-rearing modes when the adult reached the furthest degree of separation and started turning to the child as an interlocutor. In fact it was the historical moment of the invention of childhood: for the child, however negatively characterized, was now understood by adults as a crucial site for the reproduction of the new, appropriately repressed adult. Some connection with childhood as a separate form of life had been made, even if it manifested as a relation of domination over and implicit violence toward the child's form of life. The less the child resembled the adult, the more she became the object of adult attention. Said otherwise, the more the adult differentiated from the child, the more visible the child became to her. The child now had a soul (the "natives" of the colonies, not yet). In hermeneutical terms, this is the furthest moment of distanciation, the last attempt to take complete control of the other with one's projections, the moment just before the moment of negativity and the opening of the "between"—the recognition of the other as unassimilable to our own projections—which is the necessary preliminary for dialogue.

It certainly is not dialogue. As Elias said of the Intrusive adults of the early modern period, it is "incomprehensible" to them that children are not like them "by 'nature'"—the surest sign of a projective relation. Children "touch again and again on the adult threshold of delicacy, . . . they infringe the taboos of society, cross the adult shame frontier, and penetrate emotional danger zones which the adult himself can only control with difficulty." So all demands on children have an undertone of moral insistence, of "aggressive and threatening severity." The child becomes a site for unremitting work, for hypervigilance; "one must not cease toiling," our German child-rearing manual tells us, "until all willfulness is gone." The child may be an alienated, estranged being, but she has the adult's full attention.

That attention varied in emphasis. For both Renaissance humanists and Protestant reformers, not only was the ancient ideal of the *puer senex*—long applied to the legendary childhoods of saints and heroic figures—a strong guiding image in relating to children, but it was actively pursued through a passionate concern with literacy, as well as an intense preoccupation with personal religious experience. Among these classes, children of seven years of age were assumed to enter school already reading and writing and ready for classical languages, which they sometimes studied from six in the morning until five-thirty, with only short breaks, for ten or eleven months a year.[59] The sixteenth and seventeenth were the centuries of the child prodigy, and under such intensive discipline, many children reached levels of accomplishment in letters and mathematics that contemporary genetic epistemologists would not think possible, much less "developmentally appropriate." They were also the centuries of the active evangelization of children by their Calvinist parents. Children were assumed to be capable of recognizing their sinfulness—not just of act, but of intention—and of repenting and turning toward a new identity in Christ. Thus, religious education of the young became a matter of great urgency.

This early-modern attention to children of the Intrusive Mode may seem to us closer to abuse than to nurture or education, but it was just this assiduous, careful attention given to children by early moderns that provides us the first example of the active, purposeful interest in children as individuals that is much more common today. The Puritans, for example, were quite clear that their children were persons in the full Christian sense of that term—that they had "souls" that were of equal value to the souls of adults. Janeway's claim of children that "they are not too little to die, they are not too little to go to Hell, they are not too little to serve their great Master, too little to go to Heaven,"[60] can be read in two ways. From one point of view, it is an example of the extent to which the early moderns, in their obsession with transforming children into adults through rigorous spiritual and educational exercise, made of them "miniature adults"—thus completely misinterpreting them, and providing the most extreme example of adult egocentrism in regard to children. From another, it is the beginning of an unprecedented emphasis placed by adults on children and childhood as a crucial life stage, as well as a new sense of responsibility toward children on the part of adults, and an interest in them as persons in their own right. As Marcus points out, "Puritan belief in the corruption of the unregenerate child's nature led them to investigate that nature with a shrewdness of psychological insight unprecedented in earlier educational writings."[61] To make both readings at once maintains the ambiguity and ambivalence that pervades the adult's understanding of the child.

This ambiguity is a major theme of the adult-child relation in itself, and must not be avoided. It is present, not just in the pietistic tradition, but in the secular as well, and is at the origins—both chronologically and methodologically—of the modern approach to children. It is present, for example, in the originators of the two major thematic emphases of modern education, John Locke and Rousseau. Locke, whose associationist theory legitimated what could be termed the "etic" or training school of education, a behavioristic tradition that is the foundation of public, universal education, was also, as the author of a widely read child-rearing manual published in 1693, an early critic of corporeal punishment and respecter of the individuality of children. Rousseau, although correctly associated with progressive, child-centered education, in fact holds epistemological views that, apart from the prophetic undercurrent that informs *Emile*, verge on a deficit model of childhood. As for Locke the child is a cognitive *tabula rasa*, for Rousseau the child is "devoid of all morality in his actions," having a soul that is "yet blind," at an age "when the heart feels nothing yet"—"childhood is reason's sleep."[62] Even the statements which make his reputation as the *emeritus* of the progressive tradition in modern education, examined in context, signal not so much an appreciation of the child qua child as a legitimating rhetoric for an educational technique, based on the highly mechanistic French sensationalist psychology of the eighteenth century, which has distinct behavioristic characteristics, and is as intrusive and as it is manipulative.

Thus, both Locke and Rousseau, in that they were major philosophical voices of their day, offered a new legitimation for taking an interest in children. Both also reinforced for modernity an image of the child as a rudimentary condition, raw material for the new man of reason, to be produced through a systematic, theoretically driven (whether "hands on" or "hands off"), program of socialization. For both, as paradigmatic moderns, the child represents nature, an untamed wilderness to be shaped and transformed by method. That Rousseau's method is a negative rather than a positive one—"letting nature alone in everything"[63]—is, in his hands, no less a way of shaping nature. Ironically enough, *Emile* resonates more with twentieth-century behaviorist technology than Locke's *Some Thoughts Concerning Education*, although it was Locke's genetic epistemology that came to ground twentieth-century behaviorist theory. And the increasing number of child-rearing manuals of the late eighteenth century—among which was *Emile*—are testimony to the new, technological approach toward childhood characteristic of the Intrusive Mode. But the ambiguity can never be forgotten, for in fact this new approach represented an ever increasing attention to, and even absorption in, childhood. It would take the movement of which Rousseau was the first, self-contradictory and inconsistent representative—the Romantic critique of Enlightenment reason—to spawn a more widespread interest in children apart from what adults could make them into through education.

The Intrusive Mode found its most complete and lasting expression in the rise of universal, compulsory schooling—both in its institutional goals and in its forms and methods. The Intrusive Mode made alliance—as did the rise of "discipline" in general in the eighteenth and nineteenth centuries—with the interests of the hegemonic state, so perfectly exemplified in its first post-revolutionary manifestation in the modern totalitarian nation in France—the Napoleonic—where in 1808 a unified educational system was established, and instruction at all levels was devoted to the systematic training of "citizens" devoted to religion, prince, "fatherland," and family.[64] The school as an early expression of disciplinary technology carried the same assumptions and used the same techniques as did the army, the prison, and the asylum. Discipline simultaneously found its way into the emergent nuclear family in the increasingly influential theoretically driven pronouncements of the medical profession. Aries argued persuasively that as the state increased in power and influence through its ability to keep the peace and to order the social environment, the family, deprived of its role in maintaining social order, shrank to nuclear size[65] and became another state-sanctioned site for the reproduction of the worker-citizen. The patriarch-father was the administrator of this new mini-colony.

But even as the Intrusive Mode was reified in political and social institutions, it was reaching its term from within. For as the spirit of individualism increased, and the new psychological inwardness associated with modern subjectivity emerged and proliferated, and as these tendencies both reinforced and were reinforced by the rise of political liberalism, the child came increasingly to be recognized as a subject in her own right. In the case of England, Lawrence Stone associates the rise of a new "affective individualism" in adult-child relations with the conflict between Calvinistic anthropology and a growing secularism that began near the end of the socially and politically turbulent seventeenth century.[66] That century's struggles over the emergence of ideals of political and religious autonomy were isomorphic with a similar process within individual self-understanding, and with the understanding of the self's place in the universe. The conclusions and implications of the physical sciences of the age—empiricism's new direct link between science and technology in the service of "mastering nature," Newton's impersonal, clockwork universe—all served to subvert the Great Chain of Being, or the understanding of the universe as a hierarchically ordered structure to which humans were subordinated. As the normative idea of cosmic individualism in the form of Reformed Christianity, discrete, boundaried subjectivity, and political tolerance grew, it must eventually be applied, not just to the white male adult, but to every other, including the child.

As childhood is otherness, the excluded underside of adult subjectivity, it remains the wilderness of the unconscious to be subdued and cultivated, and the "white paper" upon which the modern adult, understood as the not-child, is authored. The repression of the characteristics of child subjectivity in adult self-understanding and the construction of childhood as a space for the colonization of "nature" was paralleled in early modernism by the psychosocial adventure of the discovery and colonization of the "new world" of the Americas. The "wild man," a figure that haunted the Jews and the Greeks from ancient times as a symbol of human nature "outside the city" reappeared in modern discourse as a thoroughly ambivalent figure.

The new world "savage" was, like all those who live beyond the rule of law, either an animal or a god, a prime object for projections of either good or evil by those who live within the rule. The "native" or "aboriginal" was another paradigmatic other for modern European man. He or she symbolized, with the characteristic ambivalence of the projection, either the spontaneous plenitude of a form of subjectivity still in touch with nature and the unconscious, (i.e., nature both without and within) or the original state of depravity assumed by both Hobbes and Calvin. The "savage" was offered either as a critique of our own over-socialized nature or as an ominous example of what happens to human nature when, as Erasmus insisted, it is not "at once and without delay . . . subjected to a process of intensive instruction." The ambivalence of the wild man in Western self-understanding found representative expression in Daniel Defoe, whose *Robinson Crusoe*—a narrative of the modern European adult refinding his wild man and an instant classic from its appearance in 1719—was matched by his later reflections on a real wild man: Peter the wild boy, about 15 years old, was discovered in Germany in 1724 and brought to London in 1726, where he became a sensation. Having met with Peter in person, Defoe argued at length that "Education seems to me to be the only specifick Remedy for all the Imperfections of Nature."[67]

The child is both the wild man within modernist civilization and within the civilized individual. He is a unique sort of wild man, in that for modern, repressed subjectivity, one needn't travel—even to the other side of the tracks—to encounter him. He is the enemy within the gates of civilization itself—or in the positive projection, the noble savage in one's own home, a constant reminder to the adult, either as primordial good or primordial depravity, of his own prehistory—of a subjectivity outside the gates of the city of the super-developed ego-function of the modern self. Historian Hayden White has said of the Western psychohistorical process,

> From biblical times to the present, the notion of the Wild
> Man was associated with the idea of the wilderness—the
> desert, forest, jungle, and mountains—those parts of the

physical world that had not yet been domesticated or marked
out for domestication in any significant way. As one after
another of these wildernesses was brought under control, the
idea of the Wild Man was progressively despatialized. This
despatialization was attended by a compensatory process of
psychic interiorization."[68]

In the Intrusive Mode, childhood, which represents the last wilderness for adult subjectivity, is "marked out for domestication." For those
nineteenth-century crusaders of civilization, both Christian and secular,
the domestication of childhood offered the promise of the domestication of history. But the emergence of this hope in fact heralded the terminus of the Intrusive Mode, for it was the dialectical moment in which
the psychohistorical structure manifested the internal contradictions
that would lead to its transformation. At the very moment in which the
othering of the child assumed hegemonic proportions in the ideal of
universal, compulsory education-as-discipline and in the search for a
"science" (meaning a proto-technology) of child rearing, its antithesis
emerged in Romanticism, for which the Wild Man—and the child—is
identified with that part of the self that modern subjectivity has
repressed and split off. Romanticism affirms and identifies with the
enemy. The adult has now come to the end of his rope; he turns and
faces both the child and the "primitive." He recognizes the other as
himself—he acknowledges and owns his shadow projection—and so
begins a process of dialogue.

The process is both internal and external. In recognizing the other
as himself, he recognizes himself as an other. He recognizes himself as a
composite structure, and he understands that the executive center of
this composite structure, the "ego," or Plato's "reason" is not in control
of—perhaps not even aware of—all the elements of the structure. In a
structure that has turned from vertical (hierarchical) to horizontal (dialogical), the exclusions and hierarchies that the ego has persuaded itself
are necessary to unity become dangerous schisms and hiatuses. In addition, he understands, as N.O. Brown put it, that

> Projection and introjection, the process whereby the self as dis-
> tinct from the other is constituted, is not past history, an event
> in childhood, but a present process of continuous creation.
> The dualism of self and external world is built up by a con-
> stant process of reciprocal exchange between the two. The self
> as a stable substance enduring through time, an identity, is
> maintained by constantly absorbing good parts (or people)

from the outside world and expelling bad parts from the inner world. There is a continual unconscious wandering of other personalities into ourselves. . . . Every person, then, is many persons . . . We are members of one another.[69]

So begins one aspect of the transformation from modern to post-modern subjectivity, in which the subject has become a field of multiple relationships, a subject-in-process. There is no subject as fixed essence, there is only the process of subjectivity, which in philosopher and psychologist Julia Kristeva's words, is a "field of relationships," continually "constructed and deconstructed in an interplay between his discourse and the other."[70] Two generations after the "high" Romantics, Freud began the exploration of this new self-understanding, and identified childhood—and the adult's relationship to her own childhood—as its major problematic. After Freud, childhood is understood as present and active throughout the life cycle. In keeping with the ambivalence that runs like a fault line through the history of the adult-child relation, childhood for Freud was the site both of trauma and fixation, and—in his concept of primary narcissism—a form of subject-world relationship that is the matrix of adult creativity, and therefore of the possibility for the continual transformation of subjectivity. Childhood is the place of structural transformation, both as memory and as possibility.

The child is the subject-in-process, the "field of relationships," exemplified. The dimensionality of childhood is the dimensionality of creativity, both individual and cultural, and child rearing represents for the adult the possibility of the deconstruction of the ego's monotheistic, "thematizing gaze"—the beginning of what Levinas calls "the liberation of the ego with regard to the self." It is the end of the reign of reason, if reason is understood as that form of knowledge, which, as he characterizes it, "never encounters anything truly other in the world"[71] because it assimilates, through projection, the other to its own structures of judgment. This dialectical shift in the normative meaning and significance of the adult-child relationship was isomorphic with the crisis of rationalism of the post-Enlightenment West that Romanticism inaugurated. As Merleau-Ponty put it, "the attempt to explore the irrational and integrate it into an expanded reason . . . remains the task of our [twentieth] century."[72]

It is in institutionalized education that the reorientation of adult subjectivity that begins in parenthood is carried from the family into society. The imperative for dialogue that was announced with the appearance of the child-as-subject in Romanticism was institutionalized first in the family and then in the school. In a school understood as a site for adult-child dialogue, the teacher is a paradigmatic hermeneut of childhood, for he undergoes dialogue, not just with his own interior childhood, but with the persons of many actual children, and the culture of childhood in its current historical form. In this new formulation, school remains what it has always been—a place where the child is introduced to the discourses and the forms of knowledge of adult culture, and to the culture of childhood of her own time. But when the adult enters this experience as a subject-in-process, as a "decentered" ego for whom the child is an interlocutor rather than an object of manipulation, the school is understood as the communicative space in which children *and* adults are in a process of mutual transformation. School is the cultural "between" of the dialogical relation, the space of difference, which is the space neither of the subject nor the object, the adult or the child, but where their forms of life meet and converse. It is analogous to the theater, or the artist's studio. It is a space of play and creativity, where new cultural forms, new forms of subject-object relation, and new forms of negotiation between primary and secondary process are tried out. It is the space where life and art meet in the interests of individual, cultural, and social transformation.

The adult involved in the life-cycle moment that Erik Erikson called the "generative"—the moment of turning and caring for the next generation[73]—is also the moment that Jung identifies as the onset of individuation—the process of the decentering of the ego in the interests of further self-integration. This, in turn, is identified with Levinas' "rupture of the egoist-I and its reconditioning in the face of the other," or the moment of the emergence of a new form of alterity, or being-in-relation-to-the-other. As the monotheistic, hierarchical self is deconstructed, the self understood as in a continual process of reconstruction becomes possible. The subject-in-process is a form of selfhood whose boundaries—both internal and external—have become problematized. It is the end of what Elias called the "discrete self," or *homo clausus* (closed man), the epistemological subject of classical philosophy, the self who might as well have come into the world as an adult, whose "core, his being, his true self appears . . . as something divided within him by an invisible wall from everything outside, including every other human being."[74] *Homo Clausus* is the adult self of the Intrusive adult-child relation, in whom childhood is dramatically split off, invested with ambivalent projections and identifications, and projected onto the real child.

The Intrusive form of adult subjectivity showed the first signs of its eventual transformation in the first half of the nineteenth century under the influence what deMause has called the Socializing Mode. Here the parent still understands the child as an instinctually ambivalent creature, but the element of danger has been reduced to the extent that the adult now identifies with that instinctual ambivalence, and is no longer blindsided by it in her own psychic economy. For the authors of the early-nineteenth-century form of autobiography called the Childhood, the child was denizen of a lost paradise of self-world unity, or the myth of the wild man projected backwards and placed in his original Eden. For the theologically liberal middle classes, this wildness was reappropriated and redeemed as a form of energy that did not need to be forcibly excised or repressed or suppressed in children. Certain culturally influential adults no longer felt the need to "reach into the very insides" of the child through discipline, but rather to create forms and styles of parenting and education that provided structures that shaped the "wildness" into socially acceptable forms. This is first fruits of Romanticism's affirmation of the unconscious and the irrational, contemporary with the new culture wars then raging in Christian circles over the doctrine of original sin.

At this moment in the adult-child relation, a new metaphor of childhood began to emerge in adult discourse—the child as plant, and education as gardening. The organic metaphor replaced earlier Ambivalent and Intrusive metaphors of malleable wax and *tabula rasa*. The gardener need only provide enough light, enough water, perhaps (depending on the child) some weeding, and a nutrient-rich soil for the emergence of a psychologically healthy adult. The child still represented nature, and nature still needed to be tamed—but not forcibly subdued. The plant is nature understood as endowed with an internal developmental plan, which, given the right conditions, will unfold of itself. A continuity had been established between the child and the adult. Wordsworth's phrase "the child is father to the man," which seems so obvious today as to appear tautological, was in the nineteenth century, a dawning realization. The Intrusive Mode, which constructed adulthood as completely separate from childhood—and consciousness, represented by ego, as completely separate from the unconscious— had reached its term, and the moment of the possibility of dialogue had arrived. At this furthest moment of hermeneutical distantiation, the adult turned and began to face the child.

Dialogue becomes possible at the dialectical moment of separation because it is only at this moment that there is the possibility of a critical stance toward our own projections. The projective reaction is now even further controlled, for the adult recognizes his own nature in the instinctual expression of the child—a nature that, in the Socializing Mode, still needs to be shaped, but not forcibly reconstructed. The advent of the Socializing Mode was in fact the historical moment in which the benign projection—the "divine child"—began to emerge in Romantic philosophical and literary thought. Now the stage was set for Freud and the rise of deMause's last, contemporary mode, the Empathic, beginning in the mid twentieth century; but it would be another hundred years—after nineteenth-century evolutionary theory, which annexed the child as did the doctrine of original sin a century earlier, played itself out—before adult-child dialogue as a cultural ideal on a wide scale became possible.

From a dialectical point of view, evolutionary theory's appropriation of childhood in the late nineteenth century represents a scientific (replacing the theological) reification of the separation between adult and child, and a move into even further objectification. From this, the nondialogical side of the separation, the child is connected with adults, but the connection is between a lower and a higher form of life. In evolutionary theory, the Socializing Mode's metaphor of the child as plant is transformed into an even more radically organismic doctrine, based on the new biology, which takes more primitive forms of life as its explanatory model for the human. It is no accident that Piaget, the foremost child psychology theorist of the twentieth century, did his first research (at the age of 13) on the effects of the changing environment of Lake Geneva on the form and development of the molluscs inhabiting it.

The rise of developmental psychology in the late nineteenth century,[75] based on this organismic, objectifying model, provided the legitimating theory for the deployment of massive modern educational systems during that same period. The "science of childhood" staked out and developed by the new disciplines of psychology and sociology reified the actual marginalization of children in institutions through framing childhood in a series of regularized explanatory narratives, all of which were based on theories whose general principles were founded on the nonhuman—the first and most primary of which was (as was already implicit in Aristotle), evolutionary biology. These narratives are based on the observation of children within the world organized for them by adults, and act to legitimate that organization, thus operating in a recursive cycle. Two basic tenets of Darwin's theory, for example, lent themselves to an image of the child that neatly paralleled the latter's increasing social, cultural, and psychological colonization by institutional forces: the theory of progression, by which simple forms of life were said to precede more complex forms; and the theory of transformation, by which the more complex were said to be descended from simpler forms.[76] Both theories placed the child, with the mollusc, the ape, and the "primitive" (about whom information was, through the new science of anthropology, flooding into the West) on a lower level of a phylogenetic continuum. The conviction that the child in its ontogenesis was recapitulating the phylogenetic evolution of the race became the founding and guiding theory in child study in the late nineteenth and early twentieth centuries. As a way of seeing childhood, the law of recapitulation represents a height of adultism, in that it regards all of childhood's forms of life—whether cognitive, affective, sexual, or moral, as merely preformative states. And in defining the child as a more primitive life form, it sanctions the organization and the coercion of children, and their separation into different environments, where they are handled by "specialists." It represents the discourse of Foucaultian "discipline" reified in scientific theory.

Evolutionary doctrine annexed childhood as its proof-text for the human condition just as the doctrine of original sin had done before it. The child as deficit, wilderness, or chaos is no longer postulated as one side of an ontological split, but is assimilated into colonialist discourse as an aspect of a developmental pattern. In recapitulation theory, the child and the "native" are assimilated to each other. The latter is a manifestation of the "childhood" of the species, and hence must be treated as a child. The colonial outpost and the school become analogous. White Western bourgeois subjectivity, and its exemplar in the white adult bourgeois male, is reified as a normative ideal.[77]

Evolution's grand narrative is implicit in the thought of Piaget, who, along with Freud, was the most influential interpreter of childhood of the twentieth century. In his early book *The Child's Conception of the World,* he aligns children's implicit ontological and epistemological theories both with "primitive" mentality and with the thinking of ancient philosophers.[78] The endpoint of cognitive development for Piaget is the subject-world relation that he calls "formal operations," based on a logic of separation and objectification, and implicitly excluding the body, the unconscious, the emotions, and intersubjectivity except as the experience of entertaining multiple perspectives. Piaget reifies the modern middle-class European subject of surplus-repression as scientific theory, and reproduces the notion of the white Western male adult as an endpoint of development on the plane of cognitive psychology. Half a century later, Piaget's normative ideal for intelligence was imported into ethics in Lawrence Kohlberg's theory of moral development, in which is implicit the notion of the decentered, deracinated, male adult as a terminus of subjective and intersubjective development.

Piaget's and Kohlberg's formulations exemplify the Socializing Mode. Both cognitive and ethical/intersubjective development are constructed as unidirectional, and assume an endpoint from which the fully formed adult looks back, and toward which he brings children through childrearing and education. Freud's work shared these implicit assumptions of late-nineteenth- and early-twentieth-century evolutionism; he too postulated a series of stages—in this case psychosexual—which moved genetically in the direction of a normative adulthood. Childhood represents the unresolved elements of the adult personality. The neurotic, or the unsuccessful adult, is neurotic because he is fixated on elements of his childhood experience, and successful maturity depends on overcoming them through the distancing and resolution of the psychoanalytic process. But Freud's model, whatever its adultist clinical goals, is inherently subversive of adultism, for it introduces, not just the notion of the unconscious, which is another "Copernican Revolution" in Western self-understanding, but the child-within as interlocutor in the adult's process of achieving emotional health, and thus implicitly breaks with the notion of adulthood as a fixed state. Beginning with Freud, the adult is now understood as a process-being, whether that process is formulated as a clean-up operation of the residues of childhood or not. And the adult preoccupied with the child-within eventually turns to the child before her, for that child now evokes her own internal dialogue—which is the necessary context for the Empathic Mode.

Both ruling metaphors of the Socializing Mode—the plant in the garden and the organism recapitulating the developmental stages of the species—presume, as the Intrusive Mode did not, that the child will become an adult in the "normal" course of development. The child is still a pre-adult, but its forms of life, although still appropriated by a theory that sees them as no more than stages in a process of "growing up," are no longer considered a necessary threat to its potential future as an adult. The child is accepted as a subject, but does not yet have a voice: whatever she says is pre-understood by the adult, and can be predicted. But at least the child is no longer another species, or a projected representation of dangerous, split-off elements of the adult psyche. Although the life cycle is still understood as linear and unidirectional, a continuity between the life-phases of child and adult has been recognized. Childhood is still understood as overcome in adulthood—unless one is "neurotic," in which case one is working on overcoming it—and one does not enter into dialogue with what one has overcome. It is the entry into the final child-rearing mode of this grand psychohistorical narrative—the Empathic —which signals the onset of dialogue, for it is here that the child—both the child within and the child before me—becomes a catalyst for the adult's developmental process. The Empathic adult, in recognizing "neurosis" as a normative human condition, turns by necessity to childhood for purposes of self-reconstruction. Thus the normative ideal emerges, decades after Freud but as a central aspect of his legacy, of the mature or "realized" adult as the one who has resolved his or her childhood through integrating it into her subjective process rather than repressing it.

In the Empathic Mode, childhood is recognized as never overcome. As deMause describes it, the Empathic adult, confronted with the child's instinctual expression—or as he states it, "the child who needs something"—is able "to regress to the level of the child's need and identify with it without an admixture of the adult's own projections. The adult must be able to maintain enough distance from the need to be able to satisfy it."[79] The Empathic stance exemplifies the hermeneutical relation, in that the possibility for dialogue depends on a distanciation, followed by a disappropriation of self or "moment of negativity" followed by a "fusion of horizons," resulting in reappropriation, or reconstruction of self. It is a dialogical relation in that it is undergone in mutuality: in "regressing to the level of the child's need," the empathic adult is undergoing the crossing of the boundaries of subjectivity of the discrete self, and entering the transitional space of the "between" with the other, or the space of what I will call the "intersubject."

It is characteristic of the intersubject—as opposed to the discrete subject in interpersonal fusion—that the boundaries are crossed but not merged, melted, eradicated, or violated. The subject that recognizes itself as plural—which understands its identity as part of an integrated, field relationship with the other—enters a space in which what is mine and what is yours, what is me and what is you, what I am responsible for and what you are, do not so much collapse into each other as become the subject for discourse and negotiation.

It is just because the adult can identify with the child *and* maintain distance that she is able both to recognize and satisfy her needs. It is the absence of this capacity for psychic distance that distinguishes Aries', Huizinga's, Elias' and deMause's characterization of medieval, premodern subjectivity. It is the hypertrophy of this psychic distance that characterizes, not just Elias' description of the separated, discrete self of modernity, but the whole literature of alienation from the mid-nineteenth century on—from Kierkegaard, Nietzsche, and Dostoevsky to the sociological analysis of subjectivity initiated in Durkheim, and its dramatic philosophical expression in the existentialist tradition of the mid-twentieth century. In terms of the dialectical reconstruction of Western subjectivity through historical time, *homo clausus* is a necessary moment in the emergence of the postmodern intersubject. The

latter retains the elements of advance gained in the modern Cartesian/
Kantian/Piagetian subject, while recuperating on another level what was
lost in the shift away from the premodern, collective, or "fused" subject. And the message of the evolutionary narrative of the child-rearing
modes is that it is the relationship with that unique other among
others—the child—upon which this dialectical reconstruction of subjectivity on a broad historical-cultural level hinges. On this account, to
"regress to the level of the child's need"—which is to reexperience childhood in some form—increases rather than erodes the emotional autonomy and the capacity to make distinctions between oneself and the
other that are the normative virtues of the modern adult. But it does so,
not at the expense of the other—not through objectifying her—but
through experiencing one's own otherness. This is the form of alterity of
the postmodern subject.

The grand narrative of the six modes may seem a little less presumptive and historically naive to us—less of a myth and more of a
heuristic—if we don't insist on a linear, unilateral reading. In fact it has
been suggested[80] that all six modes—Infanticidal, Abandoning,
Ambivalent, Intrusive, Socializing, and Empathic—have always been
present in human culture, and that they undergo epochal decline and
resurgence. Each epoch defines one of the modes as normal, if not necessarily normative. Nor does this more ahistorical interpretation necessarily destroy the evolutionary implications of the theory, for it still
represents a directional movement away from a fused, projective relationship with childhood and toward a dialogical one. But the possibilities for familial expression of the modes, not just across epoch, but
across variations in culture—and within culture, across variations in
context and situation—are numerous. Two parents could operate in
different modes, for example; or a person's self-description as a
parent—her philosophy of childhood—could identify her as Intrusive,
but in critical situations she might operate empathically; or vice versa.
Or a parent might experience—and practice—all the modes throughout
his child-rearing years, depending on changing ideological persuasion,
the age of the child, the particular child in question, or all three of
these. Or a parent may experience a moment of conversion from one
mode to the other, especially as a reversal reaction to her own parents'
child-rearing mode. In addition, in our epoch, at least in the U.S., the
Intrusive, Socializing, and Empathic modes have evolved into ideological positions in those culture wars that began in the late twentieth century, and have become symbols for opposing beliefs about human
nature and of the role of change, conflict, freedom, order, desire,

autonomy, and responsibility in various competing constructions of optimum individual development and social thriving.

I have traced the history of the child's marginalization in the modernist revolution of subjectivity, and the delegitimation of the child's way of knowing by the modernist worldview. This is not to deny that the child has always been marginal, or that the tension between "adult" and "child" has always been present in some degree in every culture, or that in every age many adults have approached children dialogically, as subjects.[81] But the commonsense view, or "natural attitude" of adults, which is based on real experience interpreted by culture, still instinctively understands, and will probably always understand, childhood as a rudimentary, imperfect, immature, relatively undeveloped form of knowledge. Almost by definition, the child is seen in the context of the not-child—of what it will grow into. Moreover the story of the child's marginalization is only one part of the larger story of the Western "coming of age" in the person of the modern subject. For this coming of age also meant a crisis in the meaning of *adulthood*, or otherwise put, a crisis in subjectivity. Modernism, as a movement involving rapid, transformative change, has been one continual identity crisis for its official protagonist, the Euro-American adult. Beginning even in the mid-seventeenth century, the teleology of adulthood expressed in Baconian science, in the grave seriousness of reformed pietism, and the new idea of adult *civilité*, had come to be seen as a prison of consciousness. The *Emile* itself may be interpreted as inspired by Rousseau's radical disaffection with the adult society of his day, and a voice from a culture aware of having reached a turning point in its development.[82] For Rousseau, the crisis is expressed in the conviction that one can no longer be both "man" and "citizen." The "citizen" must exclude nature and the unconscious, both of which come increasingly to be associated with childhood. Reappropriating nature and the unconscious is analogous to reappropriating childhood, which thus becomes a powerful symbol for that return to a fundamental form of psychological integration that constantly eludes the Western adult who, through accelerating change and the modern reality principle, is increasingly cut off from his internal sources. The child has come to symbolize, in Nandy's words, "a persistent, living, irrepressible criticism of our 'rational', 'normal', 'adult' visions of desirable societies."[83]

In the deconstruction of modernism and the emergence of a new form of subjectivity, the role of childhood—and, by implication, education—in the human life-course has come to carry a new valance in cultural process. This is signaled on the objective level, not just by the religious attachment of modern, state-controlled societies to the idea of universal, compulsory, publicly funded schooling, but by the involvement of children in the new global market economies that are fed and driven by media imagery; by the emergence of the child soldier—and child casualties—in ethnic, religious, and regional wars; by the increasingly early introduction of children to sexual discourses, also a result of globalized media imagery and narrative; and by the ever-emerging, ever-retarded children's rights movement in Western societies. In none of these cases does the child have a voice—but neither does the young adult, or the retiree, or the businessman, or the parents of young children, all of whom are also the statistical targets of calculated marketing strategies and identity traps. In the "transparent society" of media-constructed globalism, the child is just another player. This is the "disappearance of childhood" predicted in the late twentieth century. Pessimistically speaking, it is just one aspect of the end of the human as we have known it— or the increasing assimilation of the human by the technologies it has created. Optimistically speaking, it is a dialectical moment of deconstruction of the human as we have known it, in the interests of a reconstructed subjectivity. Still optimistically speaking, the role of the child in this reconstruction promises the reconstruction of child rearing and education, which, in turn, promises social and cultural reconstruction. Chapter 4 will further explore the move past the modern subject for purposes of finding and delineating in Chapter 5, a practical form of education—a school—which would allow for this double promise.

4

Childhood and the Intersubject

> The most highly developed earthly man . . . is the highest
> synthetic degree of the child.
>
> —Novalis[1]

Boundary Work

Homo clausus fell slowly apart over the course of the twentieth century. The urges and tendencies that led to his deconstruction came from many quarters. The rise and ascendancy of evolutionary theory reformulated Western notions of personal/cultural development and change. The Freudian revolution coincided with the rise of multiple visions of selfhood through the findings of cultural anthropology, which in turn emerged from the ever-increasing intervisibility of cultures that followed the explosion of travel and communications technologies. That explosion has now resulted in a transformed information environment. The silent, logical cosmos of print—the cosmos of the discrete self—is rapidly giving way to the new electronic, digitized cosmos of binary code.

The new information world is as dramatically new as was the world of the book for the fifteenth and sixteenth centuries. It is different because it is a more plural world—where digital and analogical (of both voice and picture and printed word) modes meet and mix, but above all where space and time are overcome in the simulacrum, the representation, or the "virtual." Now the cultural experience of subjectivity and intersubjectivity is both immediate and removed: self is here and there, other is there and here. One is everywhere and nowhere.

The new information environment allows us to understand in a new way the extent to which subjectivity itself is a virtual reality—dependent on fantasy, projection and introjection of "unreal" contents, and hypothesis-testing—constructed as an ongoing project that travels across intersubjective boundaries, whose systemic properties include both self and other: an intersubject. As the modern, technologically mediated subject travels across boundaries of physical time and space with telephone and video and satellite and airplane and automobile, both cultural time and space and the internal, psychological time and space of the individual are in analogous situations of transgressive relations. The new time-space constructed by technology creates corresponding discourses of intersubjectivity and subjectivity. Although these discourses are generated by a certain class and economic group, their proliferation is a planetary phenomenon, for wherever this information environment touches, it creates a new situation of intervisibility.

The effects of this latest technologically induced revolution in consciousness can be mapped in widening or narrowing concentric circles, depending on whether one starts with the macro or the micro level. If we start with the macro, the changes first appear on the geopolitical and macroeconomic levels, then on the national level and within its institutions, then in the subcultures within nations, then in the life of the community, in relationships within subgroups in the community, in the family, in relations between individuals in public and in private spheres, and in the individual's understanding of herself and her relation to her immediate and far world, both in terms of possibilities for and constraints on individual thriving. The concern here is not so much to analyze these multiple levels, or the ways in which the new transcendent time-space created by the information revolution affects each, as to consider how the last two levels—the subjective and the intersubjective—are affected, and what is the role of childhood in culture and society in mediating whatever changes result.

The factors contributing to the ongoing historical reconstruction of subjectivity are causally overdetermined. The self in any given historical period or culture is a product, not just of the information environment, but of a multiplicity of other discourses—including cultural, economic, sexual, familial, political, scientific, demographic, and educational. While the bases of subjectivity are given in lived experience—in the experience of the body, the phenomena of perception, the expression and the vicissitudes of genetic predispositions, and the coherent sedimentation of intersubjective experience—historically mediated processes determine which elements of lived subjectivity are emphasized and which are deemphasized by any given culture during any given period.

One major dimension of the cultural construction of subjectivity—and one that is particularly sensitive to changes in the information environment—has to do with the extent to which the structure and experience of self is implicitly understood as part of a field structure that includes other selves, or whether the subject is considered as an atom, or discrete unit. Once we loosen the modern Western middle-class notion of a discreet, clearly boundaried self and understand subjectivity as a field phenomenon, we can interpret the relation between the elements of the field in different ways. As described in the psychosocial metaphor of cognitive field theory, elements of the field can be field-dependent or field-independent. Whatever the collective construct, field-dependence or field-independence varies along individual lines: persons are more or less constitutionally liable to the influence of others and to the psychological whole of a given moment or situation. But cultures also emphasize field-dependence or independence as normative styles of self-understanding and interaction.

Field-dependent styles are associated with traditional, collectivist cultures, and field-independence with modern or "atomized" cultures.[2] Traditional cultures are associated with an oral information environment, and modern ones with literacy. The new information environment may be thought of as a dialectical reconstruction of the two in a third form that integrates orality and literacy—the medieval and the modern—in new ways. The new information environment is constructed on digital code, like the literate, but is instantaneous, personalized, spontaneous, and interactive like the oral. Like the literate, it is representational and removed from immediate interpersonal contact, but like the oral, its speed and impression of simultaneity make of it an experience of psychological immediacy. Like the oral, it is global—it represents the world as one interactive present whole—but like the literate, that whole is entirely mediated by the individual—I have only to disconnect the telephone or videophone, turn off the television, or log off the Internet to be returned to my atomized state. It does not so much erode the personal boundaries of the modern middle-class subject as virtualize them, so that they can interpenetrate in new ways. A new sort of play with boundaries presents itself as a possibility.

Like the dweller in a large contemporary city, the postmodern subject is completely dependent on huge coordinated systems for the most basic elements of survival: food, water, energy, waste disposal, transportation, and communication. Yet he or she is isolated in the midst of this space, which is designed for separate, atomized, independent units—ensconced in crate-like buildings islanded between geometrically laid-out streets, inhabitable only by automobiles, which don't dwell in the space, but are only continually passing through it. In a society that is moving over the boundaries of the classical "modern," the elements of the collective are so inextricably interdependent that one saboteur could bring down the whole system, yet each individual unit of the system lives as if it were a completely independent individual.

Whether this is a real or only apparent paradox, the contradiction between the individual and the collective of modernism is now reaching a dialectical moment of crisis, which is both triggered and expressed through the technological development of the new kind of time-space of media, and the new information environment that results from this development. Now, wherever there is a camera or a modem connected to the vast planetary network of fiber-optic cable, a rapidly increasing number of subjects can be "there" through the simulacrum of sound and image. This new collective dimension is constructed on the basis of the subject's lived space and time, but is in fact a transcendent space-time continuum. As a space, it represents omni-presence, the possibility of being everywhere at once, which also means being nowhere in particular; temporally, it abolishes the past, and makes every representation a *now*, which also implies never. As such, it produces, as Gianni Vattimo has suggested, "a generalized cultural contamination in a world which no longer offers a sharp split between subject and object, sameness and otherness, or fiction and truth."[3] The relationship between individual and collective constructed by the new information environment confounds subjectivity itself. One can only appear in an Internet chat room, for example, through connecting with the collective virtual field; but one's appearance, unlike an appearance in the space of preliterate orality, is not an appearance at all. The I that appears is by definition a representation, and as such a "play self"—a self of infinite possibilities, none of them realizable except virtually, in the realm of "as if." Technology has developed a new way for persons to be present to each other in space and time.

From one point of view, the virtual social space of the chat room is one in which I can undertake the chief project of the subject-in-process, which is to resolve, through the play of my relations with the world and the other, the internal contradictions of my own subjectivity, as part of a process of continual reconstruction. Like the subjective play space of the young child, it is transitional, in the sense that it offers a reconfiguration of the subjective and objective poles of experience—a bridge between primary and secondary process, desire and reality. And it is itself an organon, a subject. It replaces the previous subjective organons of the family, the tribe, and the nation. As the former organons bound subjects together in a larger subjectivity, the larger subject in this case is the whole species. Virtual space is planetary hyperspace, where anybody can play.

On the other hand, this is a space in which the subject virtually disappears. The self, assimilated to its own representations, becomes a proxy of its own self-representation in anonymous cyberspace. In this case, the subject is, as Jean Baudrillard claims, "absolutely alienated in its sovereignty," in "the malefic curvature which puts an end to the horizon of meaning." He calls this "the irruption of the obscene."[4] The self can play, but the stakes have become meaningless and without issue, and quickly devolve into obsessive, narcissistic play, reinforced by the narcissistic goals of other players. In the world of the obscene there is only surface, and all relationships are commodified. The distinction between the commodified intersubjectivity of the marketplace and that of the private world of relations is blurred or confused, especially in a "service" economy. Intimacy haunts the world of hyper-reality like a possibility just recently lost, or a disappearing dimension. Or is it a new kind of intimacy emerging?

The contradiction presented here is not created by the information environment, but triggered by it. Technology changes consciousness, but it does not change consciousness into any form that is not already a possibility of consciousness, for it is consciousness that produces—expresses and develops—itself through technology. The possibilities it presents are and always have been risks as well, for any technological reification is capable of reversing the process of development and reifying the reifier in its own image—hence Jean-Francois Lyotard's intimation that the developmental trajectory of humanity is one of complexification toward the "inhuman," or the machine.[5] But it could also be argued that the mutual influence between technology and human subjectivity is part of an ontological process as old as the species itself; and that with each technological development, we are confronted more directly with the question of the relation between genetics or "instinct" and culture in the construction of subjectivity, and that this confrontation is a fruitful one.

There are certain fundamental issues of human social existence—the most obvious of which are the related ones of sexuality and child rearing—for which the possibility that culture might change or overcome biologically determined tendencies suggests the most profound implications for human thriving—even, in an age of weapons of mass destruction, for species survival. The question of human subjectivity itself is also such an issue: is it a historical phenomenon, and if so, to what degree? What can and cannot change about human "nature"? This evokes the question asked earlier: if empathic parenting requires a new sort of adult subjectivity, and if a new sort of adult subjectivity can only be produced by empathic parenting, then where does or can change enter the system?

Another major dimension of the cultural construction of subjectivity, also related to field theory, has to do with the unicity or plurality of the components of human selfhood, and by implication the extent to which the self is or is not understood as constituted by otherness. In a field theory of selfhood, the subject includes its alters, or the other selves—both internal and external—with which it is in relation, whether at the moment or as a result of past relations, as well as the collective subject, whether that be defined in terms of family, clan, tribe, nation, species, genus, or cosmos. Historically, even discrete theories of the self include internal plurality, whereas a field theory assumes plurality both within and across subjective boundaries. Plato's basic Indoeuropean formulation included, as we have seen, three components—reason (*logikos*), the passionate or the "spirited element" (*thumos*), and instinctual desire (*epithumia*)—and the successful self-structure was understood as a necessarily imposed hierarchical unity among the three. Aristotle's permutation of Plato's theory of self is an organic, biologistic one, but retains its hierarchical structure. Both are subjective structures that are held in place by reason, or, as Aristotle defined it, the "executive" function. Neither are dialectical models—that is, neither assume a transformative or reconstructive interplay between the plural elements of the self, but rather are based on an integrative model of a coming into a unitary or harmonic situation of internal "right relation."

Plato's theory of self does take intersubjectivity into account in an interesting way. As given to us in the *Republic*, the internal elements of the self are, as we have seen, writ large in the "natural" elements of social and political configuration. The appetitive or instinct-determined element is represented by the lower classes of agriculturalists and craftsmen and tradesmen—the producers (the "iron"). The level of passion or spirited will is represented by a warrior class ("silver"), and reason by an intellectual ruling class ("gold"). Here internal relations reflect and are reflected by external ones, and vice versa, but the task of subjectivity is not so much to develop or transform or to create itself as it is to find its place in the larger cosmic order of intrinsic human character and function. This, for Plato, represents *dikaiosune*—"justice," "morality," or "well-being," life lived in right relation with one's own nature. It assumes, as already pointed out, relations of hierarchical domination, not just within the polis, but within the individual. The states and activities that tend to push or displace subjectivity toward change, transformation, and development—childhood, myth, and experimental art—are dangerous for this form of subjectivity, for they trigger inquiry and dialectical change, which almost by definition represents error, danger, and social disintegration.

Plato's is a field-self to the extent that each internal dimension is represented externally, and vice versa. Although I may be a genetically determined member of the class of "iron," there is a "gold" dimension within me, and I leave that dimension to be expressed externally through those who are genetically "gold." If I am gold, then the iron part of myself is an alter, and so on. Whichever class I am a member of, I live in a social world in which members of the two other classes express genetically two elements of myself which I don't. In this part-whole relation, I see the disciplinary structure that is the normative ideal of my own subjectivity displayed and worked out in the larger social, political, and economic fabric. This suggests—albeit in a mythic formulation—a complicated situation of alterity, but a clearly demarcated and ritualized one.

Aristotle's implicit theory of subjectivity is based, not on a set of correspondences between the micro and the macro, the individual and society, but on an organismic, biological metaphor. Lower and higher forms are here represented as a developmental chain of being reaching from the vegetative soul to the animal soul to the human, all drawn toward an omega point by the unmoved mover, the teleological both origin and endpoint of an ultimately concentric cosmos. As Plato's philosopher king has the lower functions of spirited will and appetite within, so Aristotle's man has the vegetative and the animal souls within him, and in a similar hierarchical relation. But Aristotle's formulation implies change and development, if only implicitly: the movement from vegetative to animal to human implies both an evolutionary and a developmental path. And the three categories are in a nesting hierarchy—each controls the one below it, not through demanding obedience, but through sublating it.[6]

Plato's and Aristotle's are founding theoretical models of self in the Western tradition—first and enduring formulations. They were carried forward in a practical, applied way by the Stoic/Epicurean tradition, associated with the rise of pan-Hellenism through the vehicle of empire—both Alexandrian and Roman—where they were cashed in in the form of techniques and attitudes designated as "care of the self." Care of the self implies what Foucault called "technologies of the self." This second term is a semantic intensification of the first that captures this crucial moment in the evolution of the Western subject in which the Platonic/Aristotelian self turned on itself with tools—the private diary, the daily meditation during which one accounts for one's thoughts and

actions, the daily walk, the ritual of self-admonition.⁷ The Stoic/Epi-
curean self became its own therapist or pastor. The relation between
reason and desire was constructed as a structural transcendence within
the subject: a space, a split, a distance had opened in the self.

In Plato's utopia, the tripartite subject was ruled both intra- and
intersubjectively by the philosopher king. In the real world of Hellenistic cosmopolitanism—a world of cultural boundary crossings and emergent social change—the philosopher king lost his fantasied city state
and was left with only himself to rule. He became everyman (with, of
course, emphasis on "man"). Even the slave had the potential for exercising the psychotechnology of the care of the self, for Stoic subjectivity
had begun to escape its class determinism and to standardize on the
new "world citizen" class of empire (in Stoic terms, the "empire" of
cosmos itself). Understood in this sense, the Stoic subject was a precursor of the rising middle-class subject of modernism identified in Chapter
3. He was also, as characterized by Hegel, the moment in the history of
Western subjectivity of the rise of "unhapy consciousness," a fragmented self polarized between finitude and infinitude. Hegel said of the
Stoic/Skeptic formulation, "one is driven back in himself, should find
satisfaction in himself. In this independence, this rigidity of being-with-
self, this accord with himself, one is to find happiness; one should rest
in this abstract, present, self-conscious inwardness."⁸

The operationalization of the Platonic subject in Stoicism represents self as a structure characterized by potentially dangerous and alien
distances, by internal relations of potential obsession and polarization,
by the recognition of alterity—of otherness within—and above all as a
problem. In this humanistic formulation, self is not a problem to be
eradicated through flight to an absolute, to a collective, or through colonization in a class structure like the iron or the silver or the gold that
determines its expectations and possibilities, but through an ongoing
inquiry. The technologies of the self are not just therapeutic but psychoanalytic: one understands oneself as an experiment, a project, and as
capable of reconstruction. An open dialogue between reason and desire
had not yet been initiated, but the structure necessary for that dialogue
had: the Greco-Roman self had unfused and differentiated both from
the collective and within itself. Internally, it had become an interlocutive
community. Externally, it had moved toward field-independence—a
movement that would only be completed with the reprise of this form
of subjectivity in European modernism in *homo clausus*.

Historically, the Stoic self was both a trigger for and a reaction to
the emergent historical change in the individual-collective relation from
field dependence to field independence. The emergence of an "individu-

alistic upsurge and the social and political process that would have detached individuals from their traditional affiliations" during the period of late Roman Empire[9] is a historical pattern that we also find associated with the rise of middle-class individualism in the European early modern period, and which in late modern Western culture reaches crisis proportions, in paradoxical, inverse relationship with economic, technological, and infrastructural field-dependence.

In Stoicism and then Christianity, the modern Western discrete individual was, if not born, at least announced. From our perspective, it was a male patriarchal/adultist and colonialist individual. It colonized within as it colonized without. Those rejected and manipulated elements of selfhood that were projected onto the slave, the woman, and the child were—as is evidenced by the very fact of their projection—elements that represented danger to the ruling element of reason, and therefore led to the attempt to dominate those elements, both within the self and outside it. The Stoic subject, like the modern, was in a relationship of what twentieth-century psychoanalysts, following Freud's reformulation of subjectivity, would later call "splitting" with desire, or the "passions"—"the irrational power within us which refuses to obey reason."[10]

It would take a further deconstruction of subjectivity, arrived at dialectically through a developmental process of distanciation and subsequent dialogue, before the projections were in a position to be withdrawn—or, more accurately, to enter awareness as internal elements of the psyche rather than as unambiguous and socially enforced "facts" about the alien or different other. In fact in the traditional Western historical narrative, the emergent discrete individual of late antiquity disappeared along with the Roman Empire, and, as part of empire's dissolution, retreated into Christian monasticism, where it percolated in ritualized isolation as the "dark ages" swept Europe. In the psychological hothouse of the monastery, care of the self became an obsessive self-scrutiny, in which Platonic reason was associated with the gaze of God, or the absolute. The monastery was the moment of the new, private self's retreat from the world altogether, polarizing the promiscuous sociability and characteristic field-dependent subjectivity of emerging "barbarian" medieval Europe.

In Freudian terms, both Stoic and modern middle-class subjectivity put ego in a new relationship with the other elements of the psyche. The Stoic subject discovered the superego, the watcher within, who became both the analyst and the judge of the new, problematized self. Subjectivity becomes a puzzle, an unfamiliar and sometimes treacherous territory characterized by blind spots and obscurities, and subject to paradoxical and half-explained relations. Implicit even in ancient Stoicism is a recognition of the "unconscious," a dimension of subjectivity that would become the major element in Freud's reconstruction two millennia later. The unconscious is associated with the body, not just because consciousness is in a relationship of transcendence with the body, but because body is the zone in which conscious and unconscious meet. As Foucault describes Stoic practices, ". . . the focus of attention in these practices of the self is the point where the ills of the body and those of the soul can communicate with one another and exchange their distresses: where the bad habits of the soul can entail physical miseries, while the excesses of the body manifest and maintain the failings of the soul."[11] This description in fact prefigures the Freudian discourse of defense mechanisms and neuroses.

The progressive development of the socially separated, discrete self, internally divided and characterized by relations of splitting, domination/subordination and projection, had another, post-Platonic formulation—in fact a radicalization—in Descartes (1596–1650), who provided a founding metaphor for modern subjectivity. The Cartesian subject, which interplays with the two other major modernist formulations of Locke and Hume, corresponded with the crystallization of the repressed modern adult subject discussed as a psychohistorical phenomenon in Chapter 3. Here Plato's reason—"the intellect," the "thinking thing"— separated itself completely from the other two functions, which were in turn polarized by being completely associated with the body, which was understood as the seat of the "passions." Reason, the *res cogito*, was rendered a metaphysical substance inhabiting the body—or *res extensa*, the "extended thing"—as a "ghost in the machine," a dimension of permanent, ontological transcendence.

Descartes' construct is arrived at through the founding modernist project of complete and radical cognitive doubt, a clearing of the decks of anything but the evidence of the senses, combined with a developing experimental method and a strict logic of the excluded middle. But at this moment of what appears to be radical reevaluation, Platonic subjectivity was in fact recapitulated with a vengeance. Descartes reappropriated the ancient technologies of the self—in fact his *Meditations* could be read as a post-Stoic prologomena to the modern application of those technologies. The struggle between reason and desire—the "flesh," the "passions"—now became a struggle between the rational soul, the *res cogitans*, which he understands as a unity, and the body. Plato's formulation was reduced from a tripartite to a dual, binary relationship.

Seen in terms of the history of Western subjectivity, Cartesian mind-body dualism is a novel synthesis of Christian and Platonic/Stoic formulations. Descartes' polarization between body and "soul"/reason appropriated St. Paul's deadly struggle between the "flesh" and the "spirit"/logos (the element of transcendence) and assimilated it to the theory and practice of Stoic "care of the self." The result was an internal polarization more decisive than either the Christian or the Stoic, a radicalization of Hegel's unhappy consciousness, and an intensification of dialectical tension. At this moment, modern *homo clausus* had already entered his crisis: subjectivity in a condition of internal polarization so extreme that it was poised for transformation. But if we follow Hegel's Romantic narrative of the dialectic, it represented a necessary next step in the historical journey of human subjectivity, and as such an advance.

Read as a precursor to its own deconstruction, Descartes' bifurcation between mind/soul and body/desire was a last statement of the Platonic/Stoic/Christian self. As is characteristic of dialectical processes, deconstruction is initiated even as the formulation to be deconstructed emerges. Hume (1711–1776) went immediately to work: he bracketed any metaphysics of self whatsoever and undertook a consideration of subjectivity as pure immanence, in which he purposed simply to describe and explain the experience of self. The latter is dispersed into experience: a "theater" of impressions and ideas—"that succession of perceptions which we call *self*"—linked in associative contingency by relations of "resemblance, contiguity and causation."[12] Hume rejects any normatively derived conflict between higher or lower elements of the self, and thereby de-hierarchizes the experience of subjectivity. His is perhaps the first purely psychological approach to the subject. And although he speaks from a radically individualist framework, he could be said to introduce the first loosening of the chief characteristic of the modernist self—the clear boundaries of *homo clausus*. Hume enters the immanence of experience to the point where in his phenomenology of consciousness, the distinction between the experiencer and the experienced becomes, not so much ambiguous as not completely relevant. It is this loosening or bracketing of the boundaries that will lead out of the impasse of unhappy consciousness. It is preliminary to the reconstruction of the field to include both subject and world, self and other that would emerge almost two centuries later.

The social and cultural influences leading to the deconstruction of *homo clausus* are multiple and in a relationship of mutual causation, and can be traced speculatively through the nineteenth and twentieth centuries in any number of discourses—whether scientific, political, economic, technological, artistic, philosophical, cultural, demographic, familial, or sexual. In particular, the rapid ascent of the evolutionary metaphor in the latter half of the nineteenth century made of it a show-case for new images of subjectivity. It was (and is) a metaphor based on biology, and thus a materialistic one. Its most compelling and over-reaching construct—the "organism"—provided the ground for field and systems theory. This main protagonist of the evolutionary narrative stands for anything from an amoeba to Einstein. But the idea of an organism apart from an environment that supports, shapes, and is shaped by it, is by definition unthinkable: the boundaries between organism and environment cannot be thought of apart from the whole they represent. During the first half of the twentieth century, self-theory in various philosophical and scientific discourses adopted and opera-tionalized this model as the metaphysical foundation of the new disci-plines of psychology and sociology. Wertheimer's "gestalt," Piaget's equilibrative structures, Dewey's "transactionalism," Lewin's field theory and Merleau-Ponty's "chiasm" are all emblematic of the new impossibility of thinking the self apart from a ground and an interlocu-tor that it both is and is not. The dialectical prelude to the late-twenti-eth-century shift to a poststructuralist formulation of the subject was the subject's temporary disappearance in any classical sense of the term "self." In behaviorism, for example, the self as agent vanishes alto-gether, or as more than one particularly reactive element of a field in continual disturbance, shift, and reorganization.

The Ego Dethroned

The disappearance of the self into the larger structures of which it is a part that characterizes behaviorism and even gestalt theory is a correc-tive excess. Freud deconstructed the subject differently, by dethroning the Platonic executive function—the ego—and introducing a new form of transcendence or "logos" in the form of the Unconscious. Freud's overall formulation resembles Plato's—the notion of a multipartite self, with relations of tension, conflict, and negotiation between the parts. The difference is that, first, he de-hierarchizes the elements—ego, id, and superego—and sets them in relations of mutual intersection and, at least potentially, dialogue. Ego is the closest thing to Plato's reason, but ego has elements of the unconscious, from which it in fact emerges under the inexorable influence of the reality principle. It is shadowed by the superego, which, although it presents itself as the rational "con-science," is characterized by obsessive and automatistic—that is, irra-tional—tendencies. Furthermore, as the "voice within," superego is someone else's voice, an introject of parents or culturally sanctioned "oughts." Superego is "reason," but someone else's.

In Freud, ego is not, like Plato's reason, the "smallest part" that, in a realized self, must rule the larger, more unruly parts. Rather, ego is an embattled, often compromised negotiator, a classic harried middleman between the urgent and fundamental demands of id and the cold statistical world of the reality principle. Where ego can, it allows desire its search for gratification. But where and when it can pursue that search is carefully monitored by the superego, whose criteria for judgment are introjects—"tapes" that play automatically when anxiety is triggered. The Freudian is a form of reason that seeks not the purity of the *eidoi* or "forms" as templates for noble imposition on will and desire, but rather a livable balance between the invisible but ever-present forces of desire and the prevailing reality principle. Freud's subject is, in other words, an evolutionary one, modeled on an organism-in-environment in a process of continual equilibrative adaptation, ultimately identified neither with primary nor secondary processes, but with their shifting relation. Perhaps because of his clinical emphasis, Freud leaves to others the question of the cultural and historical variation possible in the relations between the pleasure principle and the reality principle—that is, the extent to which the organism changes its environment even in the process of adapting to it. The possibility that "reality" is finally, in the social realm anyway, a collective construct and therefore something that can change, is even more implicit in the interactionisms of Piaget and Dewey, and becomes explicit in Freud's left-leaning followers, whether post-Marxists like Marcuse, sex-radicals like Wilhelm Reich, or Romantics like N.O. Brown. But in fact it is just this possibility of a cultural-historical alteration in the relations between the pleasure principle and the reality principle—of a new instinctual economy—which makes of the experience of childhood and the attitudes and practices of child rearing a key element in social change.

Compared to Plato's formulation, Freuds' superego is both reason—but some mixture of *logikos* and an irrational, introjected form of "reason" as moral demand—and *thumos*, or spirited will. It is the element of self that attempts to regulate the ego's negotiations between the pleasure principle and the reality principle—a "watcher," but a frozen watcher, whose categories of judgment are ideals and prohibitions the source of which is an incalculable mixture of self and introjected others, or, in psychoanalytic parlance, "selfobjects." And as the superego is reason inflated by irrational and rationalized feeling, so the unconscious, associated with Plato's *epithumia* or pure desire for gratification, is not

just subrational as Plato held it to be, but—in Freud—also super-
rational. Dreams are the language of the unconscious, and the logical
structure of this language does not base its operations on the classical
Aristotelian elements of identity, negation, and the law of contradiction;
yet the dream could be said to be the most complex, sophisticated, and
creative narrative of which humans are capable, and that without even
trying. In this sense, the unconscious represents a "higher" reason, something it would take Jung's further development of Freudian theory to
make clear. For Jung, the unconscious is that element of subjectivity that
connects to the transpersonal, archetypal dimension usually associated
with the realms of mythology and spirituality, and thus represents the
very highest form of Platonic reason—*noesis*, or intuitive reason, knowledge immediately apprehended rather than arrived at through instrumental reason, or *logistikos*.[13]

Freud took the three fundamental dimensions of Plato's subject and
bent, stretched, and mixed them. Each dimension embodies mixed
modalities of reason and desire, the rational and the irrational. He rendered ambiguous and ambivalent the cleanly separated, ranked, and
hierarchized elements of Plato's tripartite soul. Above all he altered the
relations of power among them—and it should be remembered that for
Plato, relations of power within individuals are isomorphic with relations of power between classes, and, by extension, between persons. For
Plato, there is only one, strictly hierarchical structure of right relation
among the three dimensions—any other leads to personal and social
disorder. Reason must rule the "lower" functions. This commonsense
assumption of the necessity for an executive function in the composite
self is present in Freud as well: the ego must rule. Yet in Freud's system,
and in his actual accounts of the subjective experience of his interlocutors, ego cannot rule. Freud comes to *homo clausus* with the disturbing
message—a message that seems to throw the whole project of "Western
Civilization" into doubt—that "the ego is not master in its own house."
Its presumption to rule desire is reduced to just that—a presumption. In
order to control desire, it must revert to what he calls the "mechanisms
of defense"—projection, reaction formation, sublimation, rationalization, displacement, regression, and so on.

Yet even though ego is no longer master, and can control only
through compromise and even self-deception, and although the unconscious from which it developed as an organizing principle is as multiple
and ubiquitous and ineluctable as nature itself, yet for Freud it must
rule, even if it cannot rule well. The psychoanalytic method Freud
founded is the late modern counterpart of the Stoic technologies of the
self. In describing it, he still employs the militant Platonic vocabulary:

"Psychoanalysis is the instrument to enable the ego to achieve a progressive conquest of the id."[14] But it is the language of an erstwhile conqueror on the verge of truce and negotiation, for he knows very well that any final "conquest of the id" represents the personal and social equivalent of an Orwellian dystopia. Freud, as Nietzsche had done before him and as Max Weber was doing in the same generation, deconstructed Western rationalism by demonstrating its ambiguous underside—its alters, polarizations, shadow images, splits, compartmentalizations, and projections. The dystopia of reason had in fact already arrived by Freud's—and Weber's and Kafka's—time in the modern hegemonic, bureaucratized state and its various institutions. By the end of the twentieth century, the most naive of college students, in encountering Plato's *Republic*, reads it instinctively as a futurist nightmare. Freud, like Nietzsche and Weber, is engaged in an analysis of the fall of Western reason and its shifting role in the construction of subjectivity. He shows the inseparability of the rational and the irrational. But he also maintains a classical view of the subject as *homo clausus*, although he opens the door, through his description of what he calls "object relations"—patterns of projective and introjective relations between self and other—to a dismantling or a revision of the boundaries of self-other and self-world. This opening of the boundaries between subjects will lead to the subject-in-process, or the intersubject.

Freud wrote the first act of the historical drama of subjectivity of the twentieth century. It is the story of the deconstruction of Hegel's unhappy consciousness, and the major players are the ego, its taskmaster the superego, and the id, which is an expression of nature and the unconscious. The ego/superego is in a relationship of estrangement from and attempted domination of—through a series of progressively rearguard actions—the id/unconscious, which continually takes its revenge for its exclusion, and comes increasingly to represent the marginalized transcendent. This drama introduces what Jung in his later writings would call the "dethronement" of the ego, which he associated with the beginning of the process of reconstruction of self that leads to individuation in the emergence of the Self. The Self in his formulation is that subjective superstructure in which conscious and unconscious elements are no longer polarized, and are reconstellated as interconnecting, intercommunicative dimensions of a whole with no hegemonic executive command center, but rather a set of shifting relations governed by a transpersonal, teleological whole.[15] Jung carried forward the mediation between conscious and unconscious, reason and desire, finite and infinite, personal and transpersonal, identity and otherness, which Freud had—however reluctantly—initiated. In so doing he rejoined the great

spiritual traditions of both east and west, which understand self-realization as the reconstruction of subjectivity that follows on the deconstruction of an ego-dominated subjective and intersubjective economy.

The Emergence of the Intersubject

The ontological basis for the move from discrete subject to intersubject
had already been initiated in the paradigm change introduced by Darwinian evolutionary thought, which implicitly redefined organism and
environment—or self and world—as a unity, and their relationship as
interactive, mutually determinative, and in constant equilibrative transformation. With the emergence of gestalt psychology, field and systems
theory—already more fully developed in physics—entered the realm of
the human subject, and initiated a new subject-world, self-other boundary condition, which in turn has gradually redefined our notions of subjectivity and intersubjectivity. Gestalt theory implicitly understands the
self as a form better defined as an organism than, as was implicit in the
ancient Platonic tripartite model, a discrete unit, or in Descartes, a spiritual entity. Self-as-organism has different kinds of boundaries than self-
as-unit. First, it is permeable, in interactive exchange with what it
shares boundaries with. It moves and reshapes as the boundaries of the
other do. It takes its definition from the other as well as giving the other
its definition. Its boundaries are irregular and continually shifting, and
those shifts are determined by the need for survival and mastery, or
equilibration of structures, or "integrity"—if by that term is understood
a state in which internal/subjective and external/intersubjective subsys-
tems are in a state of integration—which in turn means that they have a
dynamic functional balance, and are not in so much disjunction that
they threaten both the organism and the environment, or self and other.
      From a field- and systems-theory perspective, the self is in contin-
ual negotiation with the other and the situation in which it finds itself
with the other, working to define itself as a diverse unity. It is both an
individual and part of a whole structure that is more than the sum of its
parts—a borderline phenomenon, which takes its identity from the
selves with which it shares boundaries as much as from some individual
teleological principle within itself. The subject-in-process is defined as
much by this border or boundary-work—the history and process of its
relations with its margins and interfaces—as by an idea of an internal
structure, or core. In its developmental vicissitudes, the subject's boundaries are explored, probed, pushed against, raised, taken down,
adjusted, and so on, in a continual process of transformation.

In contrast to the images of positive transformation or balance or thriving of the self that we find in classical formulations—images based on metaphors of distancing, exclusion, compartmentalization, hierarchy, and control—the images associated with the development of the intersubject are metaphors of interlocution, conversation, transgression, and dialogue. The psychoanalytic process itself was constructed by Freud in the form of a conversation between the elements or dimensions of the self, mediated by and interweaving with a conversation between patient and analyst. The therapist is not just an expert, but, through what psychoanalysis calls the "transference," a paradigmatic other—both an interlocutor and a partner chosen for purposes of playing out the field-relations both within the self and between self and other. The therapeutic setting is a transitional space, like the play space of the child, or the space of religious ritual or theater or art or revel or eroticism—or, as I will argue in Chapter 5, of education.

In the transitional space, the default boundaries between inner and outer are deconstructed in such a way that internal and external reality interplay, are negotiated, mediated, and reconstructed. Here the other is experienced both as an independent object in relation to my ego and as a *selfobject*, or a part of my own self-system. The selfobject is experienced as an "introject," or as part of my subjective structure. The original selfobject is the primary significant other of the infant—typically the mother—and is introjected, not as a discrete individual, but as "a class of psychological *functions* pertaining to the maintenance, restoration and transformation of self-experience."[16] In later relationships, the selfobject is projected onto the other. So the selfobject is neither self nor other, but "the *subjective* aspect of a self-sustaining function performed by a relationship of self to objects [i.e., others] who by their presence or activity evoke and maintain the self and the experience of selfhood."[17] The presence of the selfobject is, according to "self psychology"—which emerged from object relations theory in the second half of the twentieth century—essential to the infant's construction of a viable transitional space. It is the existence of this transitional space and the play within it whereby "integrity" in the sense used above—that is, a satisfactory relationship between the internal and external elements of the subjective-intersubjective system—is negotiated.

From the point of view of the intersubject, children and adults are *both* beings in continual process of development. The second half of the twentieth century was the period of the emergence of life-course developmental theory—that is, the historical moment in which adults were widely recognized as subjects-in-process. Optimal adult development also involves transitional space and the work within it with persons who are also selfobjects: this is what the play of art, ritual, eroticism, and philosophical inquiry are about. Psychoanalysis—at least following Erikson's and Jung's widening of Freud's horizon—assumes development across the life course, and thus is often referred to as a new religion for good reasons: it sets up the *temenos*—the "sacred enclosure"—of the consultation room as a transitional space where subjectivity communes and interacts with its transcendent elements—meaning those elements both within the subject herself and in the person of the other—which are "alters" or self-parts within the whole system of the intersubject. This is especially true of group therapy—and, by extension, the intensive group experience called "school"—where the systemic aspects of intersubjective experience are triggered and magnified through encounter in the transitional space with multiple others. The psychotherapeutic movement may be understood as another dialectical moment in the history of the care of the self, but it is a moment constructed on a different model of the self. It follows the moment of the radical privatization of subjectivity in *homo clausus*, and accompanies the emergence of a dialectical third term, which sublates both *homo clausus* and the form of subjectivity that preceded it, the medieval collective or fused self.

This third term, the intersubject, can also be identified with a millennial ideal that has shaped Western cultural aspirations at least since the appearance of the Christ figure. In his late work *Aion: Researches into the Phenomenology of the Self*, Jung finished his lifelong inquiry into the symbological history of Western subjectivity with the suggestion that Christ represents the implicit psychological goal of the individuation process, a subjective state he called the Self. As we have seen, the Self is for Jung a structure in which conscious and unconscious contents have undergone a reconfiguration such that they are no longer in relations of antagonism or ambivalence, or mediated by repression, defense, censorship, and consequent neurosis, but are integrated in a psychological structure that allows their optimal interplay and intervisibility. This ideal integration is an emergent system-balance achieved apart from relations of hierarchy or domination of one part of the psyche by another, which by analogical implication suggests the end of relations of hierarchy and domination between subjects. This theme is found in multiple images offered by Western post-Christian visionaries—whether in Blake's *Marriage of Heaven and Hell*, which announces (following the eighteenth-century Swedish mystic Emanuel Swedenborg) a new psychological age, or the notion among Romantic poets and philosophers of the unification of mind and nature; or Whitman's new American democratic personality of *Leaves of Grass*; or Tielhard de Chardin's notion of a collective spiritual ontogenesis leading to the development of the "noosphere"; or even the conditions of "species being" accompanying Marx's prediction of the withering of the state. Abrams, in his analysis of the Romantic vision, identifies it as "a conceptualized version of the design of Christian history":

> In this process the redemptive goal of the history of mankind was shifted from the reconciliation and reunion of man with a transcendent God to an overcoming of the opposition between ego and non-ego, or a reconciliation of subject with object, or a reunion of the spirit with its own other, and this culmination was represented as occurring in the fully developed consciousness of men living their lives in this world: the justification for the ordeal of human experience is located in experience itself.[18]

As we have seen, this mythic stratum of the Western imagination, which Blake called "the return of Adam into Paradise," is time and again associated with children and with childhood. For seekers of a golden age, childhood is both an initial and a terminal state; it represents both the beginning from which we come and the end toward which we journey.[19] One more recent appearance of the trope, appropriate for our epoch, can be recognized in the identification, as a result of Winnicott's clinical inquiry into infant psychology,[20] of the phenomenon of transitional space. As we have seen, transitional space is the space of boundary work—both within the subject and between subjects. It is the psychological space of infancy and early childhood and also of art and deep personal and interpersonal experience—the space of dream, sexuality, animality, and the divine. It is the workshop of the individuation process, which is the pursuit of the "reconciliation of subject with object" through the ongoing dialogue between conscious and unconscious elements of the personality. Successful dialogue results in the reconstellation of these elements such that the executive power of the ego is "ruptured" or decentered—which does not imply that ego surrenders its synthesizing and integrating role within the whole structure of subjectivity, but rather that it gives up its compulsive attempts to control the whole structure. It recognizes that it is not "master in its own house" and lives on.

Thus the intersubject is both an emergent historical and a perennial, even millennial normative ideal. Relative to *homo clausus*, the intersubject is subjectivity decentered, a boundary-crosser, inherently transgressive in the sense of being instinctively oriented toward dialectical transformation. For the intersubject, psychological health is indicated by the capacity to maintain an optimal moving balance in the field. The field is both the multiple and the whole, the one and the many. The whole field is my world with all its relations, near and far, present and absent. In this field, there are as many relations as are perceived by an intelligence within it—the Beijing butterfly of chaos theory is one limit-example, and the universe of omni-influence of the ancient speculative symbolic system of astrology is another. The intrasubjective field of the individual intersubject is a system of relations between parts of the self. The immediate intersubjective field of the intersubject includes others with whom she is in any kind of relation—including strangers passed on the street—and her introjections of them in her own personal field—their identity as parts of herself. The intrasubjective and the intersubjective fields make up one field, sometimes more and sometimes less distinct.

Each field is a system, and to recognize one's membership in these multiple and overlapping systems—especially when at their boundaries—is necessarily to undergo to some degree the decentering of the executive ego function. The internal balance of which Plato spoke is not attained through the imposition of principles or categories by one dimension of the self onto other dimensions, or onto an other outside oneself (who is also, through the phenomena of introjection and projection, a part of one's self-system). Rather, the balance is approached—if never arrived at except temporarily—by "remembering," or *anamnesis*, a hermeneutical process in which I in my plurality become my own text, approached interpretively. The self-work of psychoanalysis and of education is an internal and intersubjective dialogue leading to continual self-reconstruction. So in fact Freud's new technology of the self initiated the hermeneutical process that not just Merleau-Ponty but Jung as well identified as "the task" of the twentieth century: the search for the integration of the "dark" with the "light" elements of the self, and the subsequent reconstruction of the ego, and by extension, reason. Implicit in the intersubject is what Charles Taylor has called "a new synthesis of reason and desire," an "overcoming the barrier between reason and the instinctual depths," through a "decentering of subjectivity" and an "escape from the restrictions of the unitary self." For as Blake wrote, "Reason, or the ratio of all we have already known, is not the same that it shall be when we know more."[21]

The "attempt to explore the irrational and integrate it into an expanded reason," which in fact Merleau-Ponty saw as originating in

Hegel, was a project announced in early-nineteenth-century Romanticism, but that emerged in everyday discourses and popular culture in the twentieth century. Nor was it limited to the new discipline of psychology. The deconstruction of *homo clausus* was accompanied by the corresponding deconstruction of modernist epistemology, which had its final crystallization late in the nineteenth century in the logical positivism of the Vienna School. In philosophy, Alfred North Whitehead initiated a shift in metaphysics and cosmology from a theory based on substance to one based on relation and process. This was paralleled by the emergence of quantum physics and relativity theory, both of which, like Whitehead's, suggest radical new ways, as yet mostly unavailable to common perception and understanding, of constructing space, time, and their relations. The new discipline of anthropology, made possible by rapidly expanding cultural intervisibility, exposed the Western subject to alternative worldviews, which provided graphic models of diverse constructions of the relations between the rational and the irrational. Modern artists came under the influence, not just of "primitivism," but of child art as well, and Surrealism explored the semiology of the unconscious.[22] The early twentieth century was the moment of the emergence of the "stranger at the gates" of postcolonial Western civilization—the deconstruction of a hegemonic epistemology and the onset of an age of alterity. And it was at this moment in the history of the Western self—the late phase of colonialism, the proliferation of new images of subjectivity, the "discovery" of the unconscious, new theories of space-time relationships and the rise of field and systems theory, dramatically increasing intervisibility through an ever-expanding electronic, digitalized information environment—it was at this accelerated moment that the intersubject may be said to have emerged as, if not yet a viable cultural ideal, at least a thinkable one. For the lived experience of the intersubject is analogous to actually seeing/perceiving/living time and space the way relativity theory describes them. In the same way, the intersubject lives the relationship between ego and unconscious and self and other in a way that is imaginable to us, but with difficulty.

If Freud did not find his way out of the Eleatic unity of the ideal self-present and transparent ego of *homo clausus*, he prepared the way through founding the dialogical and deconstructive practice of psychoanalysis. But he certainly did not do it alone. Perhaps his most important contemporary in this regard, although relatively little known, was Max Wertheimer, who introduced field and systems theory—which was simultaneously emerging in physics—in the form of gestalt psychology. Wertheimer's basic axiom—that "there are wholes, the behavior of which is not determined by that of their individual elements, but where the part-processes are themselves determined by the intrinsic nature of the whole"[23]—is crucial to the opening of *homo clausus*. Although Freud still held implicitly to the working assumption that the borders of the self were coterminous with the borders of the organism, his introduction of the notions of projection, introjection, and identification into his description of self-processes were fundamental to the later development of a new, field-model of intersubjectivity in British and American object relations theory[24] and in continental phenomenology, most specifically in Merleau-Ponty, on whom Wertheimer was an important influence.

The intersubject emerges as a fundamental aspect of the age of alterity because it is based on the realization of what Levinas called the "fecundity of the I," or the existential experience of the multiplicity of selfhood both within and across the boundaries of the subject. The recognition of the self as a multiple structure that transcends any strict boundaries between myself and others confounds a logic based on strict identity and negation. Hegel—the grand philosopher of Romanticism— had in fact initiated the logic to describe it a century before. His *Science of Logic* of 1813 assaults the Aristotelian bedrock of the law of contradiction, not by denying it, but by embedding it in the heart of identity itself, and then putting it into motion and transformational change through time. A is A *and* not-A, being *and* nothingness, since it *is* only through positing what it *is not*. As Charles Taylor says of Hegels' logic, "not only are the properties by which we characterize things defined contrastively, but it is also an essential part of their meaning that they characterize what they apply to in part in terms of its potential causal interactions with other things."[25] In terms of a fundamental logic of the self, I as a subject come into being by distinguishing myself from what I am not. My identity is based on my relation with an other—both "within" me and "outside" me—who I am not, but without whom I would not be an identity, and whom therefore I am. This is true, originally with the other with whom I am in relation, and—as the ego forms through a process of internal division—with the other(s) "within" me. From a structural point of view then, I (the ego) am an other to my selves—both in me and in the other—and the "I" itself is by no means "master in its own house."

Applied to issues of subjectivity and intersubjectivity, Hegel's logic leads to a reordering of the ontological position of the subject and her others. The psychological implications of this logic are at least preliminarily expressed in object relations theory, for which self and other are unthinkable apart from each other. They emerge together in human infancy in a dialectical relationship, and their systemic unity remains a distinctive ontological trait. The psychotherapist David Scharf says ". . . in the inner world, we cannot conceive of our selves without invoking and relying on our objects. We see ourselves in the reflection of the other's eyes, gaze, expression, mirroring body responses and echoing sounds."[26] It is through the relationship with the other that the I emerges, is constructed and maintained; and likewise it is through the relationship with internal others that reflection itself emerges and is constructed and maintained.

The experience of recognizing that one is extended across one's own boundaries into the other and the world is, at least for the great majority of humans, not an ontological given but an ontological potential—and, when it begins to develop, a life-course event with profound ethical implications. It is realized—or not—not just through personal life-course experience, but through historical and cultural enablers and/or disenablers as well. Paradoxically, although it is a unifying process, it is triggered through the experience of alterity. One comes to recognize and identify with the whole field, or system, only by recognizing that one *is* what one also *is not*, and that the other is, not only never quite what I take him to be, but also knowable only as himself-for-me, as I am myself-for-him. This is an important recognition, for the primary ethical claim of the theory of the intersubject is that its realization in human culture acts to reduce the possibility of psychological either fusion with or (what amounts to the same thing) repudiation of the other—that it leads, on the contrary, to the increased possibility for dialogical relations, that is, relations regulated by the ability to recognize and to assume as critical an attitude toward one's own projections as toward those of the other.

On an object-relations theory account, what draws me into relation with you is that I am projecting a part of myself—whether desired or rejected—onto you, and that you are introjecting this part and "containing" it for me; you are re-presenting it as part of a constellation that is "outside" myself and which I can either reintroject as "good" rather than "bad" or threatening to my felt ego, or which I can reject as "not me." And you are doing the same with me. To understand that we are continually distributing these "split-off" parts of ourselves between each other is to realize the conditions for dialogue, for it shifts the locus of responsibility to the interaction itself, and not to one or another of the poles of the interaction. It leads us to the realization that in working with the other we are always working with parts of ourselves. It is also the condition of Levinas' notion of alterity: "Exposed to the alterity of the other person, the I's egoist capacities, its powers of synthesis, which have hitherto defined the ego . . . are 'reconditioned', 'put into question', overexposed, such that the *I* is *first* for-the-other before the very firstness of its being-for-itself."[27]

The alterity of the other is a paradoxical experience—the experience of our inextricable mutual identity as elements or members of the same field or system, played out through projection and introjection—*and* the experience of the unknowable character of the other, and therefore her ultimate transcendence. In a similar apparent paradox, the direction of positive system growth in any relationship is toward both intimacy and individuation. In recognizing that I am involved in an intersubjective process of projection and introjection, or "continual passing into each other," I recognize that what I appear to need in the other, or what I reject or accept in the other, is actually in me, and vice versa. I recognize that I am not the projections I am containing (or repudiating) for the other person, nor is she my projections, however well she may fit them. I recognize that I am as unknowable to myself as the other is, in that I can only see myself on the screen of the other. This triggers the individuation process in me, in that it prompts me to withdraw or contain my projection, having recognized it as my own. It means I am alone with my own psychic material—it means that I am the only one ultimately responsible for my thoughts and feelings about myself, the other, and the world. But at the same time it means that I am never alone. I *am* the other—we are elements of one system, located together on the boundaries of intersubjectivity.

The adult who positions herself for encounter on the boundaries is positioning herself for the potential reconstruction of those boundaries through a "reconditioning in the face of the other." The result of the reconditioning, understood as an aspect of psychological health—for boundaries can also be effaced, violated, and fatally confused—is a form of subjectivity that is both more autonomous and more connected, more independent and more relational, more capable both of empathy and of moderating its own anxiety or negative arousal, that is, "self-quieting." By implication, it is also a form of subjectivity more capable of care and justice in all its social, political, and economic relations, and therefore more in keeping with the modern Western ideal of the "democratic" personality. For the intersubject every relationship is a challenge and an opportunity for this reconditioning, and the process is never quite in one's control, since it has both conscious and unconscious dimensions. All that I control in my relationship with my interlocutor is the intention to "own" my own projections, even if that also means never knowing exactly where projection leaves off and the "real" other begins. In fact that will never be clear, since ontologically the projection will never be completely withdrawn, and the other will never be an other apart from me.

The question remains whether the intersubject so construed is a broad, epochal historical-evolutionary emergent or a condition realized by only a few, most particularly—in the modern epoch anyway—by the psychoclass of the bourgeois intelligentsia, the class with the material conditions that allow it the leisure to engage in the discourses and technologies of the self particular to this form of subjectivity. The arguments I have given from a cultural and historical point of view are obviously intended to suggest the former—that we are speaking here of the emergence of a modal personality—a form of subjectivity characteristic of a particular historical period or culture. The very term "modal personality" points to the extent to which any epochal form of subjectivity is a *subjection*—a way of being a subject that results in great degree from a collective construction, a set of legitimated discourses, of values and intentionalities shared by those with the social power to initiate and maintain them through public opinion, education, media, and even, finally, force of one kind or another. Nor does this realization necessarily conflict with an evolutionary narrative of subjectivity such as it has been offered so far: we may assume that if there is such a dialectical movement, it does not operate independently of social power and cultural politics.

Although the manner of the emergence of a modal personality such as the intersubject is unclear, it appears to have a dual movement. It shows its early signs in the privileged psychoclass which has the leisure to experiment with its forms and implications, and it is prefigured by the culturally marginalized. This is only apparently contradictory, for the two are linked by projection. And just as it has been suggested that the great artists of a given epoch "are dealing with the leading psychological problems of tomorrow,"[28] it could be hypothesized that the most pervasive personality disorders of our epoch represent fault lines in the current model of subjectivity, excesses in the system that prefigure its deconstruction and the emergence of a new balance. The most dramatic and intractable disorders of the self of the modern age as documented by contemporary psychotherapists are narcissism, borderline syndrome, and multiple personality disorder. Narcissism reflects the radical isolation of the self—the ego caught in its own mirror and unable to decenter, and as such the terminal state of *homo clausus*, and a first deconstructive moment in the transitional process. For the narcissistic personality, the possibility of a multiple self does not even exist—rather the self is split, and one part becomes alternately the involuntary worshipper or the withering critic of the other. From a psychohistorical point of view, it may be thought of as the egoist-I in its last resort—a self-structure that attempts to completely assimilate its external to its internal objects—and the modal personality of a culture of radical individualism in a situation of no exit.

Borderline personality disorder represents a dispersion, a loss of identifiable self-structure, manifested in a pervasive underlying sense that there is no "real me."[29] The borderline's selfobjects—those parts of the self that are connected with real others either past or present, but that represent and evoke one's own repressed impulses and tendencies within the economy of the self—are in a state of chaos and/or stagnation, emerging as attackers or seducers alternately of oneself or of the other onto whom one projects them.

Multiple personality disorder is a final intensification of the disintegration of the self—a condition in which internal objects no longer even recognize each other, and have turned into persona in their own right, taking turns occupying what object-relations theorists call the "central self" or "central ego." They have turned into im-personations in a psychodrama for which there is no longer a director—characters who have broken free of their author. Here the self's internal objects— what Scharff calls "the loving, hating, beckoning, accepting and rejecting objects [which] are embedded within us as cornerstones of our psyches,"[30] have become dis-integrated. In the functional self-in-process, the aggressive and the needy, the idealized, the hated and the valued parts of the self are in dynamic relation—are in dialogue—but are also in emergent, epigenetic, developmental movement toward a horizon of integration. In multiple personality disorder, each has gone its own way, and the executive function has been, not just decentered, but depotentiated.

In showing how development has gone wrong, and the elements of the self moved into overly contradictory and untenable positions, we are also shown the implicate order of subjectivity. Psychopathology clarifies the "normal"—or perhaps we should say the "acceptable," or the "liveable." For the "normal" ones, those afflicted with these fundamental disorders of the self are psychological pioneers conscripted by fate, or reluctant emigrants into the wilderness of the psyche, denizens of the psychohistorical shatter zone of the old and the new. They are the mutants of cultural evolution, if only because they are unable to fit into the prevailing normative subjectivity. As such they prefigure—at least negatively—the transition into another kind of subjectivity. They represent those weakened and damaged ones who both announce and whose struggle will be redeemed by a future culture that has figured out how to live with increased conditions of multiplicity, alterity, and difference.

The inchoate prefiguration of the intersubject by pathologies of the self implies that it is a cultural and historical task to learn how to live with this condition as a healthy phenomenon; and given the dialectical nature of psychohistorical change, it would follow that the same was the case 500 years ago for the emergent discrete modernist form of subjectivity then caught in the crossfire between the polymorphous social self of the medieval synthesis—the self living completely in the larger collective pattern—and the new form. In either case, it could also be hypothesized that, given the early histories of those characterized by these transitional pathologies, they seem most often—taking organic considerations into account—to have their etiologies in early relationships with parents. So it is—again, accounting for genetic differences—the original subjection of the self across the boundaries of subjectivity, a structural style configured through childhood experience, which determines for most of us the conditions and capacities for our own boundary work throughout our adult lives. In childhood, as Scharff says, "we live with our objects [our parents] both as real external people and as internalizations."[31]

Parents are the original selfobjects—both as real persons and as functions or virtual persons or parts of our internal structure. Our internal-external relationships with our parents are what get played out in our relations throughout adulthood. And the transitional space provided by cultural and interpersonal practices—the psychological spaces of art, philosophy, psychotherapy, eroticism, ritual, spiritual practice, and personal intimacy—is the space in which the adult has a chance, like the young child, to engage in the deep play that promises the reconfiguration of self-boundaries and functions. But as Levinas has suggested, the most profound moment of reconfiguration—and the most available to us all as well as the most grounded in everyday practice—is the prolonged life-cycle moment of rearing children. Becoming a practicing parent is the first existential experience of alterity, and the most powerful and lasting influence for understanding in a lived sense one's identity as multiple across boundaries.

In summary, the intersubject is a cultural ideal among a certain psychoclass, a future emergent construct that exists as a potential in human individuals and communities, whose origin and perennial opportunity is located in childhood, and whose emergence is greatly dependent on the kind and quality of the adult-child relation—specifically, on a form of the relation that discourages internal splitting, structural compartmentalization, and the reification of projections. The final emergence of the intersubject as an epochal norm or modal personality is dependent on multiple and ultimately uncontrollable prior external conditions that allow for its flourishing. Rather than a dispersion of individuality into mass man, or the death of the subject—which are found in separate discourses but amount to the same thing—the intersubject represents a rebalancing of the individual and collective as an ecological adaptation. It is a self-structure in which the inherently transgressive nature of intersubjectivity is recognized, and understood as a shifting dialectical and dialogical configuration that is always journeying toward an emergent integration. For subjectivity conceived as dialectical and emergent, the "successful" life-course is a continual reconstruction of a whole whose parts are in varying states of unity and contradiction, but for which contradiction is the continual incentive for further growth.

Psychogenic Theory of History and the Present Age

According to deMause's "psychogenic theory of history," ". . . because psychic structure must always be passed from generation to generation through the narrow funnel of childhood, a society's child-rearing practices . . . are the very condition for the transmission and development of all other cultural elements, and place definite limits on what can be achieved in all other spheres of history." If there is an evolution of these practices, it lies in the "'generational pressure' for psychic change," which is "spontaneous, originating in the adult's need to regress and in the child's striving for relationship." It manifests historically in what deMause calls

> a series of closer approaches between adult and child, with each closing of the distance producing fresh anxiety. The reduction of this anxiety is the main source of the child-rearing practices of each age. . . . The origin of this evolution lies in the ability of successive generations of parents to regress to the psychic age of their children and work through the anxieties of that age in a better manner the second time they encounter them than they did during their own childhood. The process is similar to that of psychoanalysis, which also involves regression and a second chance to face childhood anxieties.[32]

Every historical transformation of adult subjectivity is a result of a modal change in the experience of childhood, which in turn is a result of a change in the way adults deal with their own childhood through the experience of raising children, which in turn is a result of their experience of childhood. Although deMause insists that this change occurs "independent of social and technological change," the problem of causal circularity his formulation presents is less inexorable if other economic, political, social, class, cultural, medical, and technological variables are factored in. The onset of *homo clausus* can be traced through the rise of the modernist infrastructure—dislocation and urbanization, the advent of the middle classes and the nuclear family, capitalism, constitutional government, the printed word, the acceleration of technological innovation, and the beginnings of effective epidemiology—as well as superstructure—the Copernican cosmological revolution, Protestantism, and philosophical and scientific empiricism. The new synthesis of the intersubject is fueled, in turn, by the changes associated with postmodernism—increasing personal and cultural intervisibility through dramatic innovations in electronic communications and transportation, global economies, huge-scale urbanization, massive interdependent systems (food, water, power, transportation, etc.), global media, major advances in medicine, epidemiology and birth control, the sexual revolution and the changing roles of women, psychoanalysis, radical secularism and religious ecumenism, universal education, the Einsteinian cosmological revolution, and field and systems theory in both the natural and the human sciences.

As has been pointed out, the notion of an evolution of child-rearing modes has more empirical strength when conceived of holistically. All the child-rearing modes are present at all times in human culture, but in any given historical epoch, one mode is accepted and/or legitimated by the culturally powerful. It is easier to accept deMause's claim that advances in child-rearing modes happen whatever the historical or technological conditions if we also accept that they are all present at all times, and that a myriad of social, economic, and political conditions can influence the current balance of the modes.[33] Infanticide, abandonment, and ambivalence will always be present, and we can expect that they will increase or decrease, and even take different forms, depending on historical conditions. The Intrusive Mode may reassert itself on various levels depending on economic and social exigencies, and the Socializing Mode will always represent a fallback, or transitional mode between the Intrusive and the Empathic. Also, as already pointed out, individual differences between parents—even within the same family—will always be present, dependent on each parent's childhood history, on temperamental differences, on current conditions of social, economic, or personal stress, on culturally mediated ideological persuasions, and on particular life-cycle moments.

If this is the case, then the present moment offers an apparent paradox. On the one hand, normative or "politically correct" parental attitudes toward children are characterized by the Empathic Mode. Broad public sentiment is shocked and outraged by cases of infanticide, and numerous agencies, both public and private, are dedicated to saving children from all forms of abuse. Among the Western middle classes, spanking children is now understood as physical abuse. Liberal "experts" also commonly promulgate parenting protocols and methodologies in the popular press based on the empathic assumptions that children are to be listened to and their felt needs taken seriously. Dissatisfaction with the intrusive and/or socializing character and practices of the state-controlled public schools has reached—in the United States anyway—the status of a permanent public disposition. The pronouncements on childhood with which Rousseau astonished the world in 1763—"Childhood has its place in the scheme of human life. We must view the man as a man, and the child as a child . . . Nature wants children to be children before they are men. . . . Childhood has ways of seeing, thinking and feeling particular to itself: nothing can be more foolish than to seek to substitute our ways for them"[34]—have become common coin. If one surveyed only the popular advice literature and ignored the actual experience of children in Western cultures, one would assume that children had never been more valued by adults, or better cared for. And in one sense this is a valid assumption.

On the other hand, children are increasingly abandoned to the institutions of the state—if "state" is understood in the broader sense to include the corporate, media, and civic/legal worlds—schools, day-care centers, afterschool programs, and organized programs that act to ghettoize children within an architectural environment relentlessly designed in the image of low-level corporate office buildings—stripped-down boxes filled with ugly furniture, set in increasingly dehumanized urban and suburban landscapes bereft of the sorts of play zones and spaces traditionally associated with childhood. Children are also abandoned to the "main square" of the new information environment, the virtual space and time of the media, which both constructs and manipulates them as market-subjects, and exposes them regularly to multiple images of the two aspects of adult life the exclusion of which the traditional notion of childhood depends on—sexuality and violence. The decline of the traditional nuclear family has placed many children in a sort of demilitarized zone of familial relationships. Teachers in early-childhood settings testify to the increasing levels of knowledge of sexual information and corresponding vocabulary among young children, and homicide—including mass killings—carried out by children as young as ten years old has become a not-unexpected phenomenon.

That children are universally subjected to the disciplinary power of normalizing judgment, state coding, and surveillance in the form of traditional schooling is hardly distinctive, since adults are subjected to the same measures. And the increasing pressures on middle-class children to participate in organized "cultural activities"—whether sports, self-defense, artistic activities, or special academic tutoring—can be understood as one more aspect of the technologies of self associated with the disciplinary regime of power characteristic of the modern state and what it expects of it "citizens," whether present or future, adult or child. Following the logic of the contrastive pair adult/child, the "disappearance of childhood" that this represents can also be understood as the disappearance of adulthood, in the sense that disciplinary power infantilizes adults to the same degree to which it adultizes children. Rousseau's "citizen" is, in the modern state, also Postman's "adult-child"—the radically dumbed-down consumer—Marcuse's repressively desublimated "one-dimensional man" targeted by television sitcoms, news and extravaganzas, and commercial seductions.[35]

There is no reason that even dramatically contradictory social conditions and tendencies should not coexist in any one historical period. From a dialectical perspective, those contradictions represent the possibility for transformation. That modern childhood *and* adulthood are "disappearing" even as the Empathic Mode has become the expert-sanctioned parenting discourse of the age; that mainstream schooling still blindly and obdurately—and, in its own terms, successfully—strives to make children "citizens" before "men"; that children are more independent in the world of media and markets than ever before; that children are more manipulated by the world of media and markets than ever before; that parents hold to the value of offering their children more choice than ever before; that children are more isolated and lonely and controlled in the larger environment than before; that the nuclear family—the niche of modern childhood—is unraveling: these are indicators in which deconstructive and reconstructive elements and tendencies are ambiguously interwoven, and hint at transformation as much as at decline. For psychogenic theory, which of these are causes and which are effects in the transformation of subjectivity is not so important. What is significant is what, broadly speaking, an adult does "when faced with a child who needs something." For it is the adult for whom the voice of the child becomes the voice of a fully human other, a subject in his or her own right, who is thus triggered into a space of

intersubjectivity that is the matrix for the emergence of the intersubject. Adults are changing, children are changing, and consequently, the
adult-child relationship is changing, but it is how these changes change
adult subjectivity that will eventually make possible the reconstruction
of children's lifeworld, because it will be part and parcel of the reconstruction of the adult's.

The Dialectics of Reason and Desire

The reconstruction of Western adulthood is, as I have already repeatedly argued, a matter of the question that was implicitly posed as early
as Plato's formulation of subjectivity—the question of the relationship
between reason and desire. The problem has been posed in multiple
ways at least since the Romantic revolt against Enlightenment reason,
and Hegel's introduction of a new, dialectical logic of development.
Romanticism poses the goal as the reconciliation of reason and feeling.
Already the Romantics had announced, in Coleridge's notion of
"joy"—which might, in modern play theory, be called "flow"—a
"breaking down the boundaries of the isolated consciousness" and the
reinstatement of "the flow of a shared life between the elemental polarity of mind and nature."[36] Implicit in the Romantic formulation is the
ideal of the adult who, in Taylor's formulation, has escaped from "the
restrictions of the unitary self." As we have seen, the grand myth of
Romanticism posited a necessary division of an original unity in the
interests of a reconstructed unity. According to Taylor, "The belief
[among Romantics] was that the human destiny was to return to
nature at a higher level. . . . The original single unity makes its way
through divided paths, in reason and nature, and then comes to
fruition in a reconciliation," thus "overcoming the barrier between
reason and the instinctual depths," and "breaking down the division
between art and life."[37]

The Romantic narrative of the development of subjectivity, long
understood as a spiritual tradition, was first taken up by secular consciousness near the end of the nineteenth century in the philosophy and
science of human development, which integrates dialectical and evolutionary theory. Heinz Werner's notion of "orthogenetic development,"
presented in a classic paper in 1945, implicitly allows a theory of the
developmental pattern of biological organisms to cross over into theories of psychological development. He describes development as a
dialectical advance in which organic functions become both more centralized and more differentiated, more hierarchical and more capable of

laterality. Above all, Werner normalizes the principle of regression as necessary to development. The principle of "regression in the service of the ego" had already been announced in psychoanalysis, and is critical to deMause's explanation of the Empathic Mode, for it is "the ability to regress to the level of the child's need and correctly identify it without an admixture of the adult's own projections . . . then be able to maintain enough distance from the need to be able to satisfy it," (see p. 101 above) which is the fundamental psychological disposition of the Empathic parent.

The point for a discussion of the role both of one's own childhood and of real children in the reconstruction of adult subjectivity is that Coleridge's "joy" is emblematic of childhood, whether as experienced by children, reconstructed in adult memory, or both. The normative ideal of the dialectically transformed subject of the Romantic developmental narrative is, as put by the psychoanalyst Ernest Schactel in his definitive study of the Western "forgetting of childhood," the "person who has continued and expanded the child's openness to the world on the adult level."[38] The realized adult is the one who has not so much avoided leaving the subject-object, self-world, self-other relation of childhood, but who is continually reconstructing it in the journey into and through the "fall" signified by adult experience. The actualization of the intersubject is not a return to a historical childhood or even to specific childhood memories, but to an archetype of experience, to that "well of being," which will never be directly remembered, but only reconstructed. The adult so turned or converted to this archetype is oriented to a re-organization of lived experience, and therefore of perception itself. Bachelard refers to the character of this reorganization as the lived experience of a sense of "secret correspondence" between self and world, where "the I no longer opposes itself to the world," where "everything I look at looks at me," where "between [me] and the world there is an exchange of looks," where "everything lives with a secret life."[39] Living on the level of reconstructed childhood experience is equivalent to a realization of the self as located in an intersubjective field—the *lived* experience of subjectivity as a transitional space in which "the interpersonal and the intrapsychic realms create, interpenetrate, and transform each other in a subtle and complex manner."[40]

Given that children tend more than adults to inhabit or indwell the lived space of the intersubject, they signify doubly for adult subjectivity: they are the "before"—what the adult was before she was an adult—and also the horizonal future of a normative developmental ideal. Applied to the narrative of the dialectical reconstruction of subjectivity, they are both precursors and unconscious prophets. They represent an early and ephemeral appearance of a form of human subjectivity that may appear later in the life-course, but only if the conditions of that early appearance have been satisfied—that is, only if adults allow, as Rousseau claims that "nature wants," "children to be children before they are men." Psychologically speaking, adults who have not been allowed their own childhoods have difficulty allowing it in their own children. If this is the case, then the major question for human culture is the question of the possibility of intervention in this reproductive cycle, and thus is a question of education in the broad sense. What form of education is necessary—whether of children or adults—in order to position them for transformation into the modal adult intersubject?

As we have already seen, Levinas associates the moment of the shifting of the structure of subjectivity toward the intersubject with child rearing. Jung provides a confirming clue in his identification of a life-cycle moment with middle age, when a new subjective economy begins to emerge.[41] Finally, we have identified the experience of the intersubject with Winnicott's notion of transitional space, which in early childhood is associated, not just with play, but with the subjective field in general, in the sense that inside and outside, projection and introjection, have not been operationally dissociated—although our analysis of the intersubject would indicate that in fact they never fully are. In adulthood, the experience of transitional space is associated with play as well, and art, philosophy, and intense emotional and relational experience. To the extent that we follow Schiller's identification of the "play impulse" as the intentional state that best expresses the human impulse for transformation, we can identify play as the engine of dialectical development of the subject-in-process in its search for a harmonious integration of reason and desire, the "happy midway point between law and exigency."[42] From a phenomenological point of view, it is a refinding of the space between inside and outside, projection and introjection, which is a space of creativity and transformation, both of self and self's relations.

Because the child is a human child, born into culture and from even before first breath a cultural being, she is early conditioned by both biology and culture to the same intentional states as adults, if to varying degrees. She shares what Alfred Schutz calls the "tensions of consciousness" characteristic of all humans. What he identifies as "wide-awake consciousness"[43]—which could be defined as the primary adaptive mode of the human in her environment—is the most characteristic adult tension of consciousness. As the state adapted for biological survival, it is characterized by the clearest subject-object or subject-world demarcation, since it is the consciousness of the world of "work," which requires an instrumental manipulation of the environment by an organ-ism that is in adaptive relation to it. It is the hypertrophy of this tension of consciousness in the West, and particularly in those cultures most indoctrinated into the Protestant ethic, which has contributed to the accelerating technological advances of Europe and the United States over the last 500 years. It is also the working model for *homo clausus*, for whom self-world, self-object, and self-other separation, the perform-ance principle and surplus-repression are both functional and discursive necessities for the maintenance of the system.

On the other end of Schutz's spectrum is the tension of conscious-ness of the dream or the hallucinatory state, in which self and object are interfused and mutually transformative. This could be identified with Freud's "infantile narcissism" or "infant autism," an original human condition in which no absolutely necessary ontological or causal rela-tions in the world are operative—where, as pure pleasure principle, what one wishes happens and what happens is what one wishes. The tension of consciousness characteristic of play and the lived experience of the intersubject could be placed roughly between "wide-awake" and "dream" on Schutz's continuum. It is, as Schiller has already shown us, "everything that is neither subjectively nor objectively contingent"—and he adds, "In proportion as it [play] lessens the dynamic influence of the sensations and emotions, it will bring them into harmony with rational ideas; and in proportion as it deprives the laws of reason of their moral compulsion, it will reconcile them with the interest of the senses." [44] From a psychodynamic point of view, Schiller is here describ-ing transitional space. From the point of view of the relation between reason and desire, it represents the onset of nonrepressive sublimation, a subject-world relation that results, according to Marcuse, "from an extension rather than from a constraining deflection of the libido," and which, according to both Schiller and Marcuse, "would harmonize the feelings and affections with the ideas of reason." [45]

For the child, and most dramatically the young child, the represen-tative tension of consciousness—the default state—is one of dispersion across the boundaries between "sensations and emotions" (i.e., "desire") and "the laws of reason," a state that triggers play because the latter is the engine of their dialectical interaction. According to Win-nicott, play "is always on the theoretical line between the subjective and that which is objectively perceived . . . [it] is neither a matter of inner psychic reality nor a matter of external reality." [46] Play is the form of problem solving characteristic of this "transitional" tension of con-sciousness, as instrumental reason is for wideawake consciousness, and as the forms of symbolization that Freud described as the logic of dreams—condensation, displacement, and censorship—are for the oneiric state.[47] By this definition, and as has already been suggested, art is a form of play, as are philosophy, humor, and eroticism, and we might say, any form of "extraordinary investigations." All lead to the deconstruction-in-the-interests-of-reconstruction of boundaries between self and world and self and other, and between the pleasure principle and the reality principle, or primary and secondary process.

As a transitional being in both senses of that word, the young child lives, albeit unconsciously, that form of subjectivity I have called the intersubject. This is true as well in the realm of object relations, where the division between her real significant others and her internalizations of those others as selfobjects is still unclear and in formative process. The child is still working to arrive at what Melanie Klein called the "depressive position" (in which "depressive" evokes the emotional results of the demise of infantile narcissism and the "grandiose" self).[48] When she has worked through to this position, Winnicott says, ". . . the child can say: 'Here I am. What is inside me is me and what is outside me is not me.'"[49] But what Winnicott's inquiry—in combination with the cultural construction of the subject-in-process and its lifelong development that emerged in the second half of the twentieth century—points to in the notion of transitional space, is just the blurring of this putative boundary for purposes of creative personal and social transformation. In this sense, the developmental journey of the intersubject means the reappropriation of childhood.

If we dare apply a recapitulationist hypothesis to the relations between individual development and the development of (at least) Western culture, we might say, following Schiller, that just as the child must—because she is "a lively representation to us of the ideal, not indeed as it is fulfilled, but as it is enjoined"—"fall" from the lived experience of the intersubject into the depressive position, so earlier forms of human subjectivity were "lively representations" to us of the future ideal of the intersubject. The medieval modal personality was more of a transitional one than *homo clausus*: more emotionally immediate, less psychologically isolated, with the boundaries of the individual not yet so clearly drawn—less able to say, "What is inside me is me and what is outside me is not me." Keeping to Werner's formulation of "orthogenetic" organismic development, this personality was relatively undifferentiated, and therefore more characterized by a tendency to fusion than to dialogue, both inter- and intrapersonally. On this account, the modern modal personality that followed the medieval represents a moment of negation, a hypertrophy of individualism leading to a radical alienation and a historical "fall" into a universal "adulthood." This is reflected in the discourse of Enlightenment, whose main metaphor is the notion of "growing up" or "coming of age," with its call for human autonomy under the sign of a universal Reason. It is also, at least in its early modern beginnings, associated with the Intrusive Mode of child rearing, according to which the child must be "subjected to a process of intensive instruction." At this height of Hegel's "unhappy consciousness," of the state of being "driven back in himself," of the experience of subjectivity as "abstract, present, self-conscious inwardness," and triggered by the very material conditions that resulted from it, a synthesis emerges in a form of subjectivity dedicated to reclaiming and reintegrating the "repressed." This process is exactly equivalent to what Jung and Neumann described in the reconfiguration of conscious and unconscious elements of the personality in the emergence of Self, which is the goal of the individuation process.

At the turn of the century heralded as the "century of the child,"—the twentieth—Freud provided the final statement of *homo clausus*—unhappy consciousness, Enlightenment man, the "grown-up." In his characterization of adulthood as a condition of disillusionment and resignation to the repressive order, he endorsed the "renunciation of [the] narcissistic entitlement" that is childhood's legacy. "Infantilism," he said, "is destined to be surmounted. Men cannot remain children forever."[50] The depressive position is essential to civilization—"civilization" in Freud's terminology being code for Comte's third stage of the historical development of Western culture, the "scientific," which has displaced the "animistic" and the "religious," and which constitutes the maturity of the species in a universe that no longer affords any room for human omnipotence. "Men," said Freud, "have acknowledged their smallness and submitted resignedly to death and to the other necessities of nature."[51] Without the repression that accompanies the depressive position, none of the institutions of civilization, which are built through the sublimation of repressed drives in the form of social, familial, and economic structures, law, politics, culture, art, technology, and education, would be possible.

Freud's successors provided the historical response to his own counsel of despair, which he—positioned as he was—could not. The revolt against surplus-repression already begun in Romanticism represents the end of "Western civilization" in Freud's terms, as the civilization of *homo clausus,* and the emergence of a new ideal of maturity beyond the repressive order. Historically, the revolt against the tyranny of the depressive position has unfolded with the revelation to the West of alternative epistemologies—alternative ways of knowing and acting in the world—a revelation effected by the very information explosion that resulted from the technological advances made possible by the "tension of consciousness" of that same repressive order.

The Privileged Stranger

The child, along with the "noble savage" of modern Western colonialism, was the first to emerge to conquer—in classic theory-of-empire fashion—from within, and to initiate the culture of postcolonialism. Along with the "aboriginal" or "native," the domesticated woman, the "lower classes," the madman, and more recently the "queer," the child represents the difference overlooked and projected by *homo clausus*. The child and the woman are the most dangerously seductive of all, for they are an enemy not at but within the gates—the wild man in the bosom of the "civilized" family, repression's "savage" displacement. Along with the other "othered" ones, children carry what feminist philosopher Sandra Harding has called an "epistemic privilege." These "others" represent alternative standpoints, or ways of seeing the world based on a difference in material, class, physical, sexual—or, in the case of the mad and young children—cognitive and even perceptual reality from the dominant culture and its ways of knowing the world. Harding refers to as them "valuable 'strangers' to the social order," or "outsiders within."[52] They are those marginalized by Eurocentric, patriarchal personal, interpersonal and social constructs. As we have seen, they are typically screens for both the dark and the light projections of the dominant class—both the shadow and the ideal of freedom from repression. They are those "bondsmen" in Hegel's master-slave relationship whose identity is canceled, or put under erasure by the "desire" of the lord or master, who, ironically, only knows himself through his mastery of them—that is, through their negation—and therefore is dependent upon them for his sense of self. As Hegel says of the desire of the lord, "First, it has lost its own self, since it finds itself as an *other* being; secondly, it has thereby sublated that other, for it does not regard the other as essentially real, but sees its own self in the other."[53] As the conqueror projects his own split-off, unconscious contents onto the conquered and distances her as the profane, the untouchable, the quintessential other, so by a dialectical process, the split-off content appears in the other—in the flesh—and becomes not just an adversary but a part of one's own subjective field, a selfobject, and as such, a potential interlocutor. The slave shares in the master's power because the master defines himself in opposition to the slave, and therefore needs the slave as a dimension of his own subjectivity.

The relation of domination—of "dark" by "light," unconscious by conscious, desire by repression—which exists in the subjective economy of the master is replicated externally in colonialist and patriarchal relationships, and in the Intrusive Mode of child rearing. This has changed historically in postcolonialist reality with the "reversal"—the dialectical reappropriation through dialogue—which applies both to social history and to the history of subjectivity, and which is already implicit in any situation of domination. As Hegel said, "But just as lordship showed its essential nature to be the reverse of what it wants to be, so, too, bondage will, when completed, pass into the opposite of what it immediately is: being a consciousness repressed within itself, it will enter into itself, and change round into real and true independence."[54]

As we have seen, the child's epistemic privilege was first recognized in modernity by classical early-nineteenth-century Romanticism. Almost 100 years later, in 1891, the Romantic iconography of childhood was reinscribed in Nietzsche's *Thus Spake Zarathustra*, where he announced, along with the death of God, the death of *homo clausus* and the rise of a new form of subjectivity: "The spirit," he proclaimed, "shall become a camel, and the camel a lion, and the lion at last a child"—where child signifies "innocence and forgetfulness, a new beginning, a player, a self-propelling wheel, a first motion, a sacred Yes."[55] Nietzsche's philosophical sortie "beyond good and evil" was in fact a further development of the Romantic iconography of the child as the prophetic expression of what Judith Plotz described as a "pre-moral freedom and spontaneity in which the psyche is fully at one with itself," which prefigures the wisdom of adults unhampered by moralizing and repression.[56] It is the intuition of this form of freedom that underlies the existentialism of the first half of the twentieth century, and initiated the postmodern inquiry into what Marcuse called "a new relation between instincts and reason," "a new rationality," a "non-repressive order."[57]

The new value placed on transitional experience—which is the hallmark of childhood experience—inaugurated twentieth-century theory. Piaget's notion of cognition as a constant mediation between organism and environment—a self-regulating equilibrative process involving assimilation and accommodation—necessarily implied a continuity between internal and external structures. Dewey called this process "transaction," and his notion of "growth" as a continual reconstruction of experience permeated twentieth-century ideas of an epistemological structure that has the quality of the unfinished—with the fluidity, the permeability, the flexibility, of constant transformation—and of the inseparability of self and other. But it was twentieth-century artists who first recognized and operationalized the child's privilege, for it is in the transitional realm of art that epistemology is expressed concretely, and where its relation to actual perception is represented—for an epistemology is a way, not just of explaining, but of seeing the world. Twentieth-century art, in its project of the deconstruction of representationalism, required a related perceptual process of deconditioning of the eye, and the art of children played—along with the so-called "primitive" art and music that were beginning to find its way into European and American circles—a major role in this aesthetic revolution.[58]

Four of the twentieth century's most prominent artistic revolutionaries—Klee, Kandinsky, Picasso, and Miro—and the emergent movements they were sometimes associated with—Russian neo-primitivism, futurism, cubism, surrealism—all sat before children's art as before an unconscious generic master. Kandinsky searched it for traces of a universal visual language. Klee, when taunted by critics that his art was childish "scribbles and smears" responded "That's fine! The pictures my little Felix paints are better than mine." Picasso studied it, it is reported, with "greedy curiosity," and is said to have told Herbert Read as they toured an exhibition of child art in Paris in 1945, "When I was the age of these children I could draw like Raphael. It took me many years to learn to draw like these children." And Miro, who immersed himself in the semiotic of children's art most profoundly—its "egocentric" perspective, its style of composition built on narrative, its tendency toward highly charged single images, its bold use of color, its symbolic exaggeration, its arbitrary limiting or infinitizing of space, either heroizing or dwarfing the objects placed within it—did not just adopt child motifs and elements, but entered them. His project was not so much to appropriate the child's pictorial syntax as to internalize its perceptual universe. The result was, as the historian of art Jonathon Fineberg has put it, an "assault[ing] [on] the hierarchies of adult civilization with a subversive innocence."[59]

The persona of this subversive innocence is the "childman" of Rimbaud, ten years younger than Nietzsche—Rimbaud the child genius intent on the "disorganization of all the senses" as the chief methodology of the deconstruction of the repressive order. The reconstruction that is implicitly sought in this project is a dialectical advance of human subjectivity—a reordering of the instinctual economy that corresponds with the Romantic project of the renovation of the imagination—those for whom, as Abrams suggested, the "new earth and heaven" of Christian eschatology is "simply the ordinary world of life's everyday appearances, renovated by the interplay of mind and nature in the act of perception itself."[60] It is the bid to pass from outer revolution to a revolutionary mode of perception—a relation between self and world in which "the unconscious is . . . more unmodified and accessible." This is what Abrams called "an apocalypse by imagination,"[61] which accompanied a century of yearning for deep-structural social revolution, from the French Revolution to World War I.

Always in the vanguard of this project of renovation was the intimation and the expectation of a form of subjectivity that, in Marcuse's words, "preserves the truth of the senses and reconciles, in the reality of freedom, the 'lower' and the 'higher' faculties of man, sensuousness and intellect, pleasure and reason."[62] It represented a direct challenge to Freud's stern insistence that the repressive order is necessary to "civilization." Marcuse argued that the material conditions of existence, which have until now required it, have been transformed by that very order to a point where it is no longer necessary to species survival. Once the abundance created by the performance principle has released us from the necessity of that very principle, the reconstruction of the relation between reason and desire is possible, in the development of a "'libidinal rationality' which is not only compatible with but even promotes progress toward higher forms of civilized freedom." Marcuse expresses the vision as a transformation of subjectivity in the form of a dialectical return to the polymorphous eroticism of the young child:

> No longer used as a full-time instrument of labor, the body would be resexualized. The regression involved in this spread of the libido would first manifest itself in a reactivation of all erotogenic zones and, consequently, in a resurgence of pregenital polymorphous sexuality and in a decline of genital supremacy. The body in its entirety would become an object of cathexis, a thing to be enjoyed—an instrument of pleasure. . . . the process just outlined involves not simply a release but a *transformation* of the libido: from sexuality constrained under genital supremacy to erotization of the entire personality. It is a spread rather than explosion of libido—a spread over private and societal relations which bridges the gap maintained between them by a repressive reality principle.[63]

Elsewhere Marcuse, arguing from Schiller, analyzes this transformation as a return to the "aesthetic function" and the "play-impulse." Above all he claims that the movement does not represent mere release of impulse or instinct. Within the repressive order, movement toward release results in what he calls "repressive desublimation," or the expression of instinct in polarity with reason, where it still represents the dark, the projected, without elements of transcendence—the body apart from spirit—the obscene. The new order of subjectivity entails, on the contrary, nonrepressive sublimation, in which "the pleasure principle extends to consciousness," and "Eros redefines reason in his own terms." In the new order, "Reasonableness is what sustains the order of gratification."[64] This is an expression of the heart of the Romantic vision for dialectical reunification of the personality, stated originally in Blake's *Marriage of Heaven and Hell* during the French Revolution, where he offered three propositions on the relation between reason and desire that would preoccupy the next two centuries:

1. Man has no body distinct from his Soul; for that call'd Body is a portion of Soul discerned by the five Senses, the chief inlets of Soul in this age.
2. Energy is the only life, and is from the Body; and Reason is the bound or outward circumference of Energy.
3. Energy is Eternal Delight.[65]

Marcuse's is perhaps the latest statement of the reappropriation of childhood, articulated in terms that satisfy the fundamental questions put by both Freud and Marx to the order of modernity. Maturity here represents a reactivation of "precivilized and infantile stages," but also, in that it transforms the "perverted content of these stages," and thus does not represent regression or fixation, leads to an "attitude that experiences man and nature as joined in a non-repressive and still functioning order," where "nature is taken, not as an object of domination and exploitation, but as a 'garden' which can grow while making human beings grow."[66] It also satisfies the criteria of the intersubject as a dialectical reconstruction of the relation between subject and object, self and other such that alterity, or the progressive withdrawal of projection, is possible.

The practical question, and the question most important for those in relationship with children, is what kinds of changes in adult-child relations follow on or produce—for the causal direction is still moot—the reconstruction of normative adult maturity as a dialectical reappropriation of childhood? I have argued that the Empathic Mode of child rearing in fact represents this reappropriative ideal, and that an understanding of optimal adult development as the progressive reunification of conscious and unconscious elements of the personality and the corresponding decentering of the ego, is implicit in the Empathic Mode. Whether or not the Empathic Mode and the intersubject are becoming normative for our culture could be determined by identifying multiple criteria for evaluating changes in adult self-understanding, as well as changes in social forms among adults. How to gauge change in modal adult subjectivity is complicated by the fact that, if we stick to a dialectical interpretation of change, negative or destructive phenomena in culture may be interpreted as deconstructive moments preceding transformation. Schiller for example, writing during the French Revolution, when the impulse for social change was at a height in Europe—and even as he predicted the "new reality principle" of the Romantics—could characterize the spirit of the times as "fluctuating between perverseness and brutality, between unnaturalness and mere Nature, between superstition and moral unbelief, and it is only the equilibrium of evil that still occasionally sets bounds to it."[67] Nor does history lead us to believe that the spirit of any given time will ever present a different face, or public life ever find a balance other than the "equilibrium of evil."

The differences resulting from subjective transformation emerge most often as protest, and historically speaking, as a seed awaiting the cracking of the outer shell in order to emerge. Those who carry a new principle into the world of action typically face various forms of resistance and even martyrdom. And the emergence in adult culture of an emphasis among increasing numbers of individuals on difference, alterity and tolerance, lifelong development, multiracialism, androgyny, sexual freedom and multiplicity, environmental responsibility, human rights, social justice and world peace—amplified by the increasing intervisibility and transparency of the new information environment—represents a promise that is dialectically linked with the disorder—including the fluctuation between "perverseness and brutality"—which the dismantling of the "order of repression" entails.

The role of children and childhood in the emergence of a new order of subjectivity is multidimensional. The Empathic Mode positions parents for that moment identified by deMause that triggers the "regression in the service of the ego" which is a necessary aspect of psychological reorganization. A style of parenting that recognizes the child as a fully human other—as a form of subjectivity which, whatever its differences from the adult, carries the implicit demand that its interlocutor forego domination and assume dialogue as its normative ideal—confronts the adult with the continual necessity of deconstruction of rigid categorical structures characterized by exclusions and hierarchies. And altering the relations of power between adults and children necessarily implies altering the relations of power between the elements or dimensions of the self, and vice versa.

For the adult to purpose to listen to children means attributing reason to them, in the deepest sense of the term "reason" as a capacity and a natural tendency toward self-regulation and self-organization. Listening to children in no way implies, as it tends to do in the popular imagination, capitulating to impulse, whim, or domination, any more than it does among adults. To the extent that it recognizes the child's status as "valuable stranger" or "outsider within," this form of listening implies that each child offers the hope and possibility of the development of a new relationship between reason and desire, a new opportunity for the construction of a nonrepressive order of subjectivity, with its corresponding opportunity for the construction of a nonrepressive social order. It also implies that the child is that singular other whose unconscious vocation is to contribute to the reconstruction of adulthood through its relation to it.

Attributing self-organizing capacities to children means, on the most obvious level, ever more attention to the question of children's rights, and the transformation of child "management" methodologies from controlling, intrusive and unilateral to dialogical, collaborative, and democratic ones. On a practical level it implies a reorganization of the lifeworlds of adult and child in the direction of reintegration and deinstitutionalization in multiple domains, from the built environment to the worlds of education and work. The slogan of the Romantic pedagogue Friedrich Froebel—founder of the kindergarten—"Come let us live with our children"—perfectly expresses the urge for the reintegration of the lifeworlds that still informs those radical experiments in architecture, urban planning, and alternative schooling which have experienced perennial florescence in the West—most particularly in the Progressive educational movement of the 1920s and the counterculture movement of the 1960s. Although the reconstruction of subjectivity will not come about through any one institution, and although the family is obviously the primary institution of reproduction of the boundaries and domains of the modal self, educational institutions—most particularly the institution of the public school—play a major role, in the West anyway, in holding any particular mode of the adult-child relation in place, and thereby in the reproduction of a certain form of adulthood.

School is the place where adults and children meet for purposes of cultural and social transmission, for the production of cultural and social meanings, above all for the meanings associated with work and with the formation of collective ethics. Marcuse suggested that the reconstruction of the relation between reason and desire, or, as he put it, "the transformation of the instinctual structure" that he saw as a possible consequence of the "conquest of scarcity and alienation,"

could result in "the transformation of work into play."[68] The most logical cultural site for the institutionalization of this transformation—
which hinges on adults entering into dialogue both with their own
construction of childhood and with real children—is the school. And it
is the school to which, finally, we turn.

5

Reimagining School

. . . our social life has undergone a thorough and radical change.
If our education is to have any meaning for life, it must pass
through an equally complete transformation.

—John Dewey[1]

The Purposes of Schooling

The eminent philosopher of education John Dewey wrote these words
in 1899. If we consider the last 100 years, that "radical change" in
social life of which he spoke will be seen to have been magnified expo-
nentially. But the school has not transformed accordingly. Most of those
who work for change in public education usually satisfy themselves
with the hope that the continual assimilation—through gradual cooption of ideas and practices with which the school has been confronted at
least since the turn of the twentieth century will lead to a critical mass
of slight differences, which will eventually appear as transformation.
Whereas we in our lifetime see nothing, Rip Van Winkle might. For
others, there is no necessary expectation that slight quantitative incre-
ments will turn into qualitative change, and hence no way to imagine
the school except as "after the Revolution" whose arrival will surprise
everyone, and which will certainly not originate in the schools.

This situation presents those of us who allow ourselves to imagine
a form of schooling, universally practiced and available, which realizes
the potential of adult-child dialogue, with a danger that Dewey has

151

rightly characterized as a situation in which "the ideal is itself the product of discontent with conditions," which, instead of "serving to organ-
ize and direct effort, . . . operates as a compensatory dream."[2] This is
especially dangerous in confronting an institution that represents an
extreme case of the hardening of habits—in Dewey's broadened sense of
the word—into predetermined "ruts," which is the major problem
around which his analysis of the possibilities for social change revolves.
His succinct characterization of schooling as "largely utilized as a convenient tool of the existing nationalistic and economic regimes"[3] applies
as well today as it did at any moment in the history of public schooling.

Dewey characterizes habits as "working adaptations of personal
capacities with environing forces," "affections . . . predispositions . . .
demands for a certain kind of activity," which in fact "constitute the
self."[4] Those habits that are not flexible, and open to reconstruction
through the influence of what he calls "impulse" or the "practically
equivalent" word "instinct," are not capable of changing social conditions, and are in fact the chief causes, as he sees it, of the structural
inequalities that support both personal and social conditions of either
chaos or stagnation like economic exploitation and war. In a modern,
state-mediated polity and economy, the public school is the chief point
of application of adult habit on childish impulse. It is the point of transition between childhood—the age, in his terms, of "original modifiability" and "plasticity"—and the sort of habituated adult required for the
purposes of the state and economy. As such, it is the location in the life
cycle where the modal relation between habit and impulse, or reason
and desire, is determined through the ritual standardization of the
adult-child relation and its operationalization as the moment of transfer
or transition from childhood to adulthood.

It is this transitional moment in the life cycle, first referred to by
Freud as "latency," where the relation between impulse and habit is
normalized on an adult model: where the child is "instructed" through
the most fundamental of hidden curricula, in the role and limits, prohibitions and allowances of impulse in the reconstruction of habit. Either
we learn to use impulse, which according to Dewey is "the pivot upon
which the re-organization of activities turn," to "give new directions to
old habits and change their quality"—that is, we teach children (and
ourselves in the process) to be oriented toward continually reconstructing habits—or we reproduce the gap between old habits and present circumstances that make for what he calls, ironically enough, the
"infantilisms," the "mass of irrationalities that prevail among men of
otherwise rational tastes," which manifest "just where critical thought

is most needed—in morals, religion and politics." This reproduction of "normal" social pathology is accomplished through what he calls "training," that is, "an impatient, premature mechanization of impulsive activity after the fixed pattern of adult habits of thought and affection"[5]—in short, the adult colonization of childhood.

The school has not changed because it is the major institution for "subjection"—the social reproduction of a form of subjectivity—in the interests of modern hegemonic ideologies and economies. As such, it will never change merely through the introduction of new techniques or technologies or methodologies within the current structure of subjection, but only through a form of subjection—which amounts to a form of lived experience—based on a new set of discourses about the relation between impulse and habit. As I have already argued, the question of causality in the historical transformation or evolution of subjectivity is moot because it is both circular and overdetermined. If, as I have also argued, subjectivity is constructed to a great extent through the adult-child relation, then one must ask, what enters that system or what changes within that system in order to change the cycle of reproduction, and how? What led the premodern, collectively modulated subject to turn into the discrete subject of modernity, and what leads *homo clausus* to transition into the intersubject? Where is the path, however tortuous, from surplus-repression to a nonrepressive order?

Certainly the changes in social life of which Dewey spoke are also changes in the lived experience and self-understanding of the individual subject who participates in those changes; which, in turn, hinge on the reconstruction of habit, which in his formulation is a lifelong process. But this process shows its greatest promise in the socialization of the young, and thus is dependent on the kind and quality of the adult-child relation. Dewey's analysis is so important because he provides us with a way to imagine the transition from the modern to the postmodern subject as a dialectical process. The direction of evolution as he understands it is from an ideal of subjectivity understood as fixed habit—presented as a positive ideal in the Platonic model—to subjectivity understood as an ongoing process, which implies "a generosity of outgoing action, a liberation of power as against the close, pent in protected atmosphere of a ready-made ego"[6]—the continual reconstruction of habit, or what we have already encountered as the "subject-in-process." Dewey's ideal of the continuous reconstruction of habit as an engine for personal and social transformation is based on the deconstruction of the monological and the emergence of the dialectical self—characterized, not by exclusions and hierarchies but by plural and sometimes contradictory dimensions and attributes whose interactions implicitly aspire to a new, more differentiated and more fluid synthesis, whether that synthesis is ever completely achieved or not:

> Inconsistencies and shiftings in character are the commonest things in experience. Only the hold of a traditional conception of the singleness and simplicity of soul and self blinds us to perceiving what they mean: the relative fluidity and diversity of the constituents of selfhood. There is no one ready-made self behind activities. There are complex, unstable, opposing attitudes, habits, impulses which gradually come to terms with one another, and assume a certain consistency of configuration, ...[7]

As Dewey's analysis implies, the transition between these two ways of imagining—and therefore performing—the self, hinges on the shifting relation between reason and desire, the very binary relation that Merleau-Ponty, following a tradition at least as old as Hegel and Schiller and Romanticism in general, prophesied as the hinge of evolutionary cultural transformation, or what Dewey referred to as "a most far-reaching problem: The alterability of human nature."[8] The "nature" here identified by Dewey is in fact Marcuse's historically mediated "libidinal economy." After distinguishing between "a self taken as something already made and a self still making through action," Dewey identified the hinge of this transformation: "In the former case, action has to contribute profit or security or consolation *to* a self. In the latter, impulsive action becomes an adventure in discovery of a self which is possible but as yet unrealized, an experiment in creating a self which shall be more inclusive than the one which exists."[9]

The distinction is crucial, and made doubly so by Dewey's lifelong emphasis on the social role of education as either the reproduction of existing adult habits, or the reconstruction of those habits in a form that allows for "growth," by which he meant a form that allowed for further reconstruction. School for Dewey was the one institution—even beyond the family—which could systematically, as a *praxis*, allow "immature impulse to exercise its reorganizing potentialities." For him, ". . . the cold fact of the situation is that the chief means of continuous, graded, economical improvement and social rectification lies in utilizing the opportunities of educating the young to modify prevailing types of thought and desire."[10]

As a functional component of existing ideological and economic power and interest, universal compulsory state schooling—where by "state" is understood the regulative, hegemonic, interest-determined structure of family, law, political system, economy, and class organization—is essential to the reproduction of that form of subjectivity, that is, worker/consumer/citizen, which is necessary to maintain this structure. The school, like all analogous educational institutions in whatever age and culture, is the critical point of passage between the "wild," unsocialized being of the child and the being of the modal adult of the epoch and the culture. It is in this institution that the passage between the two states is expressed, codified, and continually enacted ritually and symbolically. The parent sends the child to school as to a site where the adult-child relation is regularized, formalized, and fitted for the construction of relations of authority in the wider adult world—the "workplace," the "moneyplace," and the "policyplace." It is in school where a process secondary to family socialization but equally powerful is initiated. Here the desires, the aspirations, the prohibitions, the fatalisms, the boundaries, and even the trangressive dreams of the modal adult—the adult with certain commonly shared tastes, aspirations, and expectations—are instilled and enforced in hegemonic form as discourses, dispositions, beliefs, and practices.

From the point of view of the psychology of ego development, school age is the moment in the life cycle when children are psychologically most available to this instillation. By "latency" Freud meant the withdrawal of libido from the bodily organs and its investment in the social relationships with mentoring adults and the tasks they demand—the expansion of eros or desire into the psychosocial sphere, with an emphasis on the world of instrumental production. Here, instinctual energy is sublimated into work energy. Erikson follows Freud in his characterization of the developmental ego "crisis" of the school-age child as the resolution of the binary psychosocial themes of "industry" and "inferiority." For Erikson, the successful (or "good-enough") resolution of each developmental crisis contributes to the epigenetic reconstruction of the ego to include a new dimension or structural element, which in this case means the awarenesses and dispositions and skills—or what Schutz, on a more fundamental psychosomatic level, called the "tension of consciousness"—appropriate to the adult world of work. In school the child learns, as Erikson put it, "to earn recognition by producing things," which is accomplished through "adjust[ing] himself to the inorganic laws of the tool world." On this social functionalist view, the expansion of the child's "ego boundaries" to "include his tools and skills," which in turn involves learning the "work principle," or "the pleasure of work completion by steady attention and persevering diligence," necessarily implies that children, in whatever culture or historical period, "receive some systematic instruction."[11]

A hermeneutics of suspicion would suggest that Freud's and Erikson's construction of latency is at least in part a theoretical reification of what deMause called the Socializing Mode, which, as we have seen, emerged in the nineteenth century. The notion of latency is a theoretical legitimation of a certain form of the adult-child relation, and thereby of a certain form of adult subjectivity. If we uncouple stage theory from purely genetic accounts and consider, as Dominick Cavallo has suggested, that "society politicizes the life cycle for its own purposes, and that one can view psycho-social development from psycho-political as well as psycho-sexual and psycho-social perspectives,"[12] we can read "latency" as a scientific legitimation of universal compulsory schooling, which was just consolidating as a hegemonic institution in the mid- to late-nineteenth century. Universal compulsory schooling is the institutionalization of the idea of latency, as Barbara Finkelstein has argued, "as a social as well as a psychological state of childhood."[13]

In spite of its anti-historical bias, it is not necessary to abandon Erikson's epigenetic theory, or even his understanding of the developmental "task" of the school-age child in order to introduce the idea of dialogue into the construction of schooling. Schools or other educational institutions in any culture are necessarily ways of what he calls "admitting the child to an understanding of meaningful roles in its technology and economy."[14] What Erikson, following Freud, has left out— and the omission is in fact the chief index of his (and Freud's) construction of childhood—is admitting the child to an understanding of meaningful roles in the construction of social and political power. If we identify the school as we now know it as an artifact of the Socializing Mode, the question becomes one of imagining the same institution fulfilling the same functions—of "admitting the child to an understanding of x"—from the point of view of the Empathic Mode. We might ask what kinds of changes that shift would bring about including, not just what technological and economical roles might or might not be understood as meaningful, but what a form of education based on dialogue— which is the basis of the Empathic Mode—would mean for the construction of relations of power.

Applied to the adult-child collective called "school," which is a community of power as much as a community of teaching and learning, a key analytic dimension in any child-rearing mode could be defined as that of both personal and collective *self-regulation*. The term evokes both developmental and political discourses. The developmental discourse of self-regulation is constructed on binaries like habit versus

impulse or instinct, internal versus external locus of control, and autonomy versus heteronomy, which in turn evoke the social and political
binaries of anarchy (in the philosophical sense of the term) versus hierarchy, self-governance versus external rule, and, at a deeper level, order
versus disorder. The notion of self-regulation, whether applied to individuals or social systems, is both about desire/reason and about power.

The Empathic construction of childhood understands the child first
as an interlocutor, and thus sees her, as described by the philosopher of
childhood Loris Malaguzzi, founder of the exemplary schools of Reggio
Emilia, as

> tak[ing]an active role in the construction and acquisition of
> learning and understanding. . . . Once children are helped to
> perceive themselves as authors or inventors, once they are
> helped to discover the pleasure of inquiry, their motivation and
> interest explode. . . The age of childhood, more than the ages
> that follow, is characterized by such expectations.[15]

Teachers in Reggio Emilia "begin by noting that it is impossible for
a culture to exist without an image of children. Children, as understood
in Reggio, are active and competent *protagonists* who seek completion
through dialogue and interaction with others, in the collective life of the
classroom, community and culture, with teachers serving as guides."[16]
Dewey understood this intuitively in his announcement of what at the
turn of the twentieth century he called "a change, a revolution, not
unlike that introduced by Copernicus"[17] in education, a revolution that
hinges on a reversal of the traditional relation between reproduction
and reconstruction. He saw the role of the school in a genuine social
and political democracy as an experimental or "embryonic" community.[18] Such a community is dedicated, not to the "citizen" but to the
"man"—or the "citizen" reconstructed as a bona fide social and political agent—in short, as the democratic personality. To believe in such a
possibility requires a new understanding of and attitude toward the
meaning and potentiality of the child's powers and impulses.

Dewey argued that the impulses—by which he means "the pivots
upon which the re-organization of activities turn, . . . agencies of deviation, for giving new directions to old habits and changing their
quality"[19]—of the young are in a different relation with their forms of
habit than is the corresponding relation in adults. In children impulses
are, because of the "original plasticity" or "modifiability" of the young,
"highly flexible starting points for activities which are diversified
according to the ways in which they are used. Any impulse may become

organized into almost any disposition according to the way it interacts with surroundings." Implicit here is the notion that any habit, bad *or* good, which has closed itself off to ongoing reconstruction by the mediation of the "pivot" of impulse, has become "arrested and incrusted." Given that "human society is always starting afresh" in the young, social transformation begins just there—in the young—and for him the central, guiding belief of a fully humanized education necessarily implies "some consciousness of the extent to which a future new society of changed purposes and desires may be created by a deliberate humane treatment of the impulses of youth."[20]

The Space of Dialogue

The argument of this book has been that, although there are many variables that contribute to the evolution of subjectivity, the final determinative causal factor is the kind and quality of the adult-child relationship itself—if only because it is through child rearing that any cultural trait is reproduced. When the latter comes to be understood as a relationship of dialogue, it is intimately associated with internal dialogue in the adult—the dialogue between the adult and his own "child"; and according to the hermeneutic principal of subjectivity, internal dialogue is the dialectical engine of subjective transformation. That is, the qualitative shifts in the adult-child relation over historical time have directly to do with the shifts in the psychic economy of the *adult* that result from internal dialogue. These shifts center in the organization and reorganization of the relations between habit and impulse, conscious and unconscious, superego (or "conscience") and ego, and in a temporal dimension, of the relations between present, past, and future (whether, for example, the adult considers himself capable of "starting again," "like a child"). To the extent to which they hinge on the ability of the various dimensions of selfhood, some of which are in contradiction, to listen to each other and to be moved by each other's "reasons," they can be understood as relations of power. On its most fundamental level, dialogue is about power, for it is based on the premise, as Martin Buber put it, that "Each must expose himself wholly, in a real way, in his humanly unavoidable partiality, and thereby experience himself in a real way as limited by the other, so that the two suffer together the destiny of our conditioned nature and meet one another in it."[21] This statement can be applied to both external and internal dialogue.

When it moves across the shifting boundaries of the subject, internal dialogue forms the basis for dialogue with the other, who on the model of the intersubject, is in fact already an element of the individual's subjective field structure through introjection and projection. The "child within"—the child the adult once was and therefore still is—is the "other" within her own libidinal economy, the "valuable stranger" or "outsider within," with whom the adult as subject-in-process is in dialogue. The child "without," the child before us, the child as presented to the adult as son or daughter or ward or student or friend or child passed on the street, is in a special relationship of dialogue and power, which Buber calls a relationship of "inclusion." In a relationship of dialogical inclusion with the child, I *assume* the existence of those powers and capacities that I as an adult find within myself either as a universal human birthright, or as products of my individual development. This means that I am committed to fostering and nurturing them, and the implicit rights, privileges, and responsibilities associated with them. In this sense I understand the child "as if" she were an ideal adult—a self-regulating subject-in-process, knowing full well that (like me) sometimes she is and sometimes she is not. When I need to protect her from her own emotionalism and poor judgment I have no qualms about doing so, but I understand these in the same way that I understand my own (usually better hidden and more controlled) emotionalism and poor judgment.

I attribute to the child the same capacities, if not the same level or consistency of their realization, for self-regulation and self-organization that I find in or attribute to myself. I attribute to the child the same needs I find in myself: for autonomous action, for personal choice, for privacy, for respect from others, for personal exploration, for moments or periods of psychological regression, for nurturance, for meaningful work, for a reasonable level of power in the personal politics of the "microsphere" or near environment, for leisure, for equal treatment in situations of dispute, for, in every case of conflict or failure, the recognition of mediating circumstances of one kind or another. When the powers and capacities I assume in the child are not realized or manifested, I take the same attitude toward that situation as I take toward myself—the same explanatory discourses and the same strategies. I understand us both to be subjects-in-process, both involved in continuous dialectical change, and both of us just as liable to system conflict, stagnation, and chaos. I understand the pattern, if not all the details or material, of our development to be the same.

This form of mutuality of attribution, which provides an interpersonal basis for dialogue, creates the same set of possibilities for my actual relation with each child-person. Buber identifies three broad categories of intentionality toward the other, or "ways in which we are able to perceive a man who is living before our eyes."[22] First, he character-izes "observing" as seeing the other as consisting of "traits," which can be cataloged and categorized.[23] This way of approaching the other is a fundamental evolutionary function that is probably brain-based and an aspect of perception itself, but as a style of personal and cultural inten-tionality it is a reification of the latter, and underlies instrumental sub-jectivity, or the "I-It" relationship, that is, the objectification of persons for purposes of security and use. Buber opposes to this the "I-Thou," or the dialogical relation.[24]

As an intentional aspect of the "everyday" tension of conscious-ness, the "I-It" relation also underlies both common sense and the sci-entific attitude. It is the basis both for the everyday rational world of use and exchange *and* for the stereotypification and subspeciation that lead to criminal behavior by whole social groups—as in cases of institu-tionalized inequalities, political and economic oppression, genocide, and ecocide. Epistemologically, it is the knowledge of what Levinas calls the egoist-I, or the situation of "totality," which "knows nothing but itself." It is a form of intentionality that has not encountered true differ-ence in the world, because it assimilates everything to its own sameness. In Jungian terms, it is a negative ego-Self axis, in which the ego denies its part-relationship with the totality of its nature, the Self, and arro-gates the whole to itself.

Elsewhere, Buber refers to it as "monologue": "He who is living the life of monologue is never aware of the other as something that is absolutely not himself and at the same time something with which he nevertheless communicates."[25] The life of monologue is the epistemo-logical basis for those attitudes we associate with adultism. It is the epistemology of schooling, which understands the child as "future citi-zen," "standing reserve," "human resource,"—as raw material for the production of an adult—in which is implicit a "deficit model" of child-hood, and the child understood as, not just an incomplete but an imper-fect form of subjectivity. In fact Gadamer specifically refers to this form of intentionality toward the other—any other—as the "educative rela-tionship," whereby "one claims to express the other's claim and even to understand the other better than the other understands himself," and thereby "seeks to calculate how the other person will behave." He calls this "the dialectic of charitable or welfare work," which "penetrates all relationships between men as a reflective form of the effort to dominate. The claim to understand the other person in advance performs the func-tion of keeping the claim of the other person at a distance."[26] This style of intentionality informs at least one dimension of mainstream develop-mental psychology that, as an instrument of state colonization, is used by institutions to categorize, control, and locate individuals within a codified system.

Buber identifies his second category, "the onlooker," with "all great artists"—which in the case of the adult-child relation, we can apply to "all great teachers." The onlooker "takes up the position which lets him see the object freely, and undisturbed awaits what will be presented to him. Only at the beginning may he be led by purpose, everything beyond that is involuntary." The onlooker is a phenomenologist—she is interested in letting the object "appear" as much as possible apart from her projections and instrumental purposes. She understands the event of her own understanding of the object as the self-structuring of the object being understood. For onlookers, the other "neither demands action from them nor inflicts destiny on them."[27] To the extent to which the teacher is an artist of soul-making, and the school her studio, she is an onlooker: epistemologically she operates in the region of *theory* in the original, etymological sense of the term. Aristotle used the word *theorein*—a way of looking translated as "to behold" or "to contemplate"— to describe what he considered the highest form of knowledge. To "behold" is to see the object, as Buber says of the onlooker, as "what is not 'character' and not 'expression',"[28] both of which are projective attributions. It is to see the world as play—as the self-structuring of the world—or, in other terms, as open, self-organizing system. For the educator-as-onlooker, the adult-child collective that we call the school is the "theater," the place of beholding, of what Gadamer calls "total presentness," in the transitional space in which the adult-child relation is played out endlessly—in which its themes and plots undergo endless recapitulation and development.[29]

Buber's final intentional category, which he calls "becoming aware," is closely associated with a key concept in his understanding of dialogue—that of "being *addressed*." In the dialogical relation, the other "says something to *me*, addresses something to me, speaks something that enters my own life."

> It can be something about this man, for instance that he needs me. But it can also be something about myself. The man himself in his relation to me has nothing to do with what is said. He has no relation to me; he has indeed not noticed me at all. It is not he who says it to me, . . . but *it* says it.[30]

What "it" says is connected for Buber with the "sign." "Signs," he says, "happen to us without respite, living means being addressed, we would need only to present ourselves and to perceive."[31] Although

Buber insists that the signs that "happen to us" cannot be predicted or categorized, we may say that the adult in dialogue with childhood and the child is in the realm of a specific order of signification, and that the sign of childhood is received across that "abyss of historical consciousness" between the adult and her childhood mentioned in Chapter 1 which characterizes the hermeneutical situation. The "it" that speaks to the adult is the child's form of life in its structure as a different relationship between habit and impulse, reason and desire—a different tension of consciousness. But this is not a *sign* unless it arrives uncategorized, not—as in the monological, "educative" relationship, as something "understood in advance"—but as a sign that triggers the appropriation of a new or rediscovered form of knowledge in the adult. Therefore it should not and in fact cannot be named or predicted, and in the end must be understood as the sign of the difference, or alterity that makes for genuine dialogue. It is the recognition of difference between adults and children that leads adults to recognize and listen to the individual voices of children, rather than to presume "to express the other's claim and even to understand the other better than the other understands himself," and thereby "seek to calculate how the other person will behave." It is the possibility of this recognition that gives the phenomenon of school its importance, and makes of it a key intercultural space of meeting and coconstruction.

Adults and children are faced with at least four kinds of concrete difference. Physical and physiological difference—in size and weight, patterns of activity level, hormonal and neuronal differences—either result in or are translated into social difference, above all differences in power, wealth, status, and degrees of independence. The existential difference between adults and children—the kind and quality of their lived experience—is an expression both of physical and physiological differences and of social difference. It is different, for example, to negotiate the world from a height of three or four feet, as opposed to five and a half or six, and neuronal differences translate into differences in perception itself. Finally, different degrees of inductive experience make for a different practical logic—the child's cognitive maps and categorical structures are typically not as complex as the adult's, simply because she has not been around as long. This is not to deny that children of five may have developed a more sophisticated and functional structure of judgment in their given life-context than some full-grown adults—especially in schools, which are designed at least partially with children in mind. In fact one of the major characteristics of adultism is the ignorant attribution of ignorance to children.

These differences between children and adults are finally no more telling or determinative or even more extreme than some cultural differences between adults. Like members of different adult cultures, the child lives in a "culture of childhood" in which there are traditions, practices, and expectations that make the culture what it is, and in which there are pathologies and virtues specific to it. The culture of childhood lives necessarily in a dependent relation to adult culture, but the style and character of that dependency can vary greatly from culture to culture, and between historical periods.

It is the reification of the four forms of difference—physical, social, existential, and experimental—by adults that makes for the basic psychosocial structure of the traditional school, which is a site for the imposition of sameness by one culture—the culture of adulthood, which is more powerful than the other—on the culture of childhood. Although the perennial conflict between these two cultures guarantees that the traditional school will always be in some sense a place of struggle, there is no reason to believe that these two cultures would not struggle in a school in which genuine dialogue took place, given the close relationship between conflict and reconstruction. A school that understands itself as in-process in no way overcomes, any more than any other institution, the vicissitudes of the relations of power, given that power is, in Foucault's classic formulation, omnipresent—"not because it has the privilege of consolidating everything under its invincible unity, but because it is produced from one moment to the next, at every point, or rather in every relation from one point to another. Power is everywhere; not because it embraces everything, but because it comes from everywhere."[32] The school as embryonic community is in fact a laboratory for relations of power—a site necessary to any collective interested in social reconstruction. As a laboratory, its goal is to resist what Foucault calls "Power," that is, hierarchy and "lordship" in whatever form, which he characterizes as ". . . permanent, repetitious, inert, and self-reproducing," yet "simply the overall effect that emerges from all these mobilities [of power with a small "p"], the concatenation that rests on each of them and seeks in turn to arrest their movement."[33]

In order to emerge, the event of dialogue requires an initial separation, a distance to be bridged, and a "will to relation," relation having been made possible only by the hermeneutical act of "setting at a distance." "Distance," according to Buber, "provides the human situation; relation provides man's becoming in that situation." Buber's ontology of intersubjectivity implies the intersubject, who as a dialectical synthesis of the collective and the discrete subject, recognizes her own radical individuality again within a dual system of self and other: the intersubject "can accomplish the act of relation in the acknowledgement of the fundamental actuality of distance."[34] Broadly speaking, the premodern, collective self is in a situation of psychological fusion with the other, and the modern, discrete self is in a situation of isolation and objectification. The intersubject is in a situation of dialogue, which sublates both terms of the binary construct in a third structure that mediates distance and relation.

Dialogue assumes the rupture of the egoist-I and the reconstellation of the ego-Self axis, which precipitates an internal reconstruction whereby the self recognizes its own multiplicity, the otherness within itself, and simultaneously that the other—who is also multiple—is a part of its intersubjective field through projection and introjection. Dialogue both causes and is caused by reconstruction across the boundaries of the self, but it emerges not as an experience of fusion or collective identification, but as the recognition of the very otherness of the other—the recognition that the other "is absolutely not myself" and that the other is "the very one she is." Dialogue implies accepting another human being in his or her particularity as "the single one," the "Thou."[35] It requires the withdrawal of the projection of the egoist-I, which, paradoxically, reveals, not just the individual who is absolutely not myself, but the intersubjective structure of subjectivity that contains us. I and the other are both more individualized through withdrawal of the projection, and more recognizable as field beings, in that the structure of intersubjectivity is clarified when its contents (projections and introjections) are distinguished from its formal structure—the structure that carries and organizes those contents.[36]

The "between" of dialogue is both the between *within* the subject—the difference that the subject finds within herself—and the between *between* subjects—the space of interlocution where self-other boundaries become mutually transgressive and thereby negotiable between persons. These two forms of alterity are in dialectical relation. Together, they establish transitional or "potential" space—the space outside the individual, but is not the external world, the space of creativity and transformative process. It is, as we have seen, the dialectical "third way of living," which mediates the inner reality of the individual and the shared reality of the world that is external to individuals. The transitional is a space of the deconstruction and reconstruction of interhuman relations of all kinds, including relations of power—which implies the dialectical overcoming of Hegel's paradigmatic master-slave relationship in the direction of equality—and relations involving the reconstruction of mutual values and accepted social and political practices. It is the space of the more fluid relation between impulse and habit that is childhood, and is marked above all by the sign of *play*, which, as Winnicott has shown, corresponds in the world of adults to the space of what he broadly calls "culture": art, philosophy, religion, intense relational experience, dreaming, envisioning.[37]

The transitional "between" is the site where the ego understood as the bearer of the "same," the "thematizing gaze," the epistemological subject who "never encounters anything truly other in the world" because it assimilates the other to its own structures of judgment—which, as we have seen, Levinas associates with Western reason—undergoes reconstruction, creating at least the possibility of "the liberation of the ego with regard to the self."[38] Philosopher Hugh Silverman calls it "the space of difference which is neither that of the subject nor that of the object"—a space of *inquiry*, in that inquiry involves "the appropriation of a space which is neither that of the interpreter nor of the interpreted, but one which uncovers what most needs to be said with respect to that which is interpreted"[39]—in which one is, in Buber's terms, "addressed" by the "sign." The interlocutors enter dialogue as a space in which the assumptions of *both* are put under interrogation, and in which therefore the outcome is uncertain and emergent. Nor is there any necessary expectation that difference will be overcome. If it is overcome it will be through a higher resolution, a sublation, which will in turn carry its own difference within it.

The School as Laboratory of the Third Way of Living

Reimagining the praxis of school on this side of the "revolution not unlike that introduced by Copernicus" means imagining an institution that creates the conditions for dialogical relations between the forms of intentionality of childhood and adulthood. As we have seen, Schiller understood "the third joyous kingdom of play" as representing a dialectical reconciliation between "rational ideas" and "the interest of the senses,"[40] or reason and desire, and—either synonymously or analogously understood—primary and secondary process, unconscious and conscious contents, impulse and habit, and ultimately, ego and Self. Understanding the school as laboratory, studio, or experimental cultural zone—the transitional space in which this reconciliation is continually and perennially undertaken, where adults invent and maintain and mediate an interactive and performative structure which "permit[s] immature impulse to exercise its reorganizing potentialities"[41]—in no way trumps the perennial function of the school as a site where, on

Erikson's account, "ego-boundaries" are expanded to include "tools and skills," where we first experience "the pleasure of work completion by steady attention and persevering diligence," or where children "receive some systematic instruction." If Freud's psychosexual theory of latency and Erikson's "industry versus inferiority" stage of epigenetic ego-formation reflect a genetic psychosocial situation and not merely a historically determined psychopolitical one, they will apply to the school as a site for cultural reconstruction as much as a site for cultural reproduction.

As it is, the implicit goals of schooling as we mostly know it are in direct contradiction with a major conditional requirement for dialogue—that it is possible only in a context of noninstrumental relations. Buber's presentation of the complex, emergent, and uncontrollable relationship between dialogical and instrumental relations in the two basic word-pairs "I-Thou" and "I-It" make it clear that instrumental and dialogical relations are mutually dependent and even mutually entraining.[42] The instrumental world of "use" is in fact what we typically mean by the "world as experience" as opposed to the "world of relation." Nevertheless, the school is currently implicitly constructed, not just as an involuntary reflection of, but as an intentional reification of that use-world—as a world of the calculated reproduction of the "citizen," "the worker," and the "consumer," in which latter is also implicit the "information-consumer," that is, someone who accepts the state media's account of the world—whether by "state" is understood the government or the corporations. Traditional state-driven educational rhetoric, with a mixture of sentimentality and instrumentalism as chillingly grotesque as it is hypocritical, refers to children as "our most precious resource," and need say no more in order to be understood. The school as we know it simply cannot understand itself as other than a colonizing arm of the state, taken in its broadest sense to include not just legal and political and economic forms, but social and cultural and relational ones—from the form of the community to the form of the family to the form of individual sexual organization and of sexual morality.

As a colonizing institution, it is the school's "job" to produce, through what Dewey describes as "converting an original docility to the new into a docility to repeat and conform," an adult subject who will maintain these forms. The way the school accomplishes this is by setting impulse and habit, reason and desire, at odds, and thereby sundering the dialectical connection between them that is the location of the potential for individual and social reconstruction. What is reproduced in the very structure and intent of traditional schooling is whatever the good intentions of its operatives, "the social divorce of routine habit from thought, of means from ends, practice from theory." In fact Dewey goes on to deconstruct the interests behind those "good intentions" in a few blunt sentences: "Those who wish a monopoly of social power find desirable the separation of habit and thought, action and soul, so characteristic of history. For the dualism enables them to do the thinking and planning, while others remain the docile, even if awkward, instruments of execution. Until this scheme is changed, democracy is bound to be perverted in realization."[43]

Although overcoming the instrumental relations that are inscribed in the school as an institution of social reproduction in no way implies doing away with the school as a preparation for the world of work, it does imply the reconstruction of the world of work as much as the world of leisure and the world of politics. The adult not subjected to "premature mechanization," like the adult of Coleridge who "retains the feelings of childhood into the powers of manhood" has learned a way of being, a pattern of coordinating means and ends, of uniting action and soul through "constantly utilizing unused impulse to effect continuous reconstruction."[44] This adult subject offers the promise of constructing, collectively and individually, new approaches to the tool world, which imply new approaches to the ethics of work, which imply new approaches to social justice, which imply new approaches to the construction of power. The index of a culture oriented to reconstruction rather than reproduction will be an educational structure that encourages a form of individual and social life that marries, as in the Romantic vision, ends and means, habits and thoughts, practice and theory.

What are the fundamental practical guidelines for such a school? Is there just one way that such a school can be constructed, or multiple ones? To affirm the former promises the imposition of yet another "one best system." The only set of criteria that can be consistently applied without the danger of totalitarianism are the principles of dialogue, which we have identified as: 1) a hermeneutical approach to self and other, that is, the recognition and acceptance of distance and relation in dialectical process; 2) the affirmation of the other as the "single one," which is identified with alterity, or the decentered psychological organization associated with the "rupture of the egoist-I"; 3) an emphasis on noninstrumental relations, which in this case imply a meticulous respect for and attention to the perceptions, interests, and goals of childhood and of individual children; 4) a continuous attention to equitable relations of power, which implies political autonomy and self-governance, both within the school—which includes the classroom itself—and in the school's relation to larger associations of which it may be a part.

Political autonomy and self-governance are fundamental requirements for the formation of social democracy.

By social democracy is understood, following Dewey's now familiar phrase, a form of "associated living, . . . of conjoint communicated experience"[45] that forms the basis for genuine political democracy. What upholds the latter is a society dedicated to two related realms of common value: values of social justice, equality, social responsibility, nonviolence and mutual care; and values of individual rights and freedoms, which is to say the social intention to allow individuals to live a relation between impulse and habit that allows for personal transformation in the interests of self-actualization. Social democracy is about the reconstruction of relations of power on the intersubjective level, and of the relation between impulse and habit on the intrasubjective level (which, as Plato's analysis of the tripartite self indicates, is also a relation of power).

Practically speaking, what Dewey noticed and encouraged in his view of the emergence of social democracy were two tendencies. First, as he put it,

> a movement toward multiplying all kinds and varieties of associations: Political parties, industrial corporations, scientific and artistic organizations, trade unions, churches, schools, clubs and societies without number, for the cultivation of every conceivable interest that men have in common. As they develop in number and importance, the state tends to become more and more a regulator and adjuster among them; defining the limits of their actions, preventing and settling conflicts.[46]

Second, the tendency toward what is now—at least on one interpretation—known as "globalism," or at least a logical transformation of the current form of it, expressed in the slow resolution of the "opposition between the claim of independent sovereignty in behalf of the territorial national state and the growth of international and what have well been called trans-national interests." This tendency connects with the first, in that the voluntary associations that form the heart of a social democracy "do not coincide with political boundaries," and therefore

> internationalism is not an aspiration but a fact, not a sentimental ideal but a force. Yet these interests are cut across and thrown out of gear by the traditional doctrine of exclusive national sovereignty. It is the vogue of this doctrine, or dogma, that presents the strongest barrier to the effective for-

mation of an international mind which alone agrees with the
moving forces of present-day labor, commerce, science, art
and religion.[47]

As an expression, then, of social democracy, the school's role is not to
be understood as an expression of or an arm or a function of state
socialization, but as a form of association protected and nurtured, but
in no way determined by the state.

A school of the "third way of living" must, then, be understood as
an autonomous and self-governing collective in its relation with larger
bodies or associations. No obligatory curricula or academic or professional standards will be handed down to it by any group that presumes
to know its goals and interests better than itself. All that the state may
provide the school is an equalized allocation of tax monies, which
belong to the people as a whole—the "people," it is assumed, being eth-
ically committed, in their own best interests and according to the two
realms of common values mentioned above, to equal educational access
and opportunity for all of its members. Beyond financial support, the
state may certainly work as a generator and disseminator of educational
ideas and materials, but none of these shall be imposed.

Parents of students are understood as part of the "committee of the
whole" of the school community, and participate directly in school governance and administration, as do teachers, students, other staff, and
anyone else who expresses a desire to be a part of the school community. There are on principle no permanent administrators, although any
member of the community, including students and parents, either individually or as parts of administrative groups, may serve in that capacity
for extended periods of time—always at the discretion of the community as a whole. Decisions about crucial dimensions of the school such
as curricula, grouping, scheduling, personnel, and even disciplinary
issues are arrived at democratically, through inquiry and mutual deliberation, and finally, the judgment of the collective, or the committee of
the whole. On a practical basis, this means that the space and time allocated to these processes, in the form of appropriately designed meeting
spaces and a schedule that allows adequate, paid time for collaborative
inquiry and deliberation is assumed to be as essential to the quality of
the life of the school as the space and time allocated to instruction.

The school is as much a community of adult inquiry—as much a
laboratory for social democracy among adults—as it is of children, and
the processes of inquiry, deliberation, and judgment are shared by both.
In places those processes intersect, in others they operate separately, or
in a parallel, or in tandem. The professional vocation of the educator is

understood as a continual inquiry into the optimal relation between theory and practice, a continual inquiry into the adult-child relation, *and*—in keeping with Dewey's suggestion that it is among the youth that society is reconstructed—into social reconstruction in collaboration with that very youth. In such an intentional community of adults and children, the two are co-learners and co-inquirers, and this co-inquiry applies both to academic and to political, or power-related, aspects of the community.

Teachers are prepared for the school of the third way through a reconstructed form of enculturation and skill-building: the academy moves to the school, which now becomes the primary site for preparation in pedagogy, curriculum development, and group process. Classes, seminars, student teaching, consultation, and mentoring take place primarily on-site, and these classes, seminars, workshops, projects, research episodes, etc. are implicitly understood as generally open to all members of the community, including children. Pre- and apprentice teachers participate in the life of the school on all levels, including organization and governance. This represents a reprise of a pattern initiated in the U.S. at the beginning of the twentieth century and abandoned in the latter half, of "laboratory schools" in universities; what is different in this case is that the school hosts the university rather than vice versa. Professors of education have assignments that include residency in particular schools, which include classroom teaching responsibilities and mentoring of children, collaboration with teachers in curriculum development and implementation, coordination and facilitation of action and grounded research, and ongoing dialogical philosophical inquiry with teachers and other staff.

The reconstruction of physical space to accommodate this reconstruction in practice and in the theory-practice relation is a crucial aspect of the shift itself. Institutional practices are shaped and determined as much by the design of the built environment as by the activities that take place within it; in fact the two are inseparable. The built environment is a reification in space—in boundary, pathway, wall and sector—of the social roles and relationships that gave rise to it—which in turn are influenced and determined by the built environment, and so on in a circle. The philosopher of architecture Yi-Fu Tuan refers to built space as "a text encoding the rules of behavior and even a whole world view," which "demarcates and intensifies the forms of social life" within it.[48] Built space shapes, identifies and determines the range of possibility of the activities of those it contains. For the child, the built environment of the school is a first definitive social text in architectural form, which forms and instructs lived experience, and creates a lifelong psychological template for the functionality, possibility, comfort, and beauty of the work environment.

A space dedicated both to children and adults and to their interaction must take into account the differences in the lived experience of space of children and of adults, identify the intersections and the developmental trajectories of the two, and balance the distinctive needs of both. The child's most fundamental project is to "master" the world—to learn to control and manipulate and preserve and enhance it with tools and emergent skills—through play, or "playfully." Play is a form of activity in which means and end are in harmony, which effectively means that they have merged, in that the activity of play is experienced as its own end. The child has not relinquished the conviction that work should be play, and that any overdrawn distinction between the two is a problematic one. In playful work, mastery is attained through participation in the world of the task, through joining it as an interlocutor in transitional space. As a result of the interaction, something is produced, and this object is both a transformation of the world and a representation of internal transformation, which in developmental terms may be understood as greater differentiation, articulation, functional integration, and centralized control, that is, mastery. In making something in an encounter with the world the child, like the artist, produces, not just objects for use, but symbols of her own interior development. The latency child is, in Erikson's words, oriented toward "adjusting himself to the inorganic laws of the tool world"—which is to say becoming an adult—through a process akin to the artist's. The result is greater distance *and* greater relation within the environment: as a result of the process of playful work, the organism is better adapted to the environment through changing the environment and in the process of changing it, being changed itself.

The modern adult's work project—unless he or she is an artist, which can be taken in the broadest sense of the term—is, as Heidegger put it, "to pursue and entrap nature as a calculable coherence of forces," which he called "enframing."[49] This is the project of a subject who is already separated from nature, or world, and represents a hypertrophy of distance, instrumentalism, and mastery and domestication of a potentially dangerous "other." From the point of view of the child or the artist, it represents a shift from Buber's ontological position of distance and relation to distance without relation, from interlocution to colonization, from communion to alienation, differentiation to fragmentation, and from normative to implicitly pathological use of the world, including the world of other people. It has resulted in an aesthetic degradation of the lived environment that has paralleled the increasingly rapid development of the technology available to manipulate that environment. To this extent, the development of human technology, at least in the case of the West and arguably universally, can be seen either as a tragic narrative, captured originally in the myth of Prometheus; or as a dialectical moment that will be followed by a sublation, or synthesis of contradictory elements. The latter is what the subject-world relation of childhood prophecies—recalling Schiller's characterization of childhood as "a lively representation to us of the ideal, not indeed as it is fulfilled, but as it is enjoined."[50]

The transitional intentionality of the child and the artist promises a reunification of work and play. Both play in a differentiated unity with world, in the interest of communion and integration. The environment with its demands and exigencies provides the challenge, or the "aliment" for this process, which is to say for its own transformation. For the child as for the artist, the product that emerges from the engagement and that represents the encounter with the environment is relatively unexpected because it has emerged through an interactive process that allows for creative outcomes. It is not a part of what Heidegger calls the "standing reserve"—the outcome of strategies of domination, to be extracted from the world and ordered and stored—but a symbol of transformation. It stands in a different meaning-relationship to the environment. It resists the status of the standing reserve, it is "unenframe-able"—a transformation rather than an colonization of the world and the self-world relation.

The intentionality of the over-instrumentalized adult—the one, to recall again Schiller's analysis, who has undergone a "dismemberment of being," for whom "nature has disappeared from humanity," and for whom the environment has become an adversary—is a Faustian hypertrophy. But if we take a dialectical view of development, this hypertrophy is a temporary one and necessary to growth, to ultimately, in the long run, being "reconciled to nature in freedom." In its current form it is dangerously out of balance. It takes a normal aspect of self-world differentiation—the strategic impulse to put things aside, to choose, to use only those parts of the world that can be regulated and secured, stored, distributed, and placed in reserve for future use—and turns it into a general principle of use, thus rendering it ecocidal. The factors contributing to its historical reconstruction are overdetermined, but it can be assumed that key among them is the reconstruction of those two institutions most directly determinative of the education of the young—the family and the school. In the family, it implies a reconstruction of the relation between culture and instinct, thought and action, order and disorder, heteronomy and autonomy in the context of intimate relationships—that is, on the most fundamental of levels. In the school, it implies a reconstruction of the world of work: the "inorganic tool world," the world of tasks.

The physical plan of a school dedicated to the realization of a space dedicated to the reunification of work and play will include spaces that are designed for various kinds both of adult and child work, play, and meeting. The configuration of classrooms, offices, seminar and conference rooms, shop and studio areas, lounges and eating areas, large and small meeting areas, must be imagined within the larger context of design variables like the overall construction of pathway or route, the interface between indoor and outdoor spaces and the concomitant construction of a combination of natural and artificial light, the juxtaposition of "open" and "closed, "noisy" and "quiet," "hard" and "soft," public, semi-public and private spaces—of spaces designed for large groups, small groups, intimate groups and individuals. These obvious, concrete principles of overall design have been virtually ignored by school architects, under the sign of economy and a spurious argument for "efficiency."[51] Such a dramatic insensitivity to the effects or the possibilities of the built environment is an index, not just of adultism, but of the function of the school as a site for colonization. The traditional school building is a reification of the Intrusive Mode, and emerged in the late eighteenth century, as Foucault has argued, with the prison, the barracks, the hospital, the asylum, and the office building in constructing an environment designed for purposes of surveillance, classification and "normalization" of the population.[52] Normalization serves social control through the production of a "docile body," "both a productive and a subjected body," a subject who has, in Dewey's same use of the word, been converted from the "true docility" of the young—which he describes as "to be eager to learn all the lessons of active, inquiring, expanding experience"—to "subjection to those instructions of others which reflect *their* current habits. . . . a willingness to follow where others points the way, into conformity, constriction, surrender of skepticism and experiment."[53] In his archeology of disciplinary practices, Foucault chronicles the emergence of an architecture designed "to permit an internal, articulated and detailed control—to render visible those who are inside it; in more general terms, an architecture that would operate to transform individuals: to act on those it shelters, to provide a hold on their conduct, to carry the effects of power right to them, to make it possible to know them, to alter them."[55] This is the architecture of the school as we know it.

The school of the third way assumes an emergent, systemic balance of multiple pedagogies and curricula, from the most open to the most closed forms of structure and organization. The overarching theoretical perspective through which this balance is determined would be based, not on an imposed unity or hierarchical continuum, but on the assumption of radical difference, or alterity. In education, this would amount to a learning—and therefore a teaching—theory based on constructivist stage theories of development and domain theories of intelligence, both of which imply a primary emphasis on the individualization of learning and instruction within a social context. The theory justifying this approach has been in place at least since the work on human intelligence and motivation began roughly one hundred years ago with Binet, was developed and articulated in Piaget, linked to drive and ego psychology in Rogers, Maslow, and Bruner, reconstructed as multiple and nonlinear through Gardner, understood as implicitly social and dialogical in Vygotsky, and operationalized by practitioners in a multitude of ways, from curricula based on individualized instructional plans in special education to curricula directly based on multiple intelligences, to inquiry-based learning of all kinds.

A school that is constructed on the learning unit of the individual in no way implies selfish individualism; in fact it could be argued that the contradictory combination of radical individualism and brute collectivism of the Intrusive structure does much more to instigate and foment selfishness than a fully individualized model because it puts the two modes in conflict, impairing both individual and community self-realization. The grouping principle of the third way is based on the assumption that the school is an intentional community rather than a forced collective or state colony designed for the production of individual and group "high achievement," or specifically for the "tooling up" of the population for the uses of the economy or the "market." As an intentional community, it is conceived normatively by definition—that is, it is both experimental and emergent *and* guided by normative ideals; it is not a community that "just happens," nor is it a community that is determined from above, by a hierarchy of power. It is a community that very consciously explores the possibilities of the relation between adults and children in the interests of the emergence of individual self-actualization and social reconstruction, which are inseparable. And the form of social reconstruction that any intentional community based on dialogue necessarily entails will be a democratic one, which implies an intentional community dedicated to the construction of the attitudes, dispositions, knowledge and skills characteristic of a social democracy.

What has so far prevented the practical realization of constructivist-developmental theory, which has only emerged as a general phenomenon during the period of the Socializing and the Empathic Modes, are curricula and a corresponding pedagogy based on the Intrusive Mode. The heritage of the latter is written, not just into classroom activity and interaction, nor just into relations of power between adults and children and adults and adults in schools, but into the physical design of schools themselves. Reconstructed curricula, pedagogy, and relations of power, and therefore patterns of governance, demand the reconstruction of the space in which they are developed, articulated, and performed. Group activities and the spaces in which they happen are mutually interactive and determinative. To begin to reimagine how groups and individuals are organized for work and for meeting in the reconstructed school is necessarily to begin to reimagine the physical, material organization of those spaces.

There is no obvious common sense or empirically proven instructional reason to *regularly* group students by age or academic performance, or to regularly put students in groups of more than fifteen or so—whether those groups be age-graded or determined by some other criterion. Where the unit of academic measurement and analysis is the individual and his or her interest and performance, to design activities and the spaces for those activities based unilaterally on a model of large group instruction is, if not counterintuitive, then simply dramatically inefficient. The principle of transitional space calls for the construction of physical spaces that lend themselves to the "between" of any encounter, whether that encounter be between members of large, mid-sized or small groups, including triads, dyads, or the intrasubjective "between" of being alone. A curriculum, a grouping plan, a system of scheduling, a system of mentoring, a system of individual, large and small group instruction and inquiry and deliberation, a system of collective self-governance and of professional development—all of these should map onto a space designed to provide to the greatest possible degree for the specific forms of these practices.

A curriculum that is both dialogical and fully individualized is best constructed operationally as a combination of individual and group projects, individual and small group skill instruction, and group inquiry of various kinds, related both to the projects underway and to the usual subject areas that can be applied to them. In terms of content area, the curriculum should embody all the traditional academic disciplines, including the arts, languages, mathematics, physical education, and the natural, physical, and human sciences. The "project method," which has been present as a concept since the early-twentieth-century progressive school movement, offers the most obvious possibility of a dialogical and emergent reconstruction of curriculum and pedagogy. It provides for multiple approaches both to the numbers of students involved in any given project, and to the extent to which the theme or topic of the project is the outcome of a negotiation between the teacher—whose interest is in communicating and transmitting the content and processes of the disciplines—and the student's interest.[55] A project may be an individual or a collaborative inquiry, and a certain proportion of each day is devoted to it. It often calls for "field trips," and requires sufficient shop, studio, laboratory, and library spaces for its implementation. As recently implemented in the schools of Reggio Emilia, projects fall naturally into three categories: those that arise directly from the interest of a child or children, those that reflect mutual interests of teachers and children, and those chosen by teachers with certain cognitive or social concepts in mind.[57]

The effect of such an emergent curriculum is to diversify grouping practices, and thereby pedagogical strategies as well. At any given point during the school day, groups ranging in size from one to twenty persons may be found assembled, not to speak of whole-school assemblies devoted to various purposes. Each of these groupings will have an appropriate space in which to meet—a space that optimally both contains, encourages, and contributes to the structure of the particular activity in which the individual or group is engaged. Teachers will be engaged in a corresponding variety of pedagogical activities—from lecture or drill to small or large group facilitation to individual, small or large group guided skills instruction. Some students will be engaged in project work, alone or in small groups, some assembled in groups of varying sizes for tutoring or skill instruction in subjects such as mathematics or foreign languages; some will be writing or engaged in cooperative editing or writing, some will be working on a dramatic production, or practicing or performing music; some will be crafting an object in shop or studio, some engaged in group critique of a work of art, some engaged in observation of cellular structures in a laboratory, and some engaged in communal literary or historical and philosophical investigation, which includes dialogical inquiry.

If there is a set of content-expectations that form the conceptual spine and the scope and sequence for curriculum, they are understood as one dimension of the structure in which students and teachers enter into dialogue in order to produce an emergent curriculum. If adults decide, for example, that certain literacy, numeracy, musical, artistic, computer, kinaesthetic, or other knowledge and skills are critical to the school's notion of a "good education," then the principle of dialogue requires that they find a way to bring that knowledge and those skills forth in the context of the interest of the students. "Interest" of the students does not necessarily imply their *pleasure* interests—there is no necessary relationship between interest and "fun"—nor does it imply that there will not be conflicts of interests between adults and children to be continually worked through. It is also understood that in certain areas of the lifeworld there is differential authority between adults and children, just as it is understood that in certain areas there is differential responsibility. The argument for this differential is given in everyday experience, and in the great majority of cases is as obvious to children as it is to adults. The points at which it is not obvious are the very points of dialogue and reconstruction, and the adult-child collective of the school, as an "embryonic community life,"[57] is the logical site for this dialogue. The school of the third way, is in Dewey's words, a "progressive community," in that it "endeavors to shape the experience of the young so that instead of reproducing current habits, better habits shall be formed, and thus the future adult society shall be an improvement of their own."[58]

If, for example, after careful, context-sensitive deliberation, adults decide that arithmetic, algebra, and geometry skills and understanding will in the estimation of their school be considered a goal, then curricular strategies will be adopted or developed that will operationalize that goal in multiple settings. These strategies can be broadly categorized into three groups: 1) strategies for incorporating the study and mastery of mathematical skills and concepts into projects. This represents the adaptation of those skills and concepts to the spontaneous and native and emergent interests of children; 2) strategies of individualized, small, and large group instruction, which may very well involve direct instruction, individual study with workbooks, computer programs and so forth; 3) strategies for collaborative critical and dialogical inquiry into the philosophical ground—in this case epistemological, ontological, and metaphysical—of mathematics.

Philosophical inquiry is of the greatest importance for the overall character and structure of a school of the third way, for when it is conducted communally and dialogically, it represents a methodology through which children are able to encounter for themselves the fundamental questions that provide a rationale for studying mathematics—or any other of the content-areas—on a level deeper than that of its practical application. The issue of the absence of practical application is usually offered as the source of children's disaffection with school, but in fact the issue is one of an absence of the presence of children's own questions in the construction of what is studied—that is, the issue of *meaning*.[59] When mathematics—or history, or art, or language or science—is approached critically in search of the inherent assumptions underlying its beliefs and its normative claims, then its identity as a static, already-accomplished body of knowledge, externally imposed, is loosened, and the extent to which each discipline is it itself is a product of previous inquiry is revealed. As a result, children are able to connect the artifact that the organized discipline represents to their own spontaneous and interest-driven inquiries. Over 100 years ago Dewey identified the gap between the two as a fundamental problem in the construction of curriculum, and searched for some way

> to get rid of the prejudicial notion that there is some gap in kind (as distinct from degree) between the child's experience and the various forms of subject-matter that make up the course of study. From the side of the child, it is a question of seeing how his experience already contains within itself elements—facts and truths—of just the same sort as those entering into the formulated study; and what is of more importance, of how it contains within itself the attitudes, the motives, and the interests which have operated in developing and organizing the subject-matter to the plane which it now occupies. From the side of the studies, it is a question of interpreting them as outgrowths of forces operating in the child's life, and of discovering the steps that intervene between the child's present experience and their richer maturity.[60]

The "attitudes, motives and interests" contained within the child's experience that identify the child and the curriculum as "simply two limits which define a single process" have, on their deepest level, *not* to do with practical application, or the issue of "how can I use this in real life?" That question is simply a child's first challenge to the pedagogy and curriculum of colonization, and a first act of cognitive rebellion against a form of education that separates work from meaning. It would not even be asked in a school that truly valued the child's interests. Rather, the attitudes, motives and interests in question revolve around *inquiry*, which—as constructivist genetic epistemology, beginning with Dewey and Piaget, increasingly indicated over the course of the twentieth century—is the fundamental category of a kind of learning that is undertaken by and not imposed on the learner. Simply put, inquiry is a response to disequilibrium in the cognitive system, and successful inquiry results in reconstruction of the system such that it is more adequate to the environment that put the system in disequilibrium in the first place.

Inquiry presents itself in the form of a question. A question is an index of system-disequilibrium. Intrusive curriculum presents itself in the form of a series of propositions. The goal of intrusive curriculum is not to put the world in question, but to affirm a series of accepted propositions about the world. But if the child is to encounter the curriculum on the level of meaning it must be with a question; for if self-initiated learning is undertaken in the interest of the reconstruction of his or her cognitive system, then reconstruction implies a prior state of disequilibrium, which is indexed by a question. We recognize that the majority of children's questions—although often fewer than the adultist interlocutor assumes—are personal ones; but each personal question is based on a question of identity—Who am I? Who are you? What is that?—or a question of relation—between self and other, other and other, or things in the world. And each of these personal questions is connected generically, in a part-whole relation, with universal questions of identity and relation (ontology and metaphysics), and also with questions of knowability (epistemology) and of ethics. Children can move very quickly from Who am I? to What is it to be a person? What is right relation between persons? What is the difference between an animal and a person? And they can move from What is that? to How can I or anyone else know if something is true? or What is the difference between believing and knowing? Such questions lead into similar ones: What is a number? Is the mind just the brain? What is justice? What is a right? What does it mean to be free? What is culture? Is there such a thing as human nature?

These fundamental questions—questions that are central to both human understanding and conduct, which are common to us all, and which are inherently contestable[61]—in short, philosophical questions—that underlie any course of study on the most fundamental level, the level of meaning. In an Intrusive model, questions are under erasure, or they come already answered, which is the same thing. In a dialogical model, questions are the hidden springs of inquiry, of "the attitudes, the motives, and the interests" that dispose one to inquire and which drive inquiry. And given that questions are common, central, and contestable, they lend themselves to collaborative inquiry in a community of normative discourse—a speech community characterized by dialogue, and oriented to a drive for deconstruction and reconstruction of the taken-for-granted answers foisted on them by a habit-driven culture.

In a school setting, to undertake such a community of discourse amounts to the introduction of philosophy as a content area. Unlike the uses of philosophy in the intrusive curriculum, which is typically not introduced until adolescence, and which consists in a course of study in the history of philosophy, the form of philosophy with children as here understood takes up the questions that the philosophical tradition has always asked, but does so as if for the very first time. The experience of communal dialogue about our most fundamental assumptions brings us face to face with the original condition of philosophy—philosophy not as didactics, and not just as conversation, but as an emergent, multivocal, and interactive oral inquiry into questions that require an answer before any further questions can be answered, yet which are in themselves unanswerable.[62]

So reconstructed, philosophy takes its place again, as in the medieval synthesis, as the "queen of the sciences," but in this case as an oral event-structure like the Socratic, implicitly dedicated to the continual reconstruction of the answers to the same questions humans have always asked, and always implicitly oriented to the underlying question, "How are we to live?" In the school of the third way, this activity is where the whole conceptual structure of the curriculum enters transitional space. It is the space between the conceptual structures of the disciplines and the conceptual structures of each child and of the community, and as such a space of interrogation and dialogue. Recalling Winnicott's characterization of transitional space as "outside the individual, but . . . not the external world," a space into which "the child gathers objects or phenomena from external reality and uses these in the service of . . . inner or personal reality,"[63] philosophy as communal dialogical inquiry is the space where our assumptions, our fundamental beliefs enter into question for purposes of reconstruction. And those beliefs are as much about ethical and moral questions as they are about metaphysical or epistemological ones.

In a school of the third way, the dimension of collaborative philosophical inquiry will be present throughout the emergent curriculum as a form of problematization of belief—a first inquiry into the epistemology, and by implication the methodology, of any discipline that is a part of that curriculum. For example, a project that undertakes to examine the architectural, economic, social, and cultural changes in a given urban neighborhood in the last 100 years will naturally involve the introduction of historical research, which in turn will call for an inquiry into principles of historiography, which in turn will involve an inquiry into the fundamental concepts that are at issue in the philosophy of history—what constitutes a historical "fact," the question of historical goal, direction, or pattern and the idea of "progress," the question of the narrative element in history (whether it can ever be anything but a "story"), and, correspondingly, questions of interpretation: can history *ever* in its very nature, be "objective"? Is all history revisionary? And moving into ethical questions—can history be responsible or irresponsible, and if so, how does one do responsible history?

The natural movement philosophy makes from the descriptive to the normative ensures that the dimension of ethical and moral inquiry is present in the curriculum as a permanent element, and is integrated into all content areas. It also defines the school as a site in which instruction serves inquiry and not vice versa. Nor will such an emphasis have any real reconstructive power unless the same sort of communal deliberative inquiry practiced throughout the curriculum is also practiced within the school community as a whole. As we have already seen, the school of the third way is the primary site for teacher training and development. University professors have offices there, and participate in groups on multiple levels—groups of children, student and apprentice teachers, and school faculty. The school as a whole is understood as a community of inquiry—inquiry into learning, teaching, curriculum construction, school governance, assessment and evaluation, and issues of order and discipline. At any given moment during the day, one might find groups of adults—which may include children—of varying sizes, one discussing a recent or classic treatise on education or some other discipline; another engaged in an innovative course of study in mathematics or literature or art; another constructing an interdisciplinary project curriculum; another deliberating on a series of observations made by teachers or apprentice teachers of a particular child or particular group of children, for the purpose of generating curriculum or some other kind of intervention in response; another discussing a recent incident of conflict or perceived violation of persons, space or routine; another assessing a project or projects in process; another discussing a chronic problem in scheduling or group dynamics; another composed of parents and teachers engaged in deliberation of some kind. These sorts of activities *must* be understood as of equal importance to "instructional time," for they are as crucial an aspect of the life of an embryonic community as any other.

A school that has deconstructed and diversified grouping patterns, decentralized and individualized learning and instruction practices, and thereby reconstructed the distribution of individuals and groups calls for a different approach to the overall design of space, time, activity and interaction than the traditional model. A school might adopt a system of supervision based on individual advisement—whereby, for example one teacher enters into a mentoring relationship with ten to fifteen children of the same or different ages, who in turn constitute a "home" group. These groups could be assembled using various criteria: on the basis of a disciplinary interest—for example the group could be interested in languages, in the arts, or science, or mathematics; on the basis of a more immediate interest such a longterm project in which they have all expressed interest; or on the basis of skill level in numeracy or literacy (which does not necessarily mean that all students would be at the same level); on the basis of a sociometric analysis; or some other. The mentor teacher would meet with this group at the beginning and at the end of the school day, and generate and/or monitor individual and small group plans for each child. And there might be other periods during the day or the week in which this group was together—for individualized instruction, for collaborative inquiry, for project work, peer-tutoring, small-group work of various kinds, or for some other sort of problem solving.

The group's "home" space would be constructed to make it possible not only to confer, but to study and eat together. Such home spaces would be spread throughout the school, and each would provide soft places (carpeted areas with couches and soft chairs), a seminar table, appropriate space for preparing food and eating, storage and display areas for materials, and individual study areas in the form of carrels. Each place would be adjoined by the mentor teacher's office, and would also access an interior or exterior courtyard or terrace, in order to maintain an indoor-outdoor relation. Over the course of the day, children would venture out from these home bases to a variety of spaces that provide studio, workshop, lab, resource, teaching, seminar, and large-group meeting functions. Some of these spaces would be enclosed, some partially enclosed, and some areas open onto the pathways that connect them all. The younger the children, the more concentrated into one area or section around the home spaces these work and meeting spaces might be, but on general principle, the territory to be mastered progressively by each child is the whole school, in all its complexity and variety. This represents a radical difference from the traditional model of understanding of the relationship between the local and the global within the school. In the latter, the child's territory is his or her classroom, and the rest is anonymous and administered space, requiring passes, exceptions, or rebellion to explore. But the space of the school should be understood on the metaphor of a village, or hive, or labyrinth, as opposed to a "disciplined" or "normalized" space, in which one principle or style of spatial organization and use is imposed on the whole. Both home groups and individuals within them are in the new school both autonomous and interdependent, local and global, within the whole system.

Finally, in a school of the third way there is simply no place for a form of evaluation or assessment that is not directly related to helping children to better meet the goals that have been negotiated between them and the adults with whom they are collaborating. The standardized test constructs knowledge as a commodity, and performance of knowledge as an act of competition, both of which are completely irrelevant to the aims of education, and are broadly pernicious in their results. The apparatus of standardized testing is, except for its possible value as a research instrument, simply an oppressive atavism, a naked instrument of colonization with no genuine educational relevance. In a reimagined school, the unit of analysis is the individual, and the criteria for analysis the ability to meet his or her own goals and objectives. All acts of assessment should on principle include the participation in some form of the one assessed, all evaluative judgments should involve multiple perspectives, all assessment should be carried out in the form appropriate to the kind of knowledge involved, and the chief goal of any assessment and evaluation procedures should be to enable those being assessed to apply those same reflective and evaluative procedures themselves. There is no reason, for example, not to evaluate performance in mathematics using purely quantitative criteria and methods, but the very algorithm by which a student's performance is evaluated should be a part of the mathematics curriculum itself, and its implicit principles of knowledge and judgment—in this case, statistics—be at some point in the mathematics curriculum a subject of philosophical inquiry. And if assessment and evaluation cannot be meaningful, let there be none, except in the forms that emerge naturally and spontaneously from the sorts of purposeful activity in which children are engaged.

The Dark and the Light

The institution of the school, even—and perhaps especially—given the priority and status and universal influence it has assumed in the modern nation state, cannot serve as the sole engine of transformation of the instinctual structure of the modal personality of our time, the search for which has been at the heart of this inquiry. To overemphasize the influence of the school in social reconstruction (or, for that matter, reproduction) would be to succumb to the very ignorance that has informed those dystopic impositions of universal "solutions" by state planners that have characterized at least the last 100 years of collective life. Nor has the central aporia that has emerged continually in this inquiry—the problem of the order and direction of causality—been resolved. In the school as in the family, as in urban planning, the question remains how one form of subjectivity can raise up its children in another.

But the fact is that images, styles, normative models, and everyday explanations of human subjectivity have changed and are still changing, and those changes are passed to the next generation through the narrow funnel of child rearing and education. The notion of finding a way to predict how the changes happen implies that one could find a way to direct and control them, which is exactly the dialectic of welfare work, where one is concerned to understand others better than they understand themselves. This is the attitude of adultism, which attempts, especially through schooling, to reconstitute the reality of the child as an adult, rather than providing a space for a transition between childhood and adulthood that allows for the dialectical preservation and presence of childhood in adulthood, which in turn is the basis for the reconstruction of subjectivity.

Not only are causal factors both reciprocal and overdetermined, but experience would seem to indicate that in the history of cultures and societies the "highest" and "lowest" forms of subjectivity and forms of relation are always present, and their interaction ambiguous and even ironic. There will always be brutalization and dehumanization and there will always be compassion and altruism; always the highest form of idealism in action and the most egregious cynicism, venality, and impoverished imagination; always surprising breakthroughs of the good and dramatic failure and misunderstanding of the most noble intentions. There will always be filial kindness and basic human solidarity in the search for peace and justice, and there will always be perversity, violence, and blind selfishness, both individual and social. To attempt to construct a system, whether of child rearing or education, which overcame this fundamental human condition would not only be totalitarian, but its success would create an entropic social condition from which the conditions for growth were removed.

Empathic parents will always in some cases inadvertently, and against their own deepest wishes, raise children who become nonempathic adults, and vice versa. To recognize multiplicity and contradiction internally—in the self—is to recognize it in the larger system of subjectivity that is the collective, and on this account, Socrates was right when he said that virtue cannot be taught.[64] But multiplicity and contradiction are the very conditions of change, and thus, logically, the kind and quality of multiplicity and contradiction themselves will change. The intellectual, moral, and aesthetic mediocrity of the post-Intrusive school is a result of institutional resistance to that change. Institutions and individuals resist change because present change—the situation visible to us at any given moment—carries contradictions and multiple possibilities that hint at alternate futures, not all of them positive. Negative and positive elements and their conflict within a system are necessary to system transformation, and in matters related to the historical construction of subjectivity, change will always hint both at the dark and light, deadly chaos and a transformed order, thanatos and eros.

The intersubject represents both the death of the subject—not just its dissolution in the discourses that constitute it but the erosion of the boundaries that, for champions of Western individualism, constitute its only ethical possibility—and the possibility of its positive transformation. On the dark side of the dialectic of change, "mass man" was already registered from the middle of the nineteenth century on by observers like Kierkegaard, Nietzsche, and Ortega y Gasset, and the rise of the discourses both of sociology and of a psychology of the unconscious at the end of that century initiated the deconstruction of the finite, punctual self. It could easily be argued that the modal subjectivity produced by the new information environment and the triumph of global ideological and economic systems represents a profound loss of dimensionality in the self, and the erosion of those necessary tensions without which the modal personality of our time becomes increasingly shallow, shortsighted, and even mildly sociopathic—a subject in whom the relationship between reason and desire called sublimation, which for Freud was what held civilization together, has disappeared, and nothing has replaced it. This is Marcuse's "one dimensional man" in whom the possibilities of the intersubject have fallen victim to "the social controls of technological reality, which extend liberty while intensifying domination."[65] In this form of subjectivity, the liberation of desire from reason is a complete chimera, presented for the benefit of the market as a series of television commercials, and actually signals the loss of autonomy, critical consciousness, social responsibility and any sense of history. One-dimensional man represents the onset of the proliferation of a new form of the totalitarian personality, the one best adapted to the various forms of economic imperialism that represent the dark side of global capitalism.

The light side of the dialectic is the promise of the reconstruction of the relationship between reason and desire in a form of subjectivity across boundaries with the other and with the "others" within oneself. The intersubject understands her identity as a field-being, not as the sign of ego dissolution or inflation, psychological chaos, magical thinking, herd politics, and ethical relativism, but as the trigger for a form of individuality made more poignant both by its recognition of its otherness within, and of its systemic connection and fundamental identification with others. In this case, the deconstruction of the boundaries of the punctual self lead to further self-actualization and greater social compassion, further capacity for solidarity in the human cry for justice and life-affirmation. The promise here is in a reconstruction that leads to the lifting of surplus-repression and the onset of a social movement dedicated to breaking down the work-play dichotomy and finding the human and social spaces in which the connections between childhood and adulthood, life and art, are maintained. This of course has always been the "social movement" of the artist, including the artist-of-one's-own-life. The artist's witness testifies that the revolution begins, as in the Romantic vision, as a revolution of perception—a marriage of the ethical and the aesthetic.

Because the school is the space where adulthood and childhood can meet and enter dialogue, those who craft and construct schools with the normative principles of the intersubject in mind, however few and lacking in power or influence, are of the utmost significance to the future emergence of a new balance. All, realistically, that can and perhaps should be expected of the school of the third way is that it remain through the necessary paroxysms of historical change an outpost—an experimental zone dedicated to that reconstruction of relations between adults and children that enable the more general emergence of dialogical relations between the two. In dark times, the school of the third way remains, like the child in modern adult subjectivity, the "valuable stranger" and the "outsider within" to the "natives" of the mainstream culture of the adult-child relation. Such schools are like those medieval monasteries that took inside their walls the seeds of the highest development of a world then falling in ruins, and nurtured them through dark ages in expectation of a new dawn—a future world in which those seeds would carry a new and expanded meaning and possibility. The dark ages, it seems, always come, for longer or shorter periods, but there are always those who would preserve what those dark ages presume to crush and obliterate, and would deliver it, in whatever apparent chaos of historical emergence, to the future. This makes of the teacher—or rather the adult who undertakes a form of dialogical relation with children that purposes to nurture and develop the possibility of a reconstructed form of adult subjectivity—a monastic of sorts. This monastic is dedicated to assist, through her relation with children, in the construction of an institution dedicated to the third joyous kingdom of play. In this sense she is midwife to the birth of a new form of reason. The new age she represents is always on the way, and the schools she joins with others to create and protect—in the dark face of technological rationality, global imperialism, terror, and the new authoritarianism—are the safe-zones, the harbingers and the prototypes of a world to come.

Notes

Preface: On How This Book Got Its Name

1. Rainer Maria Rilke, "Childhood," in *Selected Poems,* trans. Robert Bly (New York: Harper and Row, 1981).

2. Gaston Bachelard, *The Poetics of Reverie: Childhood, Language, and the Cosmos,* trans. Daniel Russell (Boston: Beacon Press, 1969), 124, 126.

Chapter One: Questioning Childhood

1. Henry Vaughan, from "Childe-hood," *The Works of Henry Vaughan,* second edition, L.C. Martin, ed. (Oxford: Clarendon Press, 1957), 520.

2. See for example, Valerie Polokow, *The Erosion of Childhood* (Chicago: University of Chicago Press, 1982), and Gareth Matthews, *The Philosophy of Childhood* (Cambridge: Harvard University Press, 1996).

3. Kenneth Keniston, "Psychological Development and Historical Change," in Rabbs, T.K. and R.I. Rotberg, eds., *The Family in History: Interdisciplinary Essays* (New York: Farrar, Straus and Giroux, 1976), 141–157.

4. Pierre Erny, *Childhood and Cosmos: The Social Psychology of the Black African Child* (Washington, DC: Black Orpheus Press, 1973),

and Mark Golden, *Children and Childhood in Classical Athens* (Baltimore: Johns Hopkins University Press, 1990).

5. William Wordsworth, *Poems*, H.J. Hall, ed. (New York: Scott Foresman, 1924); Ralph Waldo Emerson, "Nature," in *Selected Essays, Lectures, and Poems*, R.E. Spiller, ed. (New York: Washington Square Press, 1965).

6. See *The Republic of Plato*, trans. F.M. Cornford (London: Oxford University Press, 1941), 125, 138; and *Laws*, in *Plato: The Collected Dialogues*, E. Hamilton and H. Cairns, eds. (Princeton, NJ: Bollingen, 1961), 1379. For Aristotle, see *Physics*, 197b:7–10; *Eudemian Ethics*, 1224a:27–29; *Nichomachean Ethics*, 1099b:25–1100a:5, 1104b, and 1239a:1–6., in J.L. Ackrill, ed., *A New Aristotle Reader* (Princeton, NJ: Princeton University Press, 1987); M. Ostwald, trans., *Nichomachean Ethics* (New York: Bobbs-Merrill, 1962); and John Burnet, trans. and ed., *Aristotle on Education* (Cambridge: At the University Press, 1904).

7. The first historian to suggest this was Phillipe Aries, in *Centuries of Childhood*, trans. R. Baldick (New York: Knopf, 1962). The stage was set for this analysis by Johann Huizinga in *The Waning of the Middle Ages* (New York: Anchor Books, 1954).

8. Richard Coe, *When the Grass Was Taller: Autobiography and the Experience of Childhood* (New Haven: Yale University Press, 1984).

9. Dominick Cavallo, "The Politics of Latency: Kindergarten Pedagogy, 1860–1930," in *Regulated Children/Liberated Children: Education in Psychohistorical Perspective*, Barbara Finkelstein, ed. (New York: Psychohistory Press, 1979).

10. Michel Foucault, *Discipline and Punish: The Birth of the Prison*, trans. Alan Sheridan (New York: Pantheon, 1977).

11. Marx Wartofsky, "The Child's Construction of the World and the World's Construction of the Child: From Historical Epistemology to Historical Psychology," in *The Child and Other Cultural Inventions*, F.S. Kessel and A.W. Siegel, eds. (New York: Praeger, 1983), 208.

12. John Boswell, *The Kindness of Strangers: The Abandonment of Children in Western Europe from Late Antiquity to the Renaissance* (New York: Pantheon, 1988), 27.

13. Norbert Elias, *The Civilizing Process: The History of Manners* (New York: Urizen Press, 1978).

14. Neil Postman, *The Disappearance of Childhood* (New York: Delacorte, 1982), 99.

15. Robert N. Bellah, "To Kill and Survive or To Die and Become: The Active Life and the Contemplative Life as Ways of Being Adult," in Erik H. Erikson, ed., *Adulthood* (New York: Norton, 1978).

16. For popular examples of this see John Bradshaw, *Homecoming: Reclaiming and Championing Your Inner Child* (New York: Bantam, 1990), but the theme is announced in Freudian and Jungian psychoanalysis.

17. *Of Grammatology*, trans. G.C. Spivak (Baltimore: Johns Hopkins Press, 1976).

18. Aristotle, *Nichomean Ethics*, 1119a35, 1144b5; *Politics* 1260a, 9–14.

19. Golden, 7.

20. Plato, *Symposium*, 217e., in Hamilton and Cairns, *Plato: The Collected Dialogues*.

21. Golden, 44.

22. *Proverbs* 22:15.

23. *Matthew* 11:25.

24. Ibid., 18:2.

25. Ibid., 21:14–16.

26. Peter Fuller, "Uncovering Childhood," in Martin Hoyles, ed., *Changing Childhood* (London: Writers and Publishers Cooperative, 1979), 85.

27. For a summary of sources, see David Kennedy, "The Roots of Child Study: Philosophy, History, and Religion," *Teachers College Record* 102, 3 (June 2000): 514–538.

28. For a more detailed account, see David Kennedy, "Child and Fool in the Western Wisdom Tradition," *Thinking* 11, 1 (1993): 11–21.

29. See David Kennedy, "Images of the Young Child in History: Enlightenment and Romance," *Early Childhood Research Quarterly*, 3 (June 1988): 121–137.

30. Stephen Toulmin, "The Concept of 'Stages' in Psychological Development," in Theodore Mischel, ed., *Cognitive Development and Epistemology* (New York: Academic Press, 1971), 58.

31. Charles Taylor, "What is Involved in a Genetic Psychology?" in Ibid., 409–410.

32. Sigmund Freud, in *The Standard Edition of the Complete Psychological Works of Sigmund Freud*, vol. 11, trans. and ed. James Strachey (London: Hogarth Press, 1953), 48.

33. Ashis Nandy, "Reconstructing Childhood: A Critique of the Ideology of Adulthood," in *Traditions, Tyranny and Utopias: Essays in the Politics of Awareness* (Delhi: Oxford University Press, 1987), 56–76.

34. Dieter Misgeld, "Self-Reflection and Adult Maturity: Adult and Child in Hermeneutical and Critical Reflection," *Phenomenology + Pedagogy* 3, 3 (1995): 92.

35. To put ourselves back in the young child's world of scale is a shock. This has been demonstrated by Paul Ritter, who "got his students to mock-up a room two-and-a-half times actual size, just to remind us what a child's-eye-view is really like . . . it brought gasps of astonishment from the visitors." In Colin Ward, *The Child in the City* (New York: Pantheon, 1978), 22.

36. "Il est à la fois vrai que les fonctions adultes sont déjà réprésentés chez l'enfant, et qu'elles n'y ont pas le même sens que chez l'adulte." Maurice Merleau-Ponty, "Méthode en Psychologie de L'Enfant," *Bulletin de Psychologie* XVIII 3–6 (1964), 137. This is the same problem raised by Ludwig Wittgenstein in his discussion of the attempt to describe one language game in the terms of another. See his *On Certainty* (New York: Harper and Row, 1969), para. 108 and *passim*.

37. Merleau-Ponty, "Methode en Psychologie de L'Enfant," 111.

38. This argument is made in three different ways in Johan Huizinga, *The Waning of the Middle Ages*; Norbert Elias, *The Civilizing Process*; and Philippe Aries, *Centuries of Childhood*.

39. Alfred Schutz, "On Multiple Realities," in *Collected Papers,* vol. 1, I. Schutz, ed. (The Hague: Martinus Nijhoff, 1967), 231.

40. See Robert Bernasconi, "Bridging the Abyss: Heidegger and Gadamer," *Research in Phenomenology* XVI (1986), 1–24.

41. Paul Ricoeur, *Hermeneutics and the Human Sciences*, trans. and ed. J.B. Thompson (Cambridge: Cambridge University Press, 1981), 185.

42. Hans-Georg Gadamer, *Reason in the Age of Science*, trans. F.G. Lawrence (Cambridge: MIT Press, 1986), 98.

43. Martin Buber, *I and Thou*, trans. Walter Kaufmann (New York: Scribner's, 1970), 113.

44. Ricoeur, *Hermeneutics and the Human Sciences*, 105.

45. Ibid., 143, 113.

46. Hans-Georg Gadamer, *Truth and Method* (New York: Crossroad, 1975).

47. Ricoeur, *Hermeneutics and the Human Sciences*, 191.

48. For a discussion of *anamnesis* (if), see Hans-Georg Gadamer, *The Idea of the Good in Plato and Aristotle*, trans. Christopher Smith (New Haven: Yale University Press, 1986), 53–59.

49. James Risser, "Hermeneutic Experience and Memory: Rethinking Knowledge as Recollection," *Research in Phenomenology* XVI (1986), 41.

50. Gadamer, *Reason in the Age of Science*, 105–108, passim.

51. Herbert Read, *The Innocent Eye* (New York: Henry Holt, 1947), 7.

52. Gaston Bachelard, *The Poetics of Reverie*, 114, 125.

53. Rainer Maria Rilke, *Selected Works*, trans. Robert Bly (New York: New Directions, 1967).

54. Maurice Merleau-Ponty, *The Visible and the Invisible*, trans. Alphonso Lingis (Evanston, IL: Northwestern University Press, 1968), 137; and see his *Phenomenology of Perception*, trans. Colin Smith (London, Routledge and Kegan Paul, 1962).

55. Ricoeur, *Hermeneutics and the Human Sciences*, 142. And see his *Interpretation Theory: Discourse and the Surplus of Meaning* (Fort Worth: Texas Christian University Press, 1976).

56. For a profound description of the phenomenon of force, see Simone Weil, "The Iliad: The Poem of Force," in Alasdair McIntyre, ed., *Revisions* (Terre Haute: Notre Dame University Press, 1974).

57. For a discussion of adulthood, childhood, and habit, see John Dewey, *Human Nature and Conduct* (Carbondale, IL: Southern Illinois University Press, 1988 [1922]).

58. Lloyd deMause, "The Evolution of Childhood," in deMause, ed., *The History of Childhood* (New York: Harper Torchbooks, 1974). And see David Kennedy, "Empathic Child Rearing and the Adult Construction of Childhood: A Psychohistorical Look," *Childhood* 5, 1 (February 1998): 9–22.

59. Lawrence Stone, *The Family, Sex and Marriage in England 1500–1800*, abridged edition (New York: Harper, 1979).

60. Carmen Luke, *Pedagogy, Printing, and Protestantism: The Discourse on Childhood* (Albany: State University of New York Press, 1989).

61. Michel Foucault, *Discipline and Punish*.

62. Plato, *Republic*, trans. F.M. Cornford (London: Oxford, 1941).

63. Georges Dumezil, *The Destiny of the Warrior* (Chicago: University of Chicago Press, 1970).

64. For a concise overview of Freud's basic theory in his own words, see his *The Ego and the Id*, trans. Joan Riviere (New York: Norton, 1960).

65. Only implicitly acknowledged in Freud, but explored in N.O. Brown, *Life Against Death* (Middletown, CT: Wesleyan University Press, 1959), and Herbert Marcuse, *Eros and Civilization* (Boston: Beacon Press, 1966).

66. See Erik Erikson, *Childhood and Society*, second edition (New York: Norton, 1963), Chapter 7, "Eight Ages of Man."

67. Charles Taylor Coleridge, *The Friend*, vol. I, in *Collected Works*, Barbara Rooke, ed. (Princeton, NJ: Princeton University Press, 1969), 109–110.

Chapter Two: The Primordial Child

1. Eugene Ionesco, quoted in Coe, *When the Grass Was Taller*, 63.

2. G.C. Jung, and C. Kerenyi, *Essays on a Science of Mythology: The Myth of the Divine Child and the Mysteries of Eleusis* (Princeton, NJ: Bollingen, 1963), 35.

3. "Then some children were brought to Him so that He might lay His hands on them and pray; and the disciples rebuked them. But Jesus said, 'Permit the children, and do not hinder them from coming to Me; for the kingdom of heaven belongs to such as these.'" *Matthew* 19: 13, 14. New American Standard Version.

4. *1 Corinthians* 1:18–2:16.

5. For an account of this countertradition, see David Kennedy, "Child and Fool in the Western Wisdom Tradition." And see, for example, Pierre Erny, *Childhood and Cosmos: The Social Psychology of the Black African Child* (Washington, DC: Black Orpheus Press, 1973), and "Taliesin,"in Barbara Leonie Picard, *Hero-Tales from the British Isles* (New York: Criterion Books, 1966).

6. Augustine, *The Confessions of St. Augustine,* R.S. Pine-Coffin, ed. (Harmondsworth: Penguin Books, 1961), 177.

7. Jung and Kerenyi, *Essays on a Science of Mythology,* 35, 69

8. Ibid., 130.

9. Ibid., 78–79.

10. See Victor Lasareff, "Studies in the Iconography of the Virgin," *Art Bulletin* 20 (1938), 26–65.

11. Josef Kunstmann, *The Transformation of Eros* (Edinburgh: Oliver and Boyd, 1970), 13.

12. Quoted in Ibid., 10.

13. Lasareff, "Studies in the Iconography of the Virgin," 27.

14. Kunstmann, *The Transformation of Eros,* 17.

15. Ilene H. Forsyth, "Children in Early Medieval Art: Ninth Through Twelfth Centuries," *Journal of Psychohistory* 4, 1 (Summer 1976), 36.

16. Ibid., 46–47.

17. Ibid., 32, 58.

18. Boswell, *The Kindness of Strangers.* See Chapter 5, 230.

19. Mary M. McLaughlin, "Survivors and Surrogates: Children and Parents from Ninth to the Thirteenth Centuries," in Lloyd deMause, ed., *The History of Childhood* (New York: Harper, 1974), 131–133.

20. See C.S. Lewis' discussion of "Intellectus" and "Ratio" in *The Discarded Image: An Introduction to Medieval and Renaissance Literature* (Oxford: Oxford University Press, 1964), 156–161.

21. Lasareff, "Studies in the Iconography of the Virgin," 41.

22. M.H. Abrams, *Natural Supernaturalism: Tradition and Revolution in Romantic Literature* (New York: Norton, 1971). In his discussion of the Renaissance hermetic tradition, Abrams describes Christ as having "the apocolyptic function of restoring both fallen and divided man and the fallen and fragmented universe to the perfection of their original unity," 30.

23. Leo Steinberg, *The Sexuality of Christ in Renaissance Art and in Modern Oblivion* (New York: Pantheon, 1983), 127.

24. *The Philosophy of Plotinus,* trans. and ed. Joseph Katz (New York: Appleton-Century-Crofts, 1950), Book VI: 205–270, 155.

25. Steinberg, *The Sexuality of Christ,* 3, 110.

26. Ibid., 51.

27. Erich Gombrich, *Symbolic Images: Studies in the Art of the Renaissance* (London: Phaidon, 1972), 64.

28. Ibid., 153.

29. Edgar Wind, *Pagan Mysteries in the Renaissance,* revised edition (New York: Norton, 1968), 55–67 passim.

30. Gombrich, *Symbolic Images*, 159, 168, 174.

31. Jung & Kerenyi, *Essays on a Science of Mythology,* 55, 56.

32. Kunstmann, *The Transformation of Eros,* 24.

33. For a taxonomy of the "enigmatic child," see Reinhard Kuhn, *Corruption in Paradise: The Child in Western Literature* (Hanover, NH: University Press of New England, 1982), Chapter 1.

34. This child is considered in Fuller, "Uncovering Childhood" (71–108).

35. For an account of this "monumental life" see Bachelard, *The Poetics of Reverie*, Chapter 3, "Reveries Toward Childhood."

36. My primary source for the material in this section is Leah Sinangolou Marcus, *Childhood and Cultural Despair: A Theme and Variations in 17th Century Literature* (Pittsburgh: University of Pittsburgh Press, 1978).

37. From Henry Vaughan, "Childehood" and "The Retreat," quoted in Ibid., 173.

38. Robert Pattison, *The Child Figure in English Literature* (Athens: The University of Georgia Press, 1978), 33.

39. Ibid., 36.

40. Kuhn, *Corruption in Paradise*, 208.

41. Thomas Traherne, from "Innocence," in *Poetical Works*. G.I. Wade, ed. (New York: Cooper Square Publishers, 1965), 11.

42. From "The Preparative," Ibid., 12.

43. Compiled from "Wonder," 5; and "My Spirit," 28 and 29; in Ibid.

44. From "An Infant-Ey," in Ibid., 105.

45. Ernst Cassirer, *The Philosophy of Symbolic Forms*, vol. 2, *Mythical Thought*, trans. Ralph Mannheim (New Haven: Yale University Press, 1955), 99.

46. For a thorough summary of the Romantic understanding of childhood, see Judith Plotz, "The Perpetual Messiah: Romanticism, Childhood, and the Paradoxes of Human Development," in

Barbara Finkelstein, ed., *Regulated Children/Liberated Children: Education in Psychohistorical Perspective* (New York: The Psychohistory Press, 1979), 63–95.

47. Thomas Traherne, *Centuries* (New York: Harper and Brother, 1960), 141.

48. Coe, *When the Grass Was Taller*, 240. And see Friedrich von Schiller's comments on the Pastoral, which he calls the "Idyll," in *Naïve and Sentimental Poetry and On the Sublime*, trans. Julius A. Elias (New York: Frederick Ungar, 1966), 145 ff.

49. The secularization of this myth in Romantic literature and philosophy is described in Abrams' definitive study, *Natural Supernaturalism,* published at one moment of the myth's perennial reactivation in Western thought and culture—the launching of the "counterculture" of the late 1960s and early 1970s.

50. Quoted in Philip Stewart, "The Child Comes of Age," *Yale French Studies* 40 (1968), 136–137.

51. Stone, *The Family, Sex and Marriage in England 1500–1800.*

52. Quoted in Kuhn, *Corruption in Paradise*, 62.

53. Traherne, *Centuries*, 110.

54. Schiller, *Naïve and Sentimental Poetry,* 84, 85, 87.

55. Ibid., 100, 103, 104.

56. Friedrich von Schiller, *On the Aesthetic Education of Man In a Series of Letters*, trans. Reginald Snell (New York: Frederick Ungar, 1954 [1795]), 39; and *Naïve and Sentimental Poetry*, 103.

57. Schiller, *Naïve and Sentimental Poetry*, 105.

58. Ibid., 111.

59. Schiller, *On the Aesthetic Education of Man*, 43.

60. Ibid., 113.

61. Ibid., 129, 153.

62. Ibid., 153. According to Hegel, "The harmoniousness of childhood is a gift from the hand of nature: the second harmony must spring from the labor and culture of the spirit. And so the words of Christ, 'Except ye *become* as little children', etc., are very far from telling us that we must always remain children." Quoted in Abrams, *Natural Supernaturalism*, 380–381.

63. D.W. Winnicott, *Playing and Reality* (New York: Routledge, 1989 [1971]), 51.

64. Kuhn, *Corruption in Paradise*, 229.

65. Quoted in Abrams, *Natural Supernaturalism*, 227, 292, 278, 292, 337–339.

66. Quoted in Ibid., 104, 291.

67. Schiller, *Naïve and Sentimental Poetry*, 153.

68. Abrams, *Natural Supernaturalism*, 351.

69. Winnicott, *Playing and Reality*, 102, 107, 3, 14.

70. Schiller, *On the Aesthetic Education of Man*, 78.

71. From Wordsworth's *Prelude* (II, 255–276), quoted in Abrams, *Natural Supernaturalism*, 368.

72. William Wordsworth, *The Prelude, or Growth of a Poet's Mind, an Autobiographical Poem*, second edition (Oxford: Clarendon Press, 1959), 59.

73. Ibid., II: 270–271.

74. Schiller, *On the Aesthetic Education of Man*, 79.

75. Peter Coveney, *The Image of Childhood: The Individual and Society: A Study of the Theme in English Literature* (Harmondsworth: Penguin Books, 1959), 32.

76. Eugen Fink, "The Ontology of Play," *Philosophy Today* 4 (Summer 1960): 95–109. And see also Hans-Georg Gadamer, "Play as the Clue to Ontological Explanation," in *Truth and Method* (New York: The Crossroad Publishing Company, 1975), 91–119.

77. Herbert Marcuse, *Eros and Civilization* (Boston: Beacon Press, 1966), 37.

78. Ibid., 46.

79. Jean Jacques Rousseau, *Emile*, trans. and ed. William Boyd (New York: Teachers College Press, 1956), 13.

80. Ibid., 34, 38.

81. Friedrich Froebel, *The Education of Man* (Clifton, NJ: Augustus M. Kelley, 1974), 29.

82. For a discussion of what Freud called "childhood amnesia" based on the incommensurability of perceptual-cognitive structures between early childhood and adulthood, see Ernest G. Schactel, *Metamorphosis: On the Development of Affect, Perception, Attention, and Memory* (New York: Basic Books, 1959).

83. Nandy, "Reconstructing Childhood," 71.

84. Erikson presents us with a working version of this model in his epigenetic model of the life cycle. See his *Childhood and Society.*

85. Thus the poet Rilke: ". . .the child may become older and more sensible in the everyday sense of the word, in which case he becomes a budding citizen who will join the order of his historical epoch and be ordained as a member. Or, again, he may ripen quietly and simply from the depths of his being, nourished by his own existence as a child, in which case he will belong to the spirit of all epochs—he will be an artist." Quoted in George Boas, *The Cult of Childhood* (London: The Wartburg Institute, 1966), 112.

86. Quoted in Coe, *When the Grass Was Taller*, 41.

87. Quoted in Abrams, *Natural Supernaturalism*, 380.

88. Norman O. Brown, *Life Against Death: The Psychoanalytic Meaning of History* (Middletown, CT: Wesleyan University Press, 1959), 31–34, passim.

89. Winnicott, *Playing and Reality*, 41.

90. Brown, *Life Against Death*, 30.

91. A clear example of this influence can be found in the institution of art, which was dramatically influenced by children's art over the course of the twentieth century. See Jonathon Fineberg, *The Innocent Eye: Children's Art and the Modern Artist* (Princeton: Princeton University Press, 1997).

Chapter Three: The Invention of Adulthood

1. Paul Eluard, from *Oevres Complete*, Bibliotheque de la Pleiade (Paris: Gallimard, 1968), 4: 419.

2. Aries, *Centuries of Childhood.*

3. Aristotle, *De Anima (On the Soul)*, trans. Hugh Lawson-Tancred (Harmondsworth: Penguin, 1986).

4. For a vintage example of this approach, see the developmental theory of the first dean of American psychology, George Stanley Hall, *Adolescence: Its Psychology and Its Relations to Physiology, Anthropology, Sociology, Sex, Crime, Religion and Education* (New York: Ayer, 1970 [1904]).

5. For an interesting argument for radically child-centered education based on recapitulationist theory, see J. Gary Bernhard, *Primates in*

the Classroom: An Evolutionary Perspective on Children's Education (Amherst: University of Massachusetts Press, 1988).

6. Aristotle, *Eudemian Ethics*, in H. Rackman, ed., Aristotle, vol. 20, book 8, chapter 1: 1224a and 1236a.

7. Ibid., 1239a:1.

8. *The Republic of Plato*, 125, 138; and *Laws*, in Hamilton and Cairns, eds., *The Collected Dialogues*, 1379.

9. The equivalent of Plato's "reason" as a terminal state for the philosopher king is Piaget's "formal operations," which (along with Kohlberg's "post-conventional" moral reasoning), is stated as a developmental ideal for the modern patriarchal West.

10. Plato, *Republic,* 102, 141.

11. L. Martin, H. Gutman, and P.H. Hutton, eds., *Technologies of the Self: A Seminar with Michael Foucault* (Amherst: University of Massachusetts Press, 1988).

12. Georges Dumezil, *The Destiny of the Warrior* (Chicago: University of Chicago Press, 1970).

13. Aristotle, *Nichomachean Ethics*, 1104b, in Akrill, *A New Aristotle Reader,* 379.

14. Michel Foucault, *The History of Sexuality,* vol. 3: *The Care of the Self*, trans. Robert Hurley (New York: Vintage Books, 1986), 45.

15. Julian Jaynes, *The Origins of Consciousness in the Breakdown of the Bicameral Mind* (Boston: Houghton Mifflin, 1976). See also Jan Bremmer, *The Early Greek Concept of the Soul* (Princeton: Princeton University Press, 1983).

16. Michel Foucault, "On the Geneology of Ethics," in Hubert Dreyfus and Paul Rabinow, *Michel Foucault: Beyond Structuralism and Hermeneutics*, second edition (Chicago: University of Chicago Press, 1983), 245.

17. *James* 1:17.

18. Nandy, "Reconstructing Childhood," 57.

19. C.G. Jung, *The Archetypes and the Collective Unconscious*, trans. R.F.C. Hall, Bollingen Series XX, vol. 9, i (Princeton: Princeton University Press, 1980), 284.

20. C.G. Jung, *Aion.* In *Collected Works*, trans. R.F.C. Hull, Bollingen Series XX, vol. 9, ii (Princeton: Princeton University Press, 1980). And see Erich Neumann, "Reflections on the Shadow," in *Depth*

Psychology and a New Ethic, trans. Eugene Rolfe (New York: Harper, 1973[1948]), 137–147.

21. Neumann, *Depth Psychology and a New Ethic*, 124. And see Jung and Kerenyi, *Essays on a Science of Mythology*, 100.

22. Levinas, Emmanuel. *Time and the Other*, trans. Richard A. Cohen (Pittsburgh: Dusquesne University Press, 1987), 18.

23. Neumann, *Depth Psychology and a New Ethic*, 81. And see Erich Neumann, *The Origins and History of Consciousness*, trans. R.F.C. Hull (Princeton: Princeton University Press, 1954), 414 ff.

24. Emmanuel Levinas, *Totality and Infinity*, trans. Alphonso Lingis (Pittsburgh: Duquesne University Press, 1969), 277.

25. Levinas, *Time and the Other*, 17.

26. For the beginnings of an approach to the variables involved, see, e.g., Aage B. Sorensen, Frana E. Weinert, and Lonnie R. Sherrod, eds., *Human Development and the Life Course: Multidisciplinary Perspectives* (Hillside, NJ: Lawrence Erlbaum Associates, 1986); and Glen H. Elder Jr., John Modell, and Ross D. Parke, eds., *Children in Time and Place: Developmental and Historical Insights* (Cambridge: Cambridge University Press, 1993).

27. Boswell, *The Kindness of Strangers*, 202, 27, 31, 32.

28. Aries, *Centuries of Childhood*, 411.

29. Aries, *Centuries of Childhood*; Johan Huizinga, *The Waning of the Middle Ages*; and Norbert Elias, *The Civilizing Process and State Formation and Civilization*, trans. Edmund Jephcott (Oxford: Blackwell, 1994 [1939]).

30. Elias, *The Civilizing* Process, 115–116.

31. Ibid., 117, 115.

32. Ibid., 475.

33. Ibid., 211.

34. Ibid., 209.

35. For an erudite account of the philosophical lineaments of premodern cosmology, see C.S. Lewis, *The Discarded Image*. For a more psychohistorical view, see Walter Ong, *The Presence of the Word: Some Prologomena for Cultural and Religious History* (Minneapolis: University of Minnesota Press, 1967).

36. Elias, *The Civilizing Process*, 209.

37. Hans Jonas, *The Phenomenon of Life: Toward a Philosophical Biology* (Chicago: University of Chicago Press, 1966), 7.

38. See Walter Ong, *The Presence of the Word*; and his *Orality and Literacy: Technologizing the Word* (London: Methuen, 1982).

39. Ong, *Orality and Literacy*, 81.

40. Ong, *The Presence of the Word*, 6 ff.

41. Ong, *Orality and Literacy*, Chapter 3, passim. For an application to young children's intentional style, see David Kennedy, "The Lifeworld of the Young Child," in *Young Children's Thinking: An Interpretation from Phenomenology.* Doctoral Dissertation (Lexington: University of Kentucky, 1986).

42. Ibid., Chapter 4, passim.

43. Ong, *The Presence of the Word*, 221.

44. For a discussion of *theoria* as a form of "ecstatic self-forgetfulness," a "being totally involved in and carried away by what one sees," see Gadamer, *Truth and Method*, 111.

45. Nancy Chodorow, *The Reproduction of Mothering: Psychoanalysis and the Sociology of Gender* (Berkeley: University of California Press, 1978).

46. Jonas, *The Phenomenon of Life*, 10.

47. Ibid., 124, 196, 59.

48. See Marcus, *Childhood and Cultural Despair*, 92; and David Kennedy, "Fools, Young Children, Animism, and the Scientific World Picture," *Philosophy Today* 33 (Winter), 1989: 374–381.

49. Elias, *The Civilizing Process*, 137.

50. Foucault, *Discipline and Punish*, 136.

51. For accounts from both sides of the Atlantic, see Mary Jo Maynes, "The New Pedagogy," in *Schooling in Western Europe: A Social History* (Albany: State University of New York Press, 1990), Chapter 4; and Barbara Finkelstein, "Casting Networks of Good Influence: The Reconstruction of Childhood in the United States, 1790–1870," in J.M. Hawes and N.R. Hiner, eds., *American Childhood: A Research Guide and Historical Handbook* (Westport, CT: Greenwood Press, 1985), 111–152.

52. Postman, *The Disappearance of Childhood*, 13.

53. Ashis Nandy, "Reconstructing Childhood," 59.

54. Neumann, *The Origins and History of Consciousness*, 413.

55. This account is found in Lloyd deMause, "The Evolution of Childhood," 1–73.

56. Erasmus, from *On Education for Children*, in E. Rummel, ed., *The Erasmus Reader* (Toronto: University of Toronto Press, 1990), 69.

57. deMause, "The Evolution of Childhood," 52.

58. J. Sulzer, from *An Essay on the Education and Instruction of Children*, 1748. Quoted in Alice Miller, *For Your Own Good: Hidden Cruelty in Child-Rearing and the Roots of Violence* (New York: Farrar Straus Giroux, 1983), 10–11, 13.

59. Marcus, *Childhood and Cultural Despair*, 27–28.

60. Quoted in Ibid., 51. And see C. John Sommerville, "English Puritans and Children: A Social Cultural Explanation," *The Journal of Psychohistory* 6, 1 (Summer 1978): 113–137. He claims that the Puritans "were the first to write books exclusively for children, and the first to show an awareness of the difficulties involved in communicating with them" (115). See also his *The Discovery of Childhood in Puritan England* (Athens: The University of Georgia Press, 1992).

61. Marcus, *Childhood and Cultural Despair*, 55.

62. Jean Jacques Rousseau, *Emile, Or On Education*, trans. Alan Bloom (New York: Basic Books, 1979), 92, 93, 104, 107.

63. Ibid., 131.

64. Gerald L. Gutek, *A History of the Western Educational Experience*, second edition (Prospect Heights, IL: Waveland Press, 1995), 188–191.

65. Aries, "From the Medieval Family to the Modern Family," in *Centuries of Childhood*, Part III, Chapter 2.

66. Stone, *The Family, Sex and Marriage in England 1500–1800*.

67. From Daniel Defoe, *Mere Nature Delineated* (London, 1726) quoted in Maxmillian E. Novak, "The Wild Man Comes to Tea," in Edward Dudley and Maximillian E. Novak, eds., *The Wild Man Within: An Image in Western Thought from the Renaissance to Romanticism* (Pittsburgh: University of Pittsburgh Press, 1972), 209.

68. Hayden White, "The Forms of Wildness," in Dudley and Novak, eds., *The Wild Man Within*, 7.

69. N.O. Brown, *Love's Body* (Berkeley: University of Califormia Press, 1966), 146–147.

70. Quoted in Catherine Marchak, "The Joy of Transgression: Bataille and Kristeva," *Philosophy Today* 34, 4 (Winter 1990): 357.

71. Levinas, *Time and the Other*, 92, 68.

72. Maurice Merleau-Ponty, "Hegel's Existentialism," in *Sense and Non-Sense*, trans. H.L. and P.A. Dreyfus (Evanston, IL: Northwestern University Press, 1964), 63.

73. Erikson, *Childhood and Society*, 266–268.

74. Elias, *The Civilizing Process*, 203, 204.

75. For a brief but incisive account of this historical moment, see Chapter 1, "Origins," in Erica Burman, *Deconstructing Developmental Psychology* (London: Routledge, 1994), 9–20. And for another look at origins, see Klaus F. Riegel, "The Influence of Economic and Political Ideologies on the Development of Developmental Psychology," *Psychological Bulletin* 78, 2 (1977): 129–141.

76. See Harvey Green, "Scientific Thought and the Nature of Children in America, 1820–1920," in Mary Heininger et al., *A Century of Childhood, 1820–1920* (Rochester, NY: Margaret Woodbury Strong Museum, 1984), 126.

77. See Nandy, "The Reconstruction of Childhood."

78. Jean Piaget, *The Child's Conception of the World*, trans. Joan and Andrew Tomlinson (London: Routledge and Kegan Paul, 1929).

79. deMause, "The Evolution of Childhood," 7.

80. Peter Petschauer, "Intrusive to Socializing Modes: Transitions in Eighteenth-Century Germany and Twentieth Century Italy," *The Journal of Psychohistory* 14, 3 (Winter 1987): 257–270; and "The Childrearing Modes in Flux: An Historian's Reflection," *The Journal of Psychohistory* 17, 1 (Summer 1989): 1–41.

81. For a well-argued perennialist view of the history of adult-child relations, see Linda A. Pollock, *Forgotten Children: Parent-Child Relations from 1500–1900* (Cambridge: Cambridge University Press, 1983); and her *A Lasting Relationship: Parents and Children Over Three Centuries* (Hanover, NH: University Press of New England, 1987).

82. Arnold Hauser, *The Social History of Art*, vol. 2 (New York: Vintage, 1951), 167. And see Joseph Featherstone, "Rousseau and Modernity," *Daedalus* 107 (Summer 1978): 167–192.

83. Nandy, "Reconstructing Childhood," 58.

Chapter Four: Childhood and the Intersubject

1. Novalis, *Pollen and Fragments*, trans. A. Versluis (Grand Rapids, MI: Phanes Press, 1989).

2. H.A. Witkin et al., *Psychological Differentiation* (London: Wiley, 1962).

3. Gianni Vattimo, *The End of Modernity: Nihilism and Hermeneutics in Postmodern Culture*, trans. Jon R. Snyder (Baltimore: Johns Hopkins University Press, 1988), xlvi. See also Guy Debord, *The Society of the Spectacle* (Detroit: Black and Red, 1983), who refers to the "spectacle" of the new information environment as "the heart of the unrealism of the real society," in which "everything that was directly lived has moved away into a representation" (2, 3).

4. Jean Baudrillard, *Revenge of the Crystal: Selected Writings on the Modern Object and its Destiny, 1968–1983*, trans. and ed. Paul Foss and Julian Pefanis (London: Pluto Press, 1990), 214, 163.

5. Jean-Francois Lyotard, *The Inhuman: Reflections on Time*, trans. Geoffrey Bennington and Rachel Bowlby (Stanford, CA: Stanford University Press, 1991).

6. Aristotle, *De Anima*.

7. Foucault, *The History of Sexuality*, vol. 3, *The Care of the Self*.

8. G.W.F Hegel, *Phenomenology of Spirit*, trans. A.V. Miller (New York: Oxford University Press, 1977), 124–125, 156–157.

9. Foucault, *The Care of the Self*, 41.

10. Quoted from the Greek physician Galen, in Ibid, 56.

11. Ibid.

12. David Hume, *A Treatise of Human Nature*, vol. 2, (London: J.M. Dent and Sons, 1911), 5; and Ibid., vol. 1, 65.

13. C.G. Jung, *Aion*; and "The Psychology of the Unconscious," in *Collected Works* 7, trans. R.F.C. Hull (Princeton: Princeton University Press, 1980).

14. "The Ego's Dependent Relations," in *The Ego and the Id*, 46.

15. For a Jungian account of the relations between the ego and the Self from infancy, see Erich Neumann, *The Child: Structure and Dynamics of the Nascent Personality*, trans. Ralph Manheim (New York: G.P. Putnam, 1973).

16. Robert Stolorow, "Critical Reflections on the Theory of Self Psychology: An Inside View," *Psychoanalytic Inquiry* 6 (1986): 389. The term "selfobject" was introduced by the psychoanalyst Heinz Kohut in his *The Analysis of the Self* (New York: International Universities Press, 1971).

17. E. Wolf, *Treating the Self: Elements of Clinical Self Psychology* (New York: Guilford, 1988), 184.

18. Abrams, *Natural Supernaturalism,* 187.

19. For a short but inclusive summary of the perennial myth of the golden age, see Kathleen Raines, "The Myth of the Great Year," in *Blake and Antiquity* (Princeton: Bollingen, 1977), 51–70.

20. Winnicott, *Playing and Reality.*

21. Charles Taylor, *Sources of the Self: The Making of the Modern Identity* (Cambridge: Harvard University Press, 1989), 386, 471, 465, 462; William Blake, *There Is No Natural Religion* [Second Series], in Geoffrey Keynes, ed., *Blake: Complete Writings* (Oxford University Press, 1966), 97.

22. Jonathan Fineberg has described and illustrated the intersection of these three alternative universes of art in his *The Innocent Eye: Child Art and the Modern Artist*. And see David Kennedy, "Subversive Innocence," *Childhood* 6, 2 (May 1999): 389–399.

23. Max Wertheimer, "Gestalt Theory," trans. W.D. Ellis, in Ellis, ed., *Source Book of Gestalt Psychology* (New York, Harcourt Brace & Co., 1938 [1924]).

24. The foremost representatives of this school are Melanie Klein, D.W. Winnicott, Ronald Fairbairn, Wilfrid Bion, Michael Balint, Henry Guntrip, Edith Jacobson, and Otto Kernberg. Heinz Kohut's "self psychology" also offers a perspective on subjectivity based on object relations. For an historical overview of object relations theory, see Otto F. Kernberg, *Object-Relations Theory and Clinical Psychoanalysis* (New York: Jason Aronson, 1976).

25. Charles Taylor, *Hegel* (Cambridge: Cambridge University Press, 1975), 235.

26. David E. Scharf, *Refinding the Object and Reclaiming the Self* (Northvale, NJ: Jason Aronson, 1992), 24–25.

27. Richard A. Cohen, from the Introduction to Levinas, *Time and the Other*, 16.

28. Heinz Kohut, "The Self in History," in *Self Psychology and the Humanities*: Reflections on a New Psychoanalytic Approach (New York: Norton, 1985), 168.

29. Russell Meares, *The Metaphor of Play: Disruption and Restoration in the Borderline Experience* (Northvale, NJ: Jason Aronson, 1993), 127.

30. Scharff, *Refinding the Object and Reclaiming the Self*, 25.

31. Ibid., 17.

32. deMause, "The Evolution of Childhood," 3.

33. Peter Petschauer, "The Childrearing Modes in Flux: An Historian's Reflections," *Journal of Psychohistory* 17,1 (Summer 1989): 1–41.

34. Rousseau, *Emile, Selections*, trans. and ed. William Boyd (New York: Teachers College Press, 1956), 34, 38.

35. Postman, "The Adult-Child," in *The Disappearance of Childhood*, 98–119.

36. Abrams, *Natural Supernaturalism*, 276, 277.

37. Taylor, *Sources of the Self*, 386, 471.

38. Schactel, *Metamorphosis*, 183.

39. Bachelard, *The Poetics of* Reverie, 167, 185, 188.

40. S. A. Mitchell, *Radical Concepts in Psychoanalysis: An Integration* (Cambridge: Harvard University Press, 1988), 9.

41. C.G. Jung, "The Stages of Life," in *The Structure and Dynamics of the Psyche*, trans. R.F.C. Hull (New York: Pantheon Books, 1980), 387–403.

42. Schiller, *On the Aesthetic Education of Man*, 75.

43. Schutz, "On Multiple Realities," 230.

44. Schiller, *On the Aesthetic Education of Man*, 78, 75.

45. Marcuse, *Eros and Civilization*, 170, 182.

46. Winnicott, *Playing and Reality*, 50, 96.

47. Sigmund Freud, *On Dreams*, trans. James Strachey (New York: Norton, 1989).

48. Melanie Klein, *The Psycho-Analysis of Children*, third revised edition, trans. Alix Strachey (London: The Hogarth Press, 1980), xiii, xiv.

49. *Playing and Reality*, 130.

50. Quoted in Joel Whitebook, "Reflections on the Autonomous Individual and the Decentered Subject," *American Imago* 49, 1 (1992): 111.

51. Ibid., 107.

52. Sandra G. Harding, *Whose Science? Whose Knowledge? Thinking from Women's Lives* (Ithaca, NY: Cornell University Press, 1991).

53. *Hegel: The Essential Writings*, Frederick G. Weiss, ed. (New York: Harper and Row, 1974), 71.

54. Ibid., 76.

55. Friedrich Nietzsche, *Thus Spake Zarathustra*, trans. R.J. Hollingdale (Baltimore: Penguin Books, 1971), 54, 55.

56. Plotz, "The Perpetual Messiah," 74.

57. Herbert Marcuse, *Eros and Civilization*, 197, 198, 199.

58. Fineberg, *The Innocent Eye.*

59. Ibid., 120, 100, 133, 151.

60. Abrams, *Natural Supernaturalism*, 334.

61. Ibid., 182, 334. And see Kennedy, "Subversive Innocence."

62. Marcuse, *Eros and Civilization*, 174.

63. Ibid., 199, 201.

64. Ibid., 224.

65. William Blake, *The Marriage of Heaven and Hell*, in *Blake: Complete Writings*, 148.

66. Marcuse, *Eros and Civilization*, 216.

67. Schiller, *On the Aesthetic Education of Man*, 37.

68. Marcuse, *Eros and Civilization*, 215.

Chapter Five: Reimagining School

1. John Dewey, *The School and Society*, in M.S. Dworkin, ed., *Dewey on Education: Selections* (New York: Teachers College Press, 1959), 49.

2. John Dewey, *Human Nature and Conduct*, 179.

3. Ibid., 89.

4. Ibid., 16.

5. Ibid., 67, 71, 70.

6. Ibid., 97.

7. Ibid., 96.

8. Ibid., 79.

9. Ibid., 97.

10. Ibid., 70, 89.

11. Erikson, *Childhood and Society,* 259.

12. Dominick Cavallo, "The Politics of Latency: Kindergarten Pedagogy, 1860–1930," 159.

13. Barbara Finkelstein, "Schooling and the Discovery of Latency in Nineteenth-Century America," *The Journal of Psychohistory* 13,1 (Summer 1985), 3. See also her "Casting Networks of Good Influence: The Reconstruction of Childhood in the United States, 1790–1870."

14. Erikson, *Childhood and Society,* 260.

15. Loris Malaguzzi, "History, Ideas, and Basic Philosophy," in Carolyn Edwards, Leila Gandini, and George Forman, eds. *The Hundred Languages of Children* (Norwood, NJ: Ablex, 1993), 64.

16. Carolyn Edwards, "Partner, Nurturer, and Guide: The Roles of the Reggio Teacher in Action." In Ibid., 152.

17. Dewey, *The School and Society*, 52. Dewey adds, "In this case, the child becomes the sun about which the appliances of education revolve; he is the center about which they are organized."

18. Ibid., 49.

19. Dewey, *Human Nature and Conduct*, 67.

20. Ibid., 69, 70, 75.

21. Martin Buber, *Between Man and Man* (New York: Macmillan, 1965), 6.

22. Martin Buber, "Dialogue," in *Between Man and Man*, 8.

23. Ibid.

24. Buber, *I and Thou.*

25. Buber, *Between Man and Man*, 20.

26. Gadamer, *Truth and Method*, 322, 323.

27. Buber, *Between Man and Man*, 9.

28. Ibid.

29. For a discussion the original Greek idea of *theoria*, see Gadamer, *Truth and Method*, 111.

30. Buber, *Between Man and Man*, 9.

31. Ibid., 10.

32. Michel Foucault, *The History of Sexuality* (New York: Pantheon, 1978), 93.

33. Ibid.

34. Martin Buber, "Distance and Relation," in *The Knowledge of Man: A Philosophy of the Interhuman,* trans. Maurice Friedman and R.G. Smith (New York: Harper, 1965), 64.

35. Buber, *Between Man and Man,* 51; and *The Knowledge of Man,* 79.

36. For a further development of the philosophy of dialogue, see Michael Theunissen, *The Other: Studies in the Social Ontology of Husserl, Heidegger, Sartre, and Buber,* trans. Christopher Macann (Cambridge: MIT Press, 1986), especially his "Postscript: The Transcendental Project of Social Ontology and the Philosophy of Dialogue," 361–384.

37. Winnicott, *Playing and Reality,* 51, 64.

38. Levinas, *Time and the Other,* 17, 92, 68.

39. Hugh Silverman, "Hermeneutics and Interrogation," in *Research in Phenomonology,* vol. XVI, 1986, 88, 89, 91.

40. Schiller, *On the Aesthetic Education of Man,* 78, 75.

41. Dewey, *Human Nature and Conduct,* 70.

42. ". . . The sublime melancholy of our lot [is] that every You must become an It in our world. However exclusively present it may have been in the direct relationship—as soon as the relationship has run its course or is permeated by *means,* the You becomes an object among objects, possibly the noblest one and yet one of them, assigned its measure and boundary. The actualization of the work involves a loss of actuality. . . . Every You in the world is doomed by its nature to become a thing or at least to enter thinghood again and again. . . . The It is the chrysalis, the You the butterfly. Only it is not always as if these states took turns so neatly; often it is an intricately tangled series of events that is tortuously dual." Buber, *I and Thou,* 68–69.

43. *Human Nature and Conduct,* 50, 70, 52.

44. Ibid., 73.

45. John Dewey, *Education and Democracy* (New York: Macmillan, 1916), 87.

46. John Dewey, *Reconstruction in Philosophy,* enlarged edition (Boston: Beacon Press, 1948), 203.

47. Ibid., 204, 205.

48. Yi-Fu Tuan, *Space and Place* (Minneapolis: University of Minnesota Press, 1977), 116, 112.

49. Martin Heidegger, *The Question Concerning Technology*, trans. William Lovitt (New York: Harper and Row, 1977), 21.

50. Schiller, *Naive and Sentimental Poetry*, 87.

51. A few major works that address institutional design either directly or by strong implication are the architectural classic by Christopher Alexander, *A Pattern Language* (New York: Oxford University Press, 1977); Meyer Spivak, *Institutional Settings: An Environmental Design Approach* (New York: Human Sciences Press, 1984); and Carol Simon Weinstein and Thomas G. David, eds., *Spaces for Children: The Built Environment and Child Development* (New York: Plenum Press, 1987).

52. Foucault, *Discipline and Punish*, 26.

53. Dewey, *Human Nature and Conduct*, 47.

54. Foucault, *Discipline and Punish*, 190.

55. For two brief historical overviews of the project method, see See H. Warren Button and Eugene F. Provenzo Jr., *History of Education and Culture in America* (Englewood Cliffs, NJ: Prentice Hall, 1983), 257–259, and Lawrence A. Cremin, *The Transformation of the School: Progressivism in American Education, 1876–1957* (New York: Alfred A. Knopf, 1961), 216–220. For its initial theoretical and practical emergence, see William Heard Kilpatrick, "The Project Method," *Teachers College Record* 19, 4 (September 1918), and its elaboration in his *Foundations of Method* (New York: Macmillan, 1925). For a more recent formulation, see Lilian G. Katz and Sylvia C. Chard, *Engaging Children's Minds: The Project Approach* (Norwood, NJ: Ablex, 1991).

56. For descriptions of Reggio Emilia practice, see Carolyn Edwards, Lella Gandini, and George Forman, eds., *The Hundred Languages of Children: The Reggio Emilia Approach to Early Childhood Education*, especially chapters 10 and 11, which are detailed accounts of specific projects. See also Rebecca New, "Excellent Early Education: A City in Italy Has It," *Young Children*, 45, 6 (September 1990), 4–10.

57. Dewey, *The School and Society*, 49.

58. John Dewey, *Democracy and Education* (New York: Macmillan, 1916), 79.

59. For an eloquent argument for the priority of "meaning" and "thoughtfulness" over "rationality" in educational structure and design, see Matthew Lipman, Ann Margaret Sharp, and Frederick S. Oscanyon, *Philosophy in the Classroom*, second edition (Philadelphia: Temple University Press, 1980), 4–11.

60. John Dewey, *The Child and the Curriculum*. In M.S. Dworkin, *Dewey on Education: Selections* (New York: Teachers College Press, 1959), 96–97.

61. Lawrence J. Splitter and Ann Margaret Sharp, *Teaching for Better Thinking: The Classroom Community of Inquiry* (Melbourne: ACER, 1995), 130.

62. For a fuller treatment of the implications of doing philosophy with children, see David Kennedy, "Philosophy for Children and the Reconstruction of Philosophy," in *Metaphilosophy* 30, 4 (October 1999), 338–359, and "Philosophy for Children and School Reform: Dewey, Lipman, and the Community of Inquiry," in John Portolli and Ron Reed, eds., *Children, Philosophy, and Democracy* (Detselig, 1995), Chapter 8. And for a classic formulation of a methodology of doing philosophy as communal inquiry in the elementary classroom, see Lipman, Sharp and Oscanyon, *Philosophy in the Classroom*.

63. Winnicott, *Playing and Reality*, 51.

64. Plato, *Meno*, trans. G.M.A. Grube (Indianapolis: Hackett, 1976).

65. Herbert Marcuse, *One Dimensional Man: Studies in the Ideology of Advanced Industrial Society* (Boston: Beacon Press, 1964), 72.

Bibliography

Abrams, M.H. *Natural Supernaturalism: Tradition and Revolution in Romantic Literature*. New York: Norton, 1971.

Adan, Jane. *The Children in Our Lives: Knowing and Teaching Them.* Albany: State University of New York Press, 1991.

Alexander, Christopher. *A Pattern Language*. New York: Oxford University Press, 1977.

Arditi, Jorge. *A Genealogy of Manners: Transformations of Social Relations in France and England from the Fourteenth to the Eighteenth Centuries*. Chicago: University of Chicago Press, 1998.

Aries, Phillipe. *Centuries of Childhood: A Social History of Family Life.* Trans. Robert Baldick. New York: Knopf, 1962.

Aristotle. *Aristotle*. In 23 volumes. Trans. H. Rackham. Cambridge: Harvard University Press, 1981.

Aristotle. *Nichomachean Ethics*. Trans. M. Ostwald. New York: Bobbs-Merrill, 1962.

Aristotle. *A New Aristotle Reader*. Ed. J.L. Ackrill. Princeton: Princeton University Press, 1987.

Aristotle. *De Anima (On the Soul)*. Trans. Hugh Lawson-Tancred. Harmondsworth: Penguin, 1986.

Augustine. *The Confessions of St. Augustine*. Ed. R.S. Pine-Coffin. Harmondsworth: Penguin Books, 1961.

Bachelard, Gaston. *The Poetics of Reverie: Childhood, Language, and the Cosmos*. Trans. Daniel Russell. Boston: Beacon Press, 1971.

Baudrillard, Jean. *Revenge of the Crystal: Selected Writings on the Modern Object and its Destiny, 1968–1983*. Tran. and ed. Paul Foss and Julian Pefanis. London: Pluto Press, 1990.

Bellah, Robert, "To Kill and Survive or To Die and Become: The Active Life and the Contemplative Life as Ways of Being Adult." In *Adulthood*, ed. Erik H. Erikson. New York: Norton, 1978.

Bernasconi, Robert. "Bridging the Abyss: Heidegger and Gadamer." *Research in Phenomenology* 16 (1986): 1–24.

Bernhard, J. Gary. *Primates in the Classroom: An Evolutionary Perspective on Children's Education*, Amherst: University of Massachusetts Press, 1988.

Blake, William. *The Marriage of Heaven and Hell*. In *Blake: Complete Writings*, edited by Geoffrey Keynes. Oxford: Oxford University Press, 1966.

Blake, William. *There Is No Natural Religion* [Second Series]. In *Blake: Complete Writings*, ed. Geoffrey Keynes. Oxford: Oxford University Press, 1966.

Blum, Harold P. "The Conceptual Development of Regression." In *The Psychoanalytic Study of the Child,* vol. 49, 60–76, ed. A.J. Solnit. New Haven: Yale University Press, 1994.

Boas, George. *The Cult of Childhood*. London: The Wartburg Institute, 1966.

Boswell, John. *The Kindness of Strangers: The Abandonment of Children in Western Europe from Late Antiquity to the Renaissance*. New York: Pantheon, 1988.

Bradshaw, John. *Homecoming: Reclaiming and Championing Your Inner Child*. New York: Bantam, 1990.

Bremmer, Jan. *The Early Greek Concept of the Soul*. Princeton: Princeton University Press, 1983.

Brinker-Gabler, Gisela, ed. *Encountering the Other(s): Studies in Literature, History, and Culture*. Albany: State University of New York Press, 1995.

Broughton, John, ed. *Critical Theories of Child Development*. New York: Plenum Press, 1987.

Brown, N.O. *Life Against Death: The Psychoanalytic Meaning of History*. Middletown, CT: Wesleyan University Press, 1959.

Brown, N.O. *Love's Body*. Berkeley: University of California Press, 1966.

Buber, Martin. *The Knowledge of Man: A Philosophy of the Interhu-man*. Trans. Maurice Friedman and R. G. Smith. New York: Harper, 1965.

Buber, Martin. *Between Man and Man*. Trans. R.G. Smith. New York: Macmillan, 1965.

Buber, Martin. *I and Thou*. Trans. Walter Kaufmann. New York: Scribner's, 1970 [1922].

Buchmann, Marlis. *The Script of Life in Modern Society: Entry into Adulthood in a Changing World*. Chicago: University of Chicago Press, 1989.

Burman, Erica. *Deconstructing Developmental Psychology*. London: Routledge, 1994.

Burrow, J.A. *The Ages of Man: A Study in Medieval Writing and Thought*. Oxford: Clarendon Press, 1998.

Button, H. Warren, and Eugene F. Provenzo Jr. *History of Education and Culture in America*. Englewood Cliffs, NJ: Prentice Hall, 1983.

Caillois, Roger. *Man, Play, and Games*. New York: Free Press, 1961.

Cassirer, Ernst. *The Philosophy of Symbolic Forms*. Vol. 2: *Mythical Thought*. Trans. Ralph Mannheim. New Haven: Yale University Press, 1955.

Cavallo, Dominick. "The Politics of Latency: Kindergarten Pedagogy, 1860–1930." In *Regulated Children/Liberated Children: Education in Psychohistorical Perspective*, ed. Barbara Finkelstein. New York: Psychohistory Press, 1979.

Chartier, Roger, ed. *A History of Private Life III: The Passions of the Renaissance*. Trans. Arthur Goldhammer. Cambridge: Harvard University Press, 1989.

Chodorow, Nancy. *The Reproduction of Mothering: Psychoanalysis and the Sociology of Gender*. Berkeley: University of California Press, 1978.

Coe, Richard N. *When the Grass Was Taller: Autobiography and the Experience of Childhood*. New Haven: Yale University Press, 1984.

Coleridge, Charles Taylor. *The Friend*. Vol. I. In *Collected* Works, ed. Barbara Rooke. Princeton: Princeton University Press, 1969.

Coveney, Peter. *The Image of Childhood: The Individual and Society: A Study of the Theme in English Literature*. Harmondsworth: Penguin Books, 1959.

Cremin, Lawrence A. *The Transformation of the School: Progressivism in American Education, 1876–1957*. New York: Alfred A. Knopf, 1961.

Cunningham, Hugh. *Children and Childhood in Western Society Since 1500*. New York: Longman, 1995.

Cunningham, Hugh. "Histories of Childhood." *American Historical Review* 103 (October 1998): 1195–1208.

Debord, Guy. *The Society of the Spectacle*. Detroit: Black and Red, 1983.

deMause, Lloyd, ed. *The History of Childhood*. New York: Harper Torchbooks, 1974.

Derrida, Jacques. *Of Grammatology*. Trans. G.C. Spivak. Baltimore: Johns Hopkins Press, 1976.

Dewey, John. *Democracy and Education*. New York: Macmillan, 1916.

Dewey, John. *Reconstruction in Philosophy*. Enlarged Edition. Boston: Beacon Press, 1948.

Dewey, John. *The School and Society*. In *Dewey on Education: Selections*, ed. M.S. Dworkin. New York: Teachers College Press, 1959.

Dewey, John. *The Child and the Curriculum*. In *Dewey on Education: Selections*, ed. M.S. Dworkin. New York: Teachers College Press, 1959.

Dewey, John. *Human Nature and Conduct*. Carbondale: Southern Illinois University Press, 1988 [1922]).

Duby, Georges, ed. *A History of Private Life, II: Revelations of the Medieval World*. Trans. Arthur Goldhammer. Cambridge: Harvard University Press, 1988.

Dudley, Edward, and Maximillian E. Novak, eds. *The Wild Man Within: An Image in Western Thought from the Renaissance to Romanticism*. Pittsburgh: University of Pittsburgh Press, 1972.

Dumezil, Georges. *The Destiny of the Warrior*. Chicago: University of Chicago Press, 1970.

Edwards, Carolyn, Gandini, Leila, and George Forman, eds. *The Hundred Languages of Children: The Reggio Emilia Approach to Early Childhood Education*. Norwood, NJ: Ablex, 1993.

Elder, Glen H. Jr., Modell, John, and Ross D. Parke, eds. *Children in Time and Place: Developmental and Historical Insights*. Cambridge: Cambridge University Press, 1993.

Elias, Norbert. *The Civilizing Process and State Formation and Civilization.* Trans. Edmund Jephcott. Oxford: Blackwell, 1994 [1939].

Elias, Norbert. "The Civilizing of Parents." In *The Norbert Elias Reader*, ed. Johan Goudsblom and Stephen Mennell. Oxford: Blackwell, 1998.

Eluard, Paul. *Oevres Complete.* Paris: Bibliotheque de la Pleiade, Gallimard, 1968.

Emerson, Ralph Waldo. "Nature." In *Selected Essays, Lectures, and Poems*, ed. R.E. Spiller. New York: Washington Square Press, 1965.

Erasmus. *On Education for Children.* In *The Erasmus Reader*, ed. E. Rummel. Toronto: University of Toronto Press, 1990.

Erikson, Erik H. *Childhood and Society.* Second ed. New York: Norton, 1963.

Erikson, Erik. H. *Insight and Responsibility.* New York: Norton, 1964.

Erny, Pierre. *Childhood and Cosmos: The Social Psychology of the Black African Child.* Washington, DC: Black Orpheus Press, 1973.

Featherstone, Joseph. "Rousseau and Modernity." *Daedalus* 107 (Summer 1978): 167–192.

Fineberg, Jonathon. *The Innocent Eye: Children's Art and the Modern Artist.* Princeton: Princeton University Press, 1997.

Fink, Eugen. "The Ontology of Play." *Philosophy Today* 4 (Summer 1960): 95–109.

Finkelstein, Barbara. "Pedagogy as Intrusion: Teaching Values in Popular Primary Schools in 19th Century America." *Journal of Psychohistory* 2, 3 (Winter 1975).

Finkelstein, Barbara. "In Fear of Childhood: Relationships Between Parents and Teachers in Popular Primary Schools in the 19th Century." *Journal of Psychohistory* 3, 3 (Winter 1976).

Finkelstein, Barbara. "Casting Networks of Good Influence: The Reconstruction of Childhood in the United States, 1790–1870." In *American Childhood: A Research Guide and Historical Handbook,* eds. J.M. Hawes and N.R. Hiner. Westport, CT: Greenwood Press, 1985.

Finkelstein, Barbara. "Schooling and the Discover of Latency in Nineteenth-Century America," *The Journal of Psychohistory* 13, 1 (Summer 1985), 3.

Forsyth, Ilene H. "Children in Early Medieval Art: Ninth Through Twelfth Centuries." *Journal of Psychohistory* 4, 1 (Summer 1976)

Foucault, Michel. *Discipline and Punish: The Birth of the Prison*. Trans. Alan Sheridan. New York: Pantheon, 1979.

Foucault, Michel. "On the Geneology of Ethics." In *Michel Foucault: Beyond Structuralism and Hermeneutics*, second ed. Eds. Hubert Dreyfus and Paul Rabinow. Chicago: University of Chicago Press, 1983.

Foucault, Michel. *The History of Sexuality*. Vol. 3: *The Care of the Self*. Trans. Robert Hurley. New York: Vintage Books, 1986.

Freud, Sigmund. *On Dreams*. Trans. James Strachey. New York: W.W. Norton, 1989.

Freud, Sigmund. *The Standard Edition of the Complete Psychological Works of Sigmund Freud*. Trans. and ed. James Strachey. London: Hogarth Press, 1953.

Freud, Sigmund. *The Ego and the Id*. Trans. Joan Riviere. New York: Norton, 1960.

Froebel, Friedrich. *The Education of Man*. Clifton, NJ: Augustus M. Kelley, 1974.

Fuller, Peter. "Uncovering Childhood." In *Changing Childhood*, ed. Martin Hoyles. London: Writers and Publishers Cooperative, 1979.

Gadamer, Hans-Georg. *Truth and Method*. New York: Crossroad, 1975.

Gadamer, Hans-Georg. *Reason in the Age of Science*. Trans. F.G. Lawrence. Cambridge: MIT Press, 1982.

Gadamer, Hans-Georg. *Dialogue and Dialectic: Eight Hermeneutical Studies on Plato*. Trans. P. Christopher Smith. New Haven: Yale University Press, 1980.

Gadamer, Hans Georg. *The Idea of the Good in Plato and Aristotle*. Trans. P. Christopher Smith. New Haven: Yale University Press, 1986.

Gallagher, Shaun. *Hermeneutics and Education*. Albany: State University of New York Press, 1992.

Golden, Mark. *Children and Childhood in Classical Athens*. Baltimore: Johns Hopkins University Press, 1990.

Gombrich, Erich. *Symbolic Images: Studies in the Art of the* Renaissance. London: Phaidon, 1972.

Gottlieb, Barbara. *The Family in the Western World from the Black Death to the Industrial Age.* New York: Oxford University Press, 1993.

Green, Harvey. "Scientific Thought and the Nature of Children in America, 1820–1920." In Mary Heininger et al., *A Century of Childhood, 1820–1920.* Rochester, NY: Margaret Woodbury Strong Museum, 1984.

Gutek, Gerald L. *A History of the Western Educational Experience.* Second edition. Prospect Heights, IL: Waveland Press, 1995.

Hall, George Stanley. *Adolescence: Its Psychology and Its Relations to Physiology, Anthropology, Sociology, Sex, Crime, Religion and Education.* New York: Ayer, 1970 [1904].

Hans, James S. *The Play of the World.* Amherst: University of Massachusetts Press, 1981.

Harding, Sandra G. *Whose Science? Whose Knowledge? Thinking from Women's Lives.* Ithaca, NY: Cornell University Press, 1991.

Hauser, Arnold. *The Social History of Art.* Vol. 2. New York: Vintage, 1951.

Hawes, J.M., and Hiner, N.R., eds. *American Childhood: A Research Guide and Historical Handbook.* Westport, CT: Greenwood Press, 1985.

Hegel, G.W.F. *Hegel: The Essential Writings.* Ed. Frederick G. Weiss. New York: Harper and Row, 1974.

Hegel, G.W.F. *Phenomenology of Spirit.* Trans. A.V. Miller. New York: Oxford University Press, 1977.

Heidegger, Martin. *The Question Concerning Technology.* Trans. William Lovitt. New York: Harper and Row, 1977.

Huizinga, Johann. *The Waning of the Middle Ages: A Study of the Forms of Life, Thought, and Art in France and the Netherlands in the 14th & 15th Centuries.* New York: Anchor Books, 1969.

Huizinga, Johann. *Homo Ludens.* Boston: Beacon Press, 1955.

Hume, David. *A Treatise of Human Nature.* 2 vols. London: J.M. Dent & Sons, 1911.

Hunt, David. *Parents and Children in History: The Psychology of Family Life in Early Modern France.* New York: Harper and Row, 1972.

Innis, Harold A. *The Bias of Communication*. Toronto: University of Toronto Press, 1951.

Innis, Harold A. *Empire and Communications*. Toronto: University of Toronto Press, 1972.

James, Allison and Alan Prout, eds. *Constructing and Reconstructing Childhood*. Basingstoke: Falmer Press, 1990.

James, Allison, Chris Jenks, and Alan Prout. *Theorizing Childhood*. New York: Teachers College Press, 1998.

Jaynes, Julian. *The Origins of Consciousness in the Breakdown of the Bicameral Mind*. Boston: Houghton Mifflin, 1976.

Jonas, Hans. *The Phenomenon of Life: Toward a Philosophical Biology*. Chicago: University of Chicago Press, 1966.

Jung, C.G. *The Relations Between the Ego and the Unconscious*. In *Collected Works*. Vol. 7. R.F.C. Hull, trans. Princeton: Princeton University Press, 1945.

Jung, C.G., and C. Kerenyi. *Essays on a Science of Mythology: The Myth of the Divine Child and the Mysteries of Eleusis*. Trans. R.F.C. Hull. Bollingen Series XXII. Princeton: Princeton University Press, 1963.

Jung, C.G. *Dreams*. Trans. R.F.C. Hull. Princeton: Princeton University Press, 1974.

Jung, C.G. *Aion*. In *Collected Works*. Trans. R.F.C. Hull. Bollingen Series XX, vol. 9, ii. Princeton: Princeton University Press, 1980.

Jung, C.G. *The Structure and Dynamics of the Psyche*. Trans. R.F.C. Hull. New York: Pantheon Books, 1980.

Jung, C.G. *The Archetypes and the Collective Unconscious*. Trans. R.F.C. Hall. Bollingen Series XX, vol. 9, i. Princeton: Princeton University Press, 1980.

Katz, Lilian G., and Sylvia C. Chard. *Engaging Children's Minds: The Project Approach*. Norwood, NJ: Ablex, 1991.

Keniston, Kenneth. "Psychological Development and Historical Change." In Theodore K. Rabbs and Robert I. Rotberg, eds., *The Family in History: Interdisciplinary Essays*, 141–157. New York: Farrar Straus and Giroux, 1976.

Kennedy, David. *Young Children's Thinking: An Interpretation from Phenomenology*. Doctoral Dissertation. Lexington: University of Kentucky, 1986.

Kennedy, David. "Images of the Young Child in History: Enlightenment and Romance," *Early Childhood Research Quarterly*, 3 (June 1988): 121–137.

Kennedy, David. "Fools, Young Children, Animism, and the Scientific World Picture." *Philosophy Today* 33 (Winter), 1989: 374–381.

Kennedy, David. "The Hermeneutics of Childhood." *Philosophy Today* 36,1 (Spring 1992): 44–60.

Kennedy, David. "Child and Fool in the Western Wisdom Tradition," *Thinking* 11, 1 (1993):11–21.

Kennedy, David. "Philosophy for Children and School Reform: Dewey, Lipman, and the Community of Inquiry." In Ron Reed, ed., *Children, Philosophy, and Democracy*, Chapter 8. Toronto: Detselig, 1995.

Kennedy, David. "Empathic Child Rearing and the Adult Construction of Childhood: A Psychohistorical Look." *Childhood* 5,1 (February 1998): 9–22 .

Kennedy, David. "Philosophy for Children and the Reconstruction of Philosophy." *Metaphilosophy* 30, 4 (October 1999): 338–359.

Kennedy, David. "Subversive Innocence." Review of *The Innocent Eye: Children's Art and the Modern Artist,* by Jonathon Fineberg. *Childhood* 6, 2 (May 1999): 389–399.

Kennedy, David. "The Roots of Child Study: Philosophy, History, and Religion." *Teachers College Record* 102, 3 (June 2000): 514–538.

Kennedy, David. "Parent, Child, Alterity, Dialogue." *Philosophy Today* (Spring 2001): 33–42.

Kennedy, David. "The Child and Postmodern Subjectivity." *Educational Theory* 52, 2 (Spring 2002): 155–168.

Kernberg, Otto F. *Object-Relations Theory and Clinical Psychoanalysis.* New York: Jason Aronson, 1976.

Kessel, F.S., and Siegel, A.W., eds. *The Child and Other Cultural Inventions*. New York: Praeger, 1983.

Kessen, William. *The Child.* New York: John Wiley and Sons, 1965.

Kierkegaard, Soren. *The Present Age and of the Difference Between a Genius and an Apostle.* Trans. Alexander Dru. New York: Harper Torchbooks, 1962.

Kilpatrick, William Heard. "The Project Method." *Teachers College Record* 19, 4 (September 1918)

Klein, Melanie. *The Psycho-Analysis of Children*. Third revised edition. Trans. Alix Strachey. London: Hogarth Press, 1980.

Kohut, Heinz. "The Self in History." In *Self Psychology and the Humanities: Reflections on a New Psychoanalytic Approach*. New York: Norton, 1985.

Kohut, Heinz. *The Analysis of the Self*. New York: International Universities Press, 1971.

Kuhn, Reinhard. *Corruption in Paradise: The Child in Western Literature*. Hanover, NH: University Press of New England, 1982.

Kunstmann, Josef. *The Transformation of Eros*. Edinburgh: Oliver and Boyd, 1970.

Lasareff, Victor. "Studies in the Iconography of the Virgin." *Art Bulletin* 20 (1938): 26–65.

Lasch, Christopher. *The Minimal Self: Psychic Survival in Troubled Times*. New York: Norton, 1984.

Levin, Jerome D. *Theories of the Self*. Washington: Hemisphere, 1992.

Levinas, Emmanuel. *Totality and Infinity*. Trans. Alphonso Lingis. Pittsburgh: Duquesne University Press, 1969.

Levinas, Emmanuel. *Time and the Other*. Trans. Richard A. Cohen. Pittsburgh: Duquesne University Press, 1987.

Lewin, Kurt. *Field Theory in Social Science: Selected Theoretical Papers*. Ed. Dorwin Cartwright. New York: Harper and Row, 1951.

Lewis, C.S. *The Discarded Image: An Introduction to Medieval and Renaissance Literature*. Oxford: Oxford University Press, 1964.

Lifton, Robert Jay, ed. *Explorations in Psychohistory: The Wellfleet Papers*. New York: Simon and Schuster, 1974.

Lindsay, Cecile. "Corporality, Ethics, Experimentation: Lyotard in the Eighties." *Philosophy Today* 36, 4 (Winter 1992): 389–401.

Lipman, Matthew, Ann Margaret Sharp, and Frederick S. Oscanyon. *Philosophy in the Classroom*. Second edition. Philadelphia: Temple University Press, 1980.

Lippitz, Wilfried. "Understanding Children, Communicating with Children: Approaches to the Child Within us, Before Us, and With Us." *Phenomenology + Pedagogy* 4, 3 (1986): 56–65.

Lloyd, Rosemary. *The Land of Lost Content: Children and Childhood in Nineteenth-Century French Literature*. Oxford: Clarendon Press, 1992.

Lorence, Bogna W. "Parents and Children in 18th Century Europe." *History of Childhood Quarterly* 2, 1 (Summer 1974).

Luke, Carmen. *Pedagogy, Printing, and Protestantism: The Discourse on Childhood*. Albany: State University of New York Press, 1989.

Lyotard, Jean-Francois. *The Inhuman: Reflections on Time*. Trans. Geoffrey Bennington and Rachel Bowlby. Stanford, CA: Stanford University Press, 1991.

Lyotard, Jean-Francois. "Mainmise." *Philosophy Today* 36, 4 (Winter 1992): 419–427.

Malaguzzi, Loris. "History, Ideas, and Basic Philosophy." In Carolyn Edwards, Leila Gandini, and George Forman, eds., *The Hundred Languages of Children*. Norwood, NJ: Ablex, 1993.

Marchak, Catherine. "The Joy of Transgression: Bataille and Kristeva." *Philosophy Today* 34, 4 (Winter 1990).

Marcus, Leah Sinangolou. *Childhood and Cultural Despair: A Theme and Variations in 17th Century Literature*. Pittsburgh: University of Pittsburgh Press, 1978.

Marcuse, Herbert. *One Dimensional Man: Studies in the Ideology of Advanced Industrial Society*. Boston: Beacon Press, 1964.

Marcuse, Herbert. *Eros and Civilization*. Boston: Beacon Press, 1966.

Martin, L., Gutman, H., and P.H. Hutton, eds. *Technologies of the Self: A Seminar with Michael Foucault*. Amherst: University of Massachusetts Press, 1988.

Matthews, Gareth B. *The Philosophy of Childhood*. Cambridge: Harvard University Press, 1994.

Maynes, Mary Jo. *Schooling in Western Europe: A Social History*. Albany: State University of New York Press, 1990.

McLaughlin, Mary M. "Survivors and Surrogates: Children and Parents from Ninth to the Thirteenth Centuries," in L. deMause, ed., *The History of Childhood*. New York: Harper, 1974.

McLuhan, Marshall. *The Gutenberg Galaxy: The Making of Typographic Man*. Toronto: University of Toronto Press, 1962.

Meares, Russell. *The Metaphor of Play: Disruption and Restoration in the Borderline Experience*. Northvale, NJ: Jason Aronson, 1993.

Merleau-Ponty, Maurice. *Phenomenology of Perception*. Trans. Colin Smith. London: Routledge and Kegan Paul, 1962.

Merleau-Ponty, Maurice. "Méthode en Psychologie de L'Enfant." *Bulletin de Psychologie* XVIII 3–6 (1964).

Merleau-Ponty, Maurice. "Hegel's Existentialism." In *Sense and Non-Sense*. Trans. H.L. and P.A. Dreyfus. Evanston, IL: Northwestern University Press, 1964.

Merleau-Ponty, Maurice. *The Primacy of Perception*. Evanston, IL: Northwestern University Press, 1964.

Merleau-Ponty, Maurice. *The Visible and the Invisible*. Trans. Alphonso Lingis. Evanston, IL: Northwestern University Press, 1968.

Meyer-Drawe, Kate. "Kaleidoscope of Experiences: The Capability to be Surprised by Children." *Phenomenology + Pedagogy* 4, 3 (1986): 48–54.

Miller, Alice. *For Your Own Good: Hidden Cruelty in Child-Rearing and the Roots of Violence*. New York: Farrar Straus Giroux, 1983.

Miller, Alice. *Thou Shalt Not Be Aware: Society's Betrayal of the Child*. Trans. Hildegarde and Hunter Hannum. New York: Meridian, 1986.

Misgeld, Deiter. "Self-Reflection and Adult Maturity: Adult and Child in Hermeneutical and Critical Reflection." *Phenomenology + Pedagogy* 3, 3 (1995): 92.

Mitchell, S.A. *Radical Concepts in Psychoanalysis: An Integration*. Cambridge: Harvard University Press, 1988.

Morss, J. *The Biologizing of Childhood: Developmental Psychology and the Darwinian Myth*. London: Lawrence Erlbaum, 1990.

Nandy, Ashis. "Reconstructing Childhood: A Critique of the Ideology of Adulthood." In *Traditions, Tyranny and Utopias: Essays in the Politics of Awareness*. Delhi: Oxford University Press, 1987.

Nasaw, David. *Schooled to Order: A Social History of Public Schooling in the United States*. Oxford: Oxford University Press, 1979.

Neumann, Erich. *The Origins and History of Consciousness*. Trans. R.F.C. Hull. Princeton: Bollingen Foundation/Princeton University Press, 1954.

Neumann, Erich. *Depth Psychology and a New Ethic*. Trans. Eugene Rolfe. New York: Harper, 1973[1948].

Neumann, Erich. *The Child: Structure and Dynamics of the Psyche*. Trans. Ralph Mannheim. New York: G.P. Putnam's Sons, 1973.

New, Rebecca. "Excellent Early Education: A City in Italy Has It." *Young Children*, 45, 6 (September 1990): 4–10.

Newman, Gail M. *Locating the Romantic Subject: Novalis with Winnicott*. Detroit: Wayne State University Press, 1997.

Nietzsche, Friedrich. *Thus Spake Zarathustra*. R.J. Hollingdale, trans. Baltimore: Penguin Books, 1971.

Novalis. *Pollen and Fragments*. Trans. A. Versluis. Grand Rapids, MI: Phanes Press, 1989.

O'Neill, Onora, and William Ruddick. *Having Children: Philosophical and Legal Reflections on Parenthood*. Oxford: Oxford University Press, 1979.

Ong, Walter. *The Presence of the Word: Some Prologomena for Cultural and Religious History*. Minneapolis: University of Minnesota Press, 1967.

Ong, Walter. *Orality and Literacy: Technologizing the Word*. London: Methuen, 1982.

Pattison, Robert. *The Child Figure in English Literature*. Athens: The University of Georgia Press, 1978.

Petschauer, Peter. "Intrusive to Socializing Modes: Transitions in Eighteenth-Century Germany and Twentieth Century Italy." *The Journal of Psychohistory* 14, 3 (Winter 1987): 257–270.

Petschauer, Peter. "The Childrearing Modes in Flux: An Historian's Reflection." *The Journal of Psychohistory* 17, 1 (Summer 1989): 1–41.

Piaget, Jean. *The Child's Conception of the World*. Trans. Joan and Andrew Tomlinson. London: Routledge and Kegan Paul, 1929.

Piaget, Jean. "Biology and Cognition." In Barbara Inhelder and H.H. Chipman, eds., *Piaget and His School*. New York: Springer Verlag, 1976.

Picard, Barbara Leonie. *Hero-Tales from the British Isles*. New York: Criterion Books, 1966.

Plato. *Meno*. Trans. G.M.A. Grube. Indianapolis: Hackett, 1976.

Plato. *Laws*. In *Collected Dialogues*. Eds. E. Hamilton and H. Cairns. Princeton: Bollingen, 1961.

Plato. *The Republic of Plato*. Trans. and ed. F.M. Cornford. London: Oxford University Press, 1941.

Plotinus. *The Philosophy of Plotinus*. Trans. and ed. Joseph Katz. New York: Appleton-Century-Crofts, 1950.

Plotz, Judith. "The Perpetual Messiah: Romanticism, Childhood, and the Paradoxes of Human Development." In Barbara Finkelstein, ed., *Regulated Children/Liberated Children: Education in Psychohistorical Perspective*, 63–95. New York: The Psychohistory Press, 1979.

Pollock, Linda A. *Forgotten Children: Parent-Child Relations from 1500–1900*. Cambridge: Cambridge University Press, 1983.

Pollock, Linda A. *A Lasting Relationship: Parents and Children Over Three Centuries*. Hanover, NH: University Press of New England, 1987.

Polokow, Valerie. *The Erosion of Childhood*. Chicago: University of Chicago Press, 1982.

Postman, Neil. *The Disappearance of Childhood*. New York: Delacorte Press, 1982.

Raines, Kathleen. *Blake and Antiquity*. Princeton, NJ: Bollingen, 1977.

Read, Herbert. *The Innocent Eye*. New York: Henry Holt, 1947.

Reardon, Bernard M.G. *Religion in the Age of Romanticism: Studies in Early Nineteenth Century Thought*. Cambridge: Cambridge University Press, 1985.

Ricoeur, Paul. *Hermeneutics and the Human Sciences*. J.B. Thompson, trans. and ed. Cambridge: Cambridge University Press, 1981.

Ricoeur, Paul. *Interpretation Theory: Discourse and the Surplus of Meaning*. Fort Worth: Texas Christian University Press, 1976.

Riegel, Klaus F. "Influence of Economic and Political Ideologies on the Development of Developmental Psychology." *Psychological Bulletin* 78, 2 (1972): 129–141.

Rilke, Rainier Maria. *Selected Works*. Trans. Robert Bly. New York: New Directions, 1967.

Risser, James. "Hermeneutic Experience and Memory: Rethinking Knowledge as Recollection." *Research in Phenomenology* 16 (1986): 41–56.

Robb, Nesca A. *Neoplatonism of the Italian Renaissance*. New York: Octagon Books, 1968.

Rousseau, Jean Jacques. *Emile, Or On Education*. Trans. Alan Bloom. New York: Basic Books, 1979.

Rousseau, Jean Jacques. *Emile*. Selections. Trans. and ed. William Boyd. New York: Teachers College Press, 1956.

Sallis, John, ed. *Phenomenology: Descriptive or Hermeneutic?* Special Issue, *Research in Phenomenology*, 14 (1984).

Sallis, John, ed. *Hermeneutics Today.* Special Issue, *Research in Phenomenology* 16 (1986).

Schactel, Ernest G. *Metamorphosis: On the Development of Affect, Perception, Attention, and* Memory. New York: Basic Books, 1959.

Scharf, David E. *Refinding the Object and Reclaiming the Self.* Northvale, NJ: Jason Aronson, 1992.

Schiller, Friedrich von. *On the Aesthetic Education of Man In a Series of Letters.* Reginald Snell, trans. New York: Frederick Ungar, 1954 [1795]).

Schiller, Friedrich von. *Naïve and Sentimental Poetry and On the Sublime.* Trans. Julius A. Elias. New York: Frederick Ungar, 1966.

Schutz, Alfred. "On Multiple Realities." In *Collected Papers,* vol. l. Ed. I. Schutz. The Hague: Martinus Nijhoff, 1967.

Shahar, Shulamith. *Childhood in the Middle Ages.* London: Routledge, 1990.

Silverman, Hugh. "Hermeneutics and Interrogation," in *Research in Phenomonology*, XVI (1986): 87–94.

Smith, Joseph H., and William Kerrigan, Eds. *Opening Texts: Psychoanalysis and the Culture of Childhood.* Baltimore: Johns Hopkins University Press, 1985.

Sommerville, C. John. "English Puritans and Children: A Social Cultural Explanation." *The Journal of Psychohistory* 6, 1 (Summer 1978): 113–137.

Sommerville, C. John. *The Rise and Fall of Childhood.* Beverly Hills, CA: Sage Publications, 1982.

Sommerville, C. John. *The Discovery of Childhood in Puritan England.* Athens: The University of Georgia Press, 1992.

Sorensen, Aage B., Weinert, Franz E., and Lonnie R. Sherrod, eds. *Human Development and the Life Course: Multidisciplinary Perspectives.* Hillside, NJ: Lawrence Erlbaum Associates, 1986.

Spivak, Meyer. *Institutional Settings: An Environmental Design Approach.* New York: Human Sciences Press, 1984.

Splitter, Lawrance and Ann Margaret Sharp. *Teaching for Better Thinking: The Classroom Community of Inquiry.* Melbourne: ACER, 1995.

Steedman, Carolyn. *Strange Dislocations: Childhood and the Idea of Human Interiority, 1780–1930.* Cambridge: Harvard University Press, 1995.

Steinberg, Leo. *The Sexuality of Christ in Renaissance Art and in Modern Oblivion.* New York: Pantheon, 1983.

Stephens, Sharon, ed. *Children and the Politics of Culture.* Princeton: Princeton University Press, 1995.

Stewart, Philip. "The Child Comes of Age." *Yale French Studies* 40 (1968), 136–137.

Stolorow, Robert. "Critical Reflections on the Theory of Self Psychology: An Inside View." *Psychoanalytic Inquiry* 6 (1986): 389.

Stone, Lawrence. *The Family, Sex and Marriage in England 1500–1800.* Abridged edition. New York: Harper, 1979.

Taylor, Charles. "What is Involved in a Genetic Psychology?" In Theodore Mischel, ed., *Cognitive Development and Epistemology.* New York: Academic Press, 1971.

Taylor, Charles. *Hegel.* Cambridge: Cambridge University Press, 1975.

Taylor, Charles. *Sources of the Self: The Making of the Modern Identity.* Cambridge: Harvard University Press, 1989.

Taylor, Charles. "The Dialogical Self." In D.R. Hiley, J.F. Bohman, and R. Schusterman, eds., *The Interpretive Turn: Philosophy, Science, and Culture,* 304–314. Ithaca: Cornell University Press, 1991.

Taylor, Mark C. *Journeys to Selfhood: Hegel and Kierkegaard.* New York: Fordham University Press, 2000.

Theunissen, Michael. *The Other: Studies in the Social Ontology of Husserl, Heidegger, Sartre, and Buber.* Trans. Christopher Macann. Cambridge: MIT Press, 1986.

Toulmin, Stephen. "The Concept of 'Stages' in Psychological Development." In Theodore Mischel, ed., *Cognitive Development and Epistemology.* New York: Academic Press, 1971.

Traherne, Thomas. *Poetical Works.* Ed. G.I. Wade. New York: Cooper Square Publishers, 1965.

Traherne, Thomas. *Centuries.* New York: Harper and Brother, 1960.

Tuan, Yi-Fu. *Space and Place.* Minneapolis: University of Minnesota Press, 1977.

Vandenberg, Donald. *Being and Education.* Englewood Cliffs, NJ: Prentice Hall, 1971.

Vattimo, Gianni. *The End of Modernity: Nihilism and Hermeneutics in Postmodern Culture*. Trans. Jon R. Snyder. Baltimore: Johns Hopkins University Press, 1988.

Vaughn, Henry, *The Works of Henry Vaughan*. Second edition. Ed. L.C. Martin. Oxford: Clarendon Press, 1957.

Veyne, Paul, ed. *A History of Private Life I: From Pagan Rome to Byzantium*. Trans. Arthur Goldhammer. Cambridge: Harvard University Press, 1987.

Walzer, Michael. *The Revolution of the Saints: A Study in the Origins of Radical Politics*. Cambridge: Harvard University Press, 1965.

Ward, Colin. *The Child in the City*. New York: Pantheon, 1978.

Wartofsky, Max. "The Child's Construction of the World and the World's Construction of the Child: From Historical Epistemology to Historical Psychology." In F.S. Kessel and A.W. Siegel, eds., *The Child and Other Cultural Inventions*. New York: Praeger, 1983.

Weil, Simone. "The Iliad: The Poem of Force." In Alasdair McIntyre, ed., *Revisions*. Terre Haute: Notre Dame University Press, 1974.

Weinstein, Carol Simon, and Thomas G. David, eds. *Spaces for Children: The Built Environment and Child Development*. New York: Plenum Press, 1987.

Werner, Heinz. *Comparative Psychology of Mental Development*. Revised edition. New York: International Universities Press, 1948.

Werner, Heinz. "The Concept of Development from a Comparative and Organismic Point of View." In Dale B. Harris, ed., *The Concept of Development*. Minneapolis: University of Minnesota Press, 1957.

Wertheimer, Max. "Gestalt Theory." Trans. and ed. W.D. Ellis. *Source Book of Gestalt Psychology*. New York: Harcourt Brace, 1938 [1924].

Whitebook, Joel. "Reflections on the Autonomous Individual and the Decentered Subject." *American Imago* 49, 1 (1992): 97–116.

Wind, Edgar. *Pagan Mysteries in the Renaissance*. Revised edition. New York: Norton, 1968.

Winnicott, D.W. *The Maturational Processes and the Facilitating Environment*. New York: International Universities Press, 1965.

Winnicott, D.W. *Playing and Reality*. New York: Routledge, 1989 [1971].

Witkin, H.A., R.B. Dyk, H.F. Faterson, D.R. Goodenough, and S.A. Karp, *Psychological Differentiation*. London: Wiley, 1962.

Wittgenstein, Ludwig. *On Certainty*. Trans. Denis Paul and G.E.M. Anscombe. New York: Harper and Row, 1969.

Wolf, E. *Treating the Self: Elements of Clinical Self Psychology*. New York: Guilford, 1988.

Wordsworth, William. *Poems*. Ed. H.J. Hall. New York: Scott Foresman, 1924.

Wordsworth, William. The Prelude, or Growth of a Poet's Mind, an Autobiographical Poem. Second edition. Oxford: Clarendon Press, 1959.

Index

Abrams, M.H., ix–x, 123, 144–145
Adult-child relation, xi, 3, 5–7,
    10–13, 14, 17, 19, 58, 61–62,
    70, 71–75, 85–104, 131, 148,
    152–161, 170, 186
Adulthood/adults, 3–6, 19, 23–24,
    33, 162–163
  "childhood amnesia" and, 15, 58,
    137
  Christian, 27–28, 33, 38, 67–69,
    115, 123, 144
  continuity with childhood, 58–60
  "disappearance" of, 6, 75,
    103–104, 134–135
  fall and division as, 38, 40, 42–46,
    48–49, 140–141
  Greek, Stoic, and Epicurean, 6,
    65–68
  history of, 62, 66–85
  ideology of, 13–15, 21–23, 62
  medieval, 16, 76, 79, 81, 101, 140
  modern, 6, 66–68, 77–85, 89,
    171–172
  reconstruction of, 14, 19, 22, 24,
    61, 136, 148
  reinvention of, 63, 66, 88
  transitional space and, 60, 72, 82,
    121–122, 123, 131, 137–140

"Adult-child" the, 6
Adultism, 62, 63 64, 67, 70–73,
    85–86, 99, 160, 162, 184
Agape, 37, 39, 41
Alterity, 8, 71–72, 96, 102, 111, 112,
    125–128, 131, 146, 147, 162,
    167, 174
Angelico, Fra, 35
Anselm, 11, 34, 45
Aries, Philippe, 63, 76, 92, 101
Aristotle, 4, 5, 6, 8–9, 18, 64–66, 98,
    110, 161. *Also see* "Subjectivity,
    Aristotelian"
Augustine, 10

Bachelard, Gaston, xi–xii, 20, 137
Baldwin, J.M., 47
Baudrillard, Jean, 109
Bernanos, Georges, 50
Bernard of Clairvoix, 11, 34, 45
Binet, Alfred, 174
Blake, William, 46, 122, 123, 124, 146
Boethius, 32
Boswell, John, 5, 76
Bret, Antoine, 49
Brown, N.O., x, 60, 94–95, 117
Bruner, Jerome, 174
Buber, Martin, 17, 158–162, 163

Caravaggio, 40
Cassirer, Ernst, 47–48
Cavallo, Dominick, 156
Childhood/children
  ambivalence toward, 6–12, 90, 93, 95
  archetype, xi, 9, 28–44, 52, 70
  androgyny and, 30, 38, 45, 60, 64, 98
  art of, 20, 144
  autobiography and, 4, 48, 97
  Calvinism and, 12, 69, 87–88, 90
  child study and, 1–2, 12–13, 64, 98–99
  Christianity and, 8, 10–11, 23, 27–28, 32, 33–34, 36–37, 45–46, 50–52, 53, 86, 92
  cultural transformation and, x, 24, 154
  culture of, 96, 163,
  differences from adults, 7, 15–16, 63, 68, 147, 162–163, 171
  disappearance of, 75, 104, 135
  divine child, 11, 29–43, 60. *Also see* "primordial child" and "*puer aeternus*"
  early modern, 63, 66, 90, 93, 141
  enigmatic child, 11, 43, 45
  evolutionary theory and, 12, 27, 64, 98–99, 105, 115–116, 120, 136
  family and, 41, 49, 92, 133, 134, 135, 148, 172
  fool and, 10, 11, 28, 29, 34
  hermeneutics of, 17–21, 45, 51
  history of, 63, 75–103
  iconography of, 31–43, 60, 143
  infans, 29, 36
  "inner child," 6, 7, 24, 31, 39, 62, 100, 159
  "invention" of, 63, 66, 76, 89
  Jesus sayings and, 10–11, 28, 33–34, 48
  limit condition as, 7, 9

latency stage and, 4, 152, 155–156, 166, 171
medieval, 4, 5, 11, 12, 33–34, 45, 76
organic metaphor and, 97–99
"polymorph" and, 15
primordial child, 28, 29, 31, 33, 44, 61, 62, 70. *Also see* "divine child" and "*puer aeternus*"
privileged stranger as, 142–149
proof text as, 8, 10, 12, 87, 99
puer aeternus, 28, 30. *Also see* "divine child" and "primordial child"
puer senex, 33, 89
Puritans and, 90
recapitulation theory and, 64, 99
Renaissance art in, 31, 34–42
Romantic understanding of, 4, 12, 25, 34, 39, 44–62, 73, 91, 143, 148. *Also see* "Romanticism"
sexuality and, 5, 8, 16, 30, 36, 38, 60, 99, 145
screens for adult projection as, 7–9, 11, 15, 142
text as, 18–20
"Childman," the, 144
Child-rearing modes, 22, 74, 85–103, 133
  Abandoning, 86–87
  Ambivalent, 87–88
  Empathic, 101–102, 135, 137, 146–148, 156–157, 174, 184
  Infanticidal, 86
  Intrusive, 88–96, 141, 143, 173, 175
  Socializing, 96–101, 133, 156, 174
Coleridge, Samuel Taylor, 25, 136, 137, 167
Colonization, 58, 84–85
  childhood and, 12, 44, 62, 64, 72, 93, 98, 153
  education/schooling and, 84, 98–99, 166, 173, 178, 183
Crashaw, Richard, 44, 45, 48

Darwin, Charles, 1, 2, 12, 64, 98, 120
daVinci, Leonardo, 40
Defoe, Daniel, 93
deMause, Lloyd, 22, 74, 86–106 passim, 132–133, 137, 147, 156
Depressive position, 140–141
Derrida, Jacques, 7–8
Descartes, Renee, 23, 82, 114–115, 120
Developmental stages, 4, 100, 155–156, 174
Dewey, John, xi, 61, 116, 117, 143, 151–154, 157–158, 166–169, 170, 173, 177, 178
Dialogue, 17–18, 55, 68, 70–71, 116, 121, 127, 140, 143, 147, 163–164
    children and childhood with, xi, 14–21, 22, 24, 71–75, 89, 94–98, 100–101, 147, 186
    communal, 180–181
    distanciation and appropriation and, 18, 101
    fusion of horizons and, 18–19, 101
    internal, 24, 69, 100, 123, 130
    I-Thou and I-It, 160, 166
    monologue and, 160
    reason and desire between, 37, 112, 148. *Also see* "Reason and desire"
    theory as, 14
Distanciation and appropriation, 18–19, 101
Dostoevsky, Fyodor, 101
Durkheim, Emile, 101

Education, 21–23, 52, 138
    dialogue and, *see* "Dialogue"
    Empathic Mode and, 156–157
    Intrusive Mode and, 88–94, 134, 173–175, 178–179
    mastery and, 15, 68, 82, 120, 142, 171

Plato and Aristotle and, 65–66, 69
    power and, 13, 58, 84, 135, 147, 154–159, 163, 164, 167–168, 173–175
    psychoanalysis and, 12, 124
    reconstruction as, xi, 22, 154–158, 163–164, 165–183
    reproduction as, 4, 21–22, 66, 92, 148, 153–155, 157, 166–167, 183
    Romantic, 56–62
    schooling and, 147–149, 151–186
    Socializing Mode and, 97–100, 156
    theory and, 13–14
    universal and compulsory, 11, 12, 4, 21, 56, 57, 84, 91, 94, 104, 133, 135, 154, 156
Ego
    defense mechanisms, 114, 118, 122
    dethronement/decentering/reposi-tioning/reconstruction of, 18, 38, 70–72, 94–96, 118–119, 123–124, 126–128, 129, 146, 164, 165–166
    developmental crises of, 155
    egocentrism, 8, 12, 47, 80, 87
    mastery and, 23, 67–69, 78, 93–94, 118, 123, 126. *Also see* "Subjec-tivity, domination"
    regression and, 137, 147
    supergo and id, relations with, 113, 116–120, 158, 160
    unconscious, relations with, 83, 86, 97, 125
Elias, Norbert, 5, 76–80, 89, 96, 101
Emerson, Ralph Waldo, 4
Erasmus, 80, 87, 93
Erikson, Erik H., 24, 96, 122, 155–156, 166, 171
Erny, Pierre, 4
Eros, 37, 39, 41, 146, 155, 185
Eroti/putti/cupids, 31–32, 34, 36, 39, 43
Erotic mode of activity the, 60, 61, 145

Eroticism, 43, 121, 122, 131, 140
  polymorphous, 8, 16, 60, 145
Evergood, Phillip, 43

Ficino, Marsilio, 37
Field theory, 47, 71, 95, 101, 107,
    110, 111, 115–116, 120–121,
    124–128 passim, 133, 137–138,
    142, 164, 185
Fineberg, Jonathon, 144
Fink, Eugen, 56
Foucault, Michel, 66, 114, 163
  "discipline" and, 22, 58, 84, 99
  power and, 163, 173
  "subjection" and, 84, 129, 131,
    153
  "technologies of the self" and, 9,
    66, 88, 111–112, 114, 118, 129
Fourier, Charles, 56
French Revolution, xi, 54, 145, 146,
    147
Freud, Sigmund, x, 2, 4, 12, 15, 23,
    42, 59, 60, 95, 98, 99, 121, 141,
    145, 146, 152, 155–156, 166,
    185
  dream logic and, 139–140
  model of subjectivity and, 23–24,
    100–101, 113, 114, 116–120,
    126
  primary narcissism and, 38, 47, 95,
    139
  psychoanalysis and, 121–122, 124,
    125
Froebel, Friedrich, xi, 58, 61, 148
Fuller, Peter, 10

Gadamer, Hans-Georg, 17–19, 160,
    161
Gainsborough, Thomas, 42
Gardner, Howard, 174
Gombrich, E.H., 37–38
Gray, Thomas, 45

Habit and impulse, 22, 152–158,
    162, 165, 167–168, 173, 177

Harding, Sandra, 142
Hegel, G.W., 53, 125, 154
  logic of, 126, 136
  master-slave relationship and,
    142–143, 164
  "unhappy consciousness" and, 112,
    115, 119, 141
Heidegger, Martin, 171–172
Herbert, George, 44
Hermeneutics, 17–21, 75, 89, 97,
    101, 124, 163, 167. *Also see*
    "Childhood/Children"
Herrick, Robert, 44
Holbein, Hans the Elder, 35
Homo clausus. See "Subjectivity"
Hooch, Pieter de, 40
Hoppner, John, 42
Huizinga, Johann, 76, 101
Hume, David, 78, 114–115

Individualism, 49, 66–68, 74, 78, 81,
    85, 88, 92, 107–108, 112–113,
    130, 132, 140, 174, 185
Inquiry
  children and, 61, 157
  dialogue and, 165
  education and, 169–170, 174–181
Instinctual economy, 58, 78, 85, 88,
    117, 144, 148, 154, 159
Intersubject, 101, 106, 119, 120–132,
    133, 136–140, 146, 153, 159,
    163–164, 185–186
Introjection, 94, 106, 124, 126–128,
    138, 159, 164

Jaynes, Julian, 67
Jonas, Hans, 79, 82
Jung, C.G., 118–119, 122, 124, 138
  child archetype and. *See* "Child-
    hood/children"
  divine child. *See* "Childhood/chil-
    dren"
  individuation and, 38, 70, 96, 119
  primordial child. *See*
    "Childhood/Children"

"Self" and, 30, 70, 86, 119, 122, 141, 160
shadow and, 70–71. *Also see* "Shadow"

Kafka, Franz, 119
Kandinsky, Vassily, 144
Keniston, Kenneth, 3
Kierkegaard, Søren, 101, 185
King Lear, 11
Klee, Paul, 144
Klein, Melanie, 47, 140
Kohlberg, Lawrence, 99
Kristeva, Julia, 95
Kuhn, Rheinhard, 53
Kunstman, Joseph, 32–33, 39

Lasaref, Victor, 35
Levinas, Emmanuel, 71–72, 73, 95, 96, 126, 127, 131, 138, 160, 165
Lewin, Kurt, 116
Lippi, Fra Filippo, 35
Locke, John, 7, 78, 90–91, 114
Lorenzetto, 35
Lyotard, Jean-Francois, 109

Malaguzzi, Loris, 157
Marcus, Leah S., 45, 90
Marcuse, Herbert, x, 60, 117, 139, 146, 154, 185
    non-repressive order and, 139, 143, 145
    non-repressive sublimation and, 61, 146
    performance principle and, 57, 61, 78, 85, 139, 145
    repressive desublimation and, 135, 145
    surplus-repression and, 57–58, 61, 78, 84–85, 99, 139, 153, 186
Marvel, Andrew, 44, 45
Marx, Karl, 10, 56, 59, 123, 146
Maslow, Abraham, 174
Massay, Quentin, 35
Matthews, Gareth, 187

Merleau-Ponty, Maurice, 15, 20, 47, 95, 116, 124, 126, 154
Michaelangelo, 35, 40
Miro, Joan, 144
Misgeld, Dieter, 15

Nandy, Ashis, 13, 69, 85, 103
Neoplatonism, 36–37
Neoteny, 24
Neumann, Erich, 70, 72, 141
Nietzsche, Friedrich, 101, 119, 143, 144, 185
Novalis, 59, 105

Object relations theory, 119, 121, 126–127, 130, 140
Ong, Walter, 80–81
Ortega y Gasset, José, 185

Panmechanism, 82
Panpsychism, 79–80
Parmigianino, 40
Pattison, Robert, 46
Piaget, Jean, 2, 12, 47, 65, 98, 99, 116, 117, 143, 174, 178
Picasso, Pablo, 144
Plasticity ("original modifiability"), 24, 152, 157
Plato, 4, 8–9, 19, 23, 32, 65–67, 70, 73, 94, 110–112, 114, 116–119, 124, 136, 168. *Also see* "Subjectivity, Platonic"
Play, 11, 20, 29, 45, 54–56, 60–61, 107–109, 121, 122, 131, 138–140 passim, 145, 149, 161, 165, 171
    work and, 57, 77–78, 171–173, 186
Plotinus, 36–37
Plotz, Judith, 143
Power, 58, 64, 66, 71, 78, 84, 87, 92, 118, 123, 129, 135, 142, 147, 154, 158–159, 162, 167–168
    schooling and, 84, 156–157, 163, 170, 174, 175
    Also see "Foucault, Michel"

Postman, Neil, 85, 135
Projection, 6–13 passim, 30, 64, 67, 70–72, 81–82, 86–98 passim, 106, 113, 118, 119, 124, 126, 137, 138, 161
  withdrawal of, 18, 70, 81, 101, 113, 127–129, 146, 164
Psychodynamics of literacy, 80–82
Psychodynamics of orality, 79–80
Psychoanalysis, 21, 71, 119, 121–122, 124, 125, 132, 133, 137

Raphael, 35, 39, 40, 144
Read, Herbert, 20, 144
Reality principle, 12, 57, 60–61, 77–78, 88, 103, 116–117, 140, 145, 147
Reason and desire, 37, 57–58, 60, 83, 112, 114, 118–119, 124, 136–142, 145–146, 148, 152, 154, 185, 162, 165, 185. *Also see* "Dialogue"
Reggio Emilia, 157, 176
Reich, Wilhelm, 117
Reynolds, Joshua, 42
Ribera, Jose, 40
Ricoeur, Paul, 17–21
Rilke, Rainier-Maria, x, 20
Rimbaud, Arthur, 144
Rogers, Carl, 174
Romanticism, ix–xi, 42, 46, 48, 52–62, 94–95, 97, 115, 122–126, 136, 141, 143, 144, 146, 147, 154. *Also see* "Childhood/Children"
Rousseau, Jean-Jacques, x–xi, 22, 52, 58, 74, 90–91, 103, 134, 135, 138
Rubens, Peter Paul, 40

Saint Paul, 10, 27–28, 115
Saint-Simon, Comte de, 56
Schactel, Ernest, 137
Scharf, Richard, 127, 130, 131

Schiller, Freidrich, 51–57 passim, 138–140 passim, 145, 147, 154, 165, 172
Schooling, 14, 95–96, 148–186
  assessment and, 182–183
  built environment and, 170–173, 175, 182, 185
  community of inquiry as, 169–170, 181
  curriculum and pedagogy and, 175–178
  dialogue and, 21–22, 61, 95–96, 149, 156–165, 167, 176–177
  "embryonic community" as, 157, 163, 177, 181
  governance and, 169, 175
  grouping and, 174–176
  "home space" and, 181–182
  inquiry and, 178–181
  intentional community as, 22, 61, 170, 174
  laboratory as, 163, 165,
  philosophical inquiry and, 177–181
  project method and, 175–176
  teacher preparation and, 170
  universal and compulsory, x–xii, 4–5, 13–14, 21–22, 56–57, 62, 85, 91–92, 104, 135, 152, 154–155, 156, 166
Schutz, Alfred, 16–17, 138–139, 155
Selfobject, 121–122, 130, 131, 140, 142
Self-regulation, 148, 156–157, 159
Shadow, 9, 69, 72, 86–88 passim, 94, 119, 142. *Also see* "Jung, C.G."
Silverman, Hugh, 165
Social democracy, 168–169, 174
Split-personality theorizing, 82
St. Francis of Assisi, 34, 44
Steinberg, Leo, 37
Stoicism, 6, 23, 27, 66, 68, 112–115, 118
Stone, Lawrence, 49, 92
Subjectivity, 23–24, 67–69
  Aristotelian, 64–65, 110–111

Christian, 68–69, 113, 114, 115, 123, 144
crisis of, 51–52, 94, 103, 115
cultural construction of, 106–110
democratic personality, 123, 128, 157
discrete vs. plural self, 55, 66–68, 92, 96, 101, 105, 107, 110, 113–115, 120–121, 124, 131, 153–154, 164
domination and, 23, 37, 59, 61, 66, 69, 110, 114, 119, 122, 143. *Also see* "Ego, mastery"
evolution of, 153–154, 158
field-dependent/ field-independent, 107, 112–113
Freudian. *See* "Freud"
history of, 109–126, 143
homo clausus and, 96, 101, 105, 112, 115–116, 118–119, 122, 125–126, 129, 133, 139, 141, 143, 153
modal personality, 73, 77–78, 80, 129, 130, 132, 183, 185
modern, 77–85, 140
monotheistic model of, 67–69, 95, 96
"organism" and, 12, 20, 49, 57, 98, 100, 111, 116–117, 120, 126, 136, 138–139, 140, 143, 171
personality disorders and, 129–131
Platonic, 23, 37, 65–67, 69, 71, 110–112, 114, 116–119, 124, 136
postmodern, 23, 95, 101–102, 107, 140, 143, 153
premodern, 67, 79–80, 101–102, 113, 122, 131, 140, 153, 164
reconstruction of, 24, 27, 56–59, 60–62, 70, 86, 95–96, 101–102, 106, 108, 112, 115, 119–120, 124, 132, 136–138, 140, 144–148, 164, 167, 183–186
Stoic and Epicurian, 111–115, 118

subject-in-process, 24, 73, 95, 96, 100, 108, 119, 120, 121, 138, 140, 159
technologies of the self. *See* "Foucault, Michel"
Sublimation, 185
Subspeciation, 63–64, 72, 160
Surplus-repression. *See* Marcuse, Herbert
Swedenborg, Emanuel, 122

Taylor, Charles, 12, 126, 136
Tielhard de Chardin, 123
Toulmin, Stephen, 12
Traherne, Thomas, 44, 46–51
Titian, 39
Transitional space, 47, 53, 55, 60–61, 72, 82, 101, 108, 121–123, 131, 137–138, 139, 140, 161, 164–165, 171, 175, 180. *Also see* "Winnicott, D.W."
"Between" the, 71, 81, 82, 89, 96, 101, 164–165, 175
Tuan, Yi-Fu, 170

Vattimo, Gianni, 108
Vaughan, Henry, 1, 44, 45, 48
Velasquez, Diego, 42–43
Vygotsky, Lev, 174

Wartofsky, Max, 5
Weber, Max, 119
Werner, Heinz, 47, 136–137, 140
Wertheimer, Max, 116, 125–126
White, Hayden, 93
Whitehead, A.N., 125
Whitman, Walt, 122
"Wild man," 63, 93–94, 97, 142
Wind, Edgar, 37
Winnicott, D.W., 47, 48, 53, 55, 60, 123, 138–140, 165, 180
Wordsworth, William, 4, 46, 53–56, 60, 97

Zorach, William, 43

Printed in Great Britain
by Amazon